Globalisation and Work in Asia

CHANDOS
ASIAN STUDIES SERIES:
CONTEMPORARY ISSUES AND TRENDS

Series Editor: Professor Chris Rowley,
Cass Business School, City University, UK
(email: c.rowley@city.ac.uk)

Chandos Publishing is pleased to publish this major Series of books entitled *Asian Studies: Contemporary Issues and Trends*. The Series Editor is Professor Chris Rowley, Cass Business School, City University, UK.

Asia has clearly undergone some major transformations in recent years and books in the Series examine this transformation from a number of perspectives: economic, management, social, political and cultural. We seek authors from a broad range of areas and disciplinary interests: covering, for example, business/management, political science, social science, history, sociology, gender studies, ethnography, economics and international relations, etc.

Importantly, the Series examines both current developments and possible future trends. The Series is aimed at an international market of academics and professionals working in the area. The books have been specially commissioned from leading authors. The objective is to provide the reader with an authoritative view of current thinking.

New authors: we would be delighted to hear from you if you have an idea for a book. We are interested in both shorter, practically orientated publications (45,000+ words) and longer, theoretical monographs (75,000–100,000 words). Our books can be single, joint or multi-author volumes. If you have an idea for a book, please contact the publishers or Professor Chris Rowley, the Series Editor.

Dr Glyn Jones   Professor Chris Rowley
Chandos Publishing (Oxford) Ltd   Cass Business School, City University
Email: gjones@chandospublishing.com   Email: c.rowley@city.ac.uk
www.chandospublishing.com   **www.cass.city.ac.uk/faculty/c.rowley**

Chandos Publishing: is a privately owned and wholly independent publisher based in Oxford, UK. The aim of Chandos Publishing is to publish books of the highest possible standard: books that are both intellectually stimulating and innovative.

We are delighted and proud to count our authors from such well known international organisations as the Asian Institute of Technology, Tsinghua University, Kookmin University, Kobe University, Kyoto Sangyo University, London School of Economics, University of Oxford, Michigan State University, Getty Research Library, University of Texas at Austin, University of South Australia, University of Newcastle, Australia, University of Melbourne, ILO, Max-Planck Institute, Duke University and the leading law firm Clifford Chance.

A key feature of Chandos Publishing's activities is the service it offers its authors and customers. Chandos Publishing recognises that its authors are at the core of its publishing ethos, and authors are treated in a friendly, efficient and timely manner. Chandos Publishing's books are marketed on an international basis, via its range of overseas agents and representatives.

Professor Chris Rowley: Dr Rowley, BA, MA (Warwick), DPhil (Nuffield College, Oxford) is Subject Group leader and the inaugural Professor of Human Resource Management at Cass Business School, City University, London, UK. He is the founding Director of the new, multi-disciplinary and internationally networked *Centre for Research on Asian Management*, Editor of the leading journal *Asia Pacific Business Review* (www.tandf.co.uk/journals/titles/13602381.asp). He is well known and highly regarded in the area, with visiting appointments at leading Asian universities and top journal Editorial Boards in the US and UK. He has given a range of talks and lectures to universities and companies internationally with research and consultancy experience with unions, business and government and his previous employment includes varied work in both the public and private sectors. Professor Rowley researches in a range of areas, including international and comparative human resource management and Asia Pacific management and business. He has been awarded grants from the British Academy, an ESRC AIM International Study Fellowship and gained a 5-year RCUK Fellowship in Asian Business and Management. He acts as a reviewer for many funding bodies, as well as for numerous journals and publishers. Professor Rowley publishes very widely, including in leading US and UK journals, with over 100 articles, 80 book chapters and other contributions and 20 edited and sole authored books.

Bulk orders: some organisations buy a number of copies of our books. If you are interested in doing this, we would be pleased to discuss a discount. Please contact Hannah Grace-Williams on email info@chandospublishing.com or telephone number +44 (0) 1865 884447.

Textbook adoptions: inspection copies are available to lecturers considering adopting a Chandos Publishing book as a textbook. Please email Hannah Grace-Williams on email info@chandospublishing.com or telephone number +44 (0) 1865 884447.

Globalisation and Work in Asia

EDITED BY
JOHN BURGESS
AND
JULIA CONNELL

Chandos Publishing
Oxford · England

Chandos Publishing (Oxford) Limited
Chandos House
5 & 6 Steadys Lane
Stanton Harcourt
Oxford OX29 5RL
UK
Tel: +44 (0) 1865 884447 Fax: +44 (0) 1865 884448
Email: info@chandospublishing.com
www.chandospublishing.com

First published in Great Britain in 2007

ISBN:
978 1 84334 217 5
1 84334 217 0

© The contributors, 2007

Produced from electronic copy supplied by the editors.
Printed in the UK and USA.

CONTENTS

ABOUT THE AUTHORS

Benedicto Bitonio obtained his B.A. and Law degrees from the University of the Philippines (UP). He also obtained a master's degree in Public Management from the National University of Singapore as a Lee Kuan Yew Fellow, during which time he also took up courses at the Kennedy School of Government, Harvard University. He has written papers on industrial and labor relations and has attended various international conferences, including as representative of the Philippines in the Governing Body of the International Labor Organization, Geneva.

John Burgess is a Professor, School of Business and Management and Director, Employment Studies Centre, Faculty of Business and Law, University of Newcastle, Australia. Research Interests include, non-standard employment, labour market policy, gender and work and an ageing workforce. John's most recently published book is "International Developments in the Call Centre Sector" which he co-edited with Julia Connell.

Sujinda Chemsripong is an Associate Professor in Economics and Associate Dean of the Faculty of Management and Information Sciences, at the Naresuan University in Phitsanulok, Thailand. Sujinda received her PhD from The University of Newcastle, Australia in 2004. Current research interests include: international trade especially in border trade between Thailand and Burma, labour immigration and logistic.

Rosalind Chew teaches Industrial Relations and Economics in the Division of Economics at the Nanyang Technological University in Singapore. She received her graduate training in Economics both in Singapore (Ph. D., NUS) and Canada (M.A and ABD, Western Ontario). She has four books to her credit, and has also published in various journals, including Computational Economics, the International Journal of Manpower, and Review of Pacific Basin Financial Markets and Policies. Awards received include Singapore National Book award. Her research interests include economics of employment, trade unions and industrial relations.

Julia Connell is an Associate Professor, Newcastle Graduate School of Business, University of Newcastle and Assistant Dean (International) for the Faculty of Business and Law. Research interests include change management, organisational effectiveness and various aspects of employment such as temporary work and call centres.

Kunio Hisano is a Professor within the Department of Industrial and Business System, Faculty of Economics at Kyushu University, Japan. Kunio holds a PhD in economics and specializes in industrial technology theory. Kunio's research areas include; the productivity structure of the Japanese capitalism, Micro electronics and Information Communication Technology (ICT) and the political economic system of the Japanese capitalism of 21 centuries.

Akhtar Hossain is a Senior Lecturer in Economics at the University of Newcastle, Australia. Dr Hossain has a B.Sc. (Honours) (1978) and a M.Sc. (1980) in Economics from Jahangirnagar University, Dhaka, Bangladesh. He has also earned M.A. (1984) and PhD (1989) in Economics from the University of Melbourne, and La Trobe University, Australia, respectively. Dr Hossain is widely published and is currently working on macroeconomic and monetary policy issues in Indonesia and Thailand. His research interests in macroeconomic and monetary policy issues in Bangladesh remain unchanged.

Hyunji Kwon is a Ph.D. candidate at the School of Industrial and Labor Relations, Cornell University. Her research interest consists of the changes of employment relations and flexible work arrangements in the service industries including call centers and banking.

Byoung-Hoon Lee is an associate professor in the Department of Sociology at Chung-Ang University, South Korea. He received the Ph.D. and M.S. degrees from the ILR school, Cornell University and the B.A degree from the Seoul National University in South Korea. His dissertation is on shopfloor politics of workplace innovation at auto plants.

Sangheon Lee is a Senior Research Officer with the International Labour Office (ILO) Conditions of Work and Employment Programme. He is specializing in analysing and monitoring changes in the quality of employment. His latest publications include "Working-hour gaps: trends and issues", "Working conditions and satisfaction at work: determinants and interactions in New EU Member States", "Working time capability: towards realizing individual choice" (with Deirdre McCann), and "Seniority as an employment norm: the case of layoffs and promotion in the US employment relationship". Dr. Lee is currently editing a book on *Globalization and Change in Employment Conditions in East Asia and the Pacific* (Chandos and ILO). He holds a PhD in economics from Cambridge University.

Amir Mahmood is the Acting Head of the Newcastle Graduate School of Business (NGSB). He completed his M.A and Ph.D. in economics from the University of Manitoba, Canada. Professor Mahmood's current work focuses on: WTO and trade liberalization issues; value-added productivity at the firm level; export promotion in the ASEAN economies; information technology and small and medium-sized enterprises; and conceptual, theoretical, and empirical issues in the theory of international competitiveness.

Cheng Ming Yu graduated from Universiti Putra Malaysia with a Ph.D. in Economics in 1999. Currently she is the Associate Dean of the Faculty of Management, at Multimedia University, Malaysia. Dr. Cheng is active in research and publication. She has published six books and many articles in international journals and conference proceedings. She is the recipient of an IRPA Research Grant from Ministry of Science, Technology and Innovation, Malaysia.

Pam Nilan is an Associate Professor lecturing in Sociology in the School of Humanities and Social Science at the University of Newcastle, Australia. She has been researching youth, education, gender and school-to-work transitions in the Asia-Pacific region since 1995. As co-editor with Dr Carles Feixa she has published Global Youth? Hybrid Identities, Plural Worlds (Routledge 2006) and is currently writing a book on Australian youth for Pearson, Melbourne. Dr Nilan is a member of a research team which received Australian Research Council funding in 2006 for a four year project on adolescents in Indonesia which will include collecting further data on school-to work transitions.

Bob Russell is an Associate Professor in the Department of Management at Griffith University. Prior to that, he worked for many years in the Department of Sociology at the University of Saskatchewan. His previous publications include 'More With Less': University of Toronto Press, 1999. Bob is currently pursuing research projects on work and employment representation in information industries and the impacts of business process outsourcing to developing countries.

Chew Soon Beng is Professor of Economics and Industrial Relations in the Division of Economics at Nanyang Technological University in Singapore. He received his Ph.D. from the University of Western Ontario, Canada. He is author of several books and he has also published in journals such as the Singapore Economic Review, the China Economic Review, Journal of Advances in Pacific Basin Business Economic and Finance, and International Journal of Human Resource Development and Management. His current research interests include labour market analysis and public policy in Singapore and China.

Mohan Thite has over 20 years of experience as HR professional both in industry and academia. He worked in the Indian manufacturing and service industries for several years before migrating to Australia and continues to research on HRM in India. He currently works as a faculty member in the Department of Management, Griffith University, Brisbane. He is a certified professional of Australian Human Resources Institute (AHRI) and an academic member of Academy of Management. He has published widely (including a recent book on Managing People in the New Economy). His research areas include aligning SHRM with knowledge economy, managing knowledge workers and HRM in Asia.

Prahastiwi Utari has worked as a journalist and as a radio broadcaster in Indonesia. Dr Utari completed her Masters Degree at the University of Indonesia and her Ph.D at the University of Newcastle. Dr Utari is currently a Lecturer in Communication Studies (Radio and Broadcasting) at Sebelas Maret University in Solo, Central Java. Her research interests are in journalism education, and women and media work.

Anne N. Vo is an Associate Lecturer at the University of Wollongong, Australia. After receiving her PhD in HRM from the Montfort Univeristy, United Kingdom in 2004, Dr Vo returned to Vietnam where she worked for a year. Dr Vo researches and publishes in the areas of international and comparative HRM, focusing on Asian countries, the transfer of multinational companies' IR/HRM policies and practices across borders and the transformation of HR systems in developing countries.

Alan Wood obtained his master's in International Policy Analysis at the University of Bath, Bath, U.K. He is a former consultant for the International Labour Organization and has worked with human rights NGOs. His research interests include rights and development, and labour market – poverty linkages with a specialism in the East Asian political economy.

James Xiaohe Zhang is Lecturer in the School of Economics, Politics and Tourism, at the Faculty of Business and Law, the University of Newcastle, specializing in international trade and finance and Asian economic development. He has published more than fifty articles, including twelve journal articles and twelve papers published as book chapters in internationally refereed books. James is a trained economist with a PhD degree obtained from the University of Adelaide in 1993, a Master degree from the Australian National University in 1988 and a Bachelor degree from the Beijing Normal University in 1982.

Chapter 1

GLOBALISATION AND WORK IN ASIA: AN INTRODUCTION

John Burgess and Julia Connell

INTRODUCTION

Currently Asia is one of the most dynamic parts of the globe in terms of its economic growth and social transformation. Recent growth in the world's global economy is being sustained by high growth rates in Asia, especially in China. That said, it is not only rapid economic growth that characterises the region, it is also the major transformation that is taking place within countries. In China, the most populous country of the region, the current rate of industrialisation matches that of 19th century Europe in terms of its impact on the economy and society. In India, the second most populous country in the region, there has been a major inflow of jobs and investment into the business services sector, particularly in call centres (Taylor and Bain, 2006). For the first time ever Asia is benefiting from the restructuring of the global service sector, with many jobs being transferred to India, the Philippines, China and Malaysia as part of the process of business process outsourcing from Europe and North America (Srivastata and Theodore, 2006). Singapore, Hong Kong, Tokyo and Shanghai are becoming key international centres in the global banking and financial services industry and, in the process, they are assuming the status of global cities (Sassen, 2001).

The process of economic growth and transformation is irregular. Indeed the Asian experience is one of heterogeneity and dissimilarity. For example, alongside countries with relatively low levels of GDP per capita (such as Bangladesh, Myinmar, Laos, Cambodia and Vietnam) there are other countries with relatively high living standards such as South Korea, Singapore and Japan. Some countries compete to attract foreign investment (Singapore and Malaysia) while others maintain a relatively closed economy (Myinmar). Concomitantly some countries grapple with the displacement and transfer of surplus labour from agriculture to manufacturing, and from rural to urban regions (Bangladesh and China) whereas others have to accommodate the loss of manufacturing jobs and the rationalisation of their service industries (South Korea and Japan). These changes have led to large flows of labour and capital within the region. For instance, while Singapore and Japan are highly dependent on guest workers to fill labour shortages – in Singapore nearly 30 per cent of the workforce are migrant workers (ILO, 2006a) – India, Pakistan, the Phillipines and Indonesia provide immigrant workers in large numbers across the region and into the Middle East. It is estimated that nearly two thirds of migrant labour in the region is made up of females from the Phillipines, Indonesia and Sri Lanka (ILO, 2006a).

In this volume the focus of discussion is on work and employment in Asia, particularly in consideration of the effects of globalization. The continent known as Asia comprises 49 countries and covers approximately 30 per cent of our planet. This edited volume includes eleven of the 49 countries which were specially selected due to their prominence in the region. While the volume does not include all Asian countries it does incorporate a representative cross section of Asian countries by population size (from China to Singapore), by economic development (from Japan to Bangladesh), by location (from India to Japan), and by ethnicity (monocultural Japan and Korea to multicultural Singapore and India). The book seeks to examine a number of key issues linked to work, employment and labour regulation in the region. Discussion conveys consciousness of the ongoing economic integration that is occurring both within Asia and between Asia and the rest of the world.

Needless to say any discussion of Asian economic development after the 1997 financial crisis has to be cognizant of the debate concerning globalisation. Specifically, how has globalisation impacted on work, job opportunities and patterns of employment exclusion? While globalisation tends to be both stereo-typed and a social construction in the literature (Munck, 2004), as Dicken (1998: 1) suggests 'there is something new and big that is going on out there'. In the overview chapter Lee and Wood point to the rapid growth in intra-Asian trade as one manifestation of globalisation. Other factors resulting from globalisation include a growing external orientation (and a growing share of trade to GDP), increases in foreign direct investment, linked processes of production and distribution (including global production chains) and the sectoral transformation of economies (Debrah and Smith, 2001). What is clear is that although globalisation offers opportunities for wealth and improved living standards, it can also lead to new forms of social and economic exclusion (Sengenberger, 2002). In addition, the benefits from globalisation tend to be unevenly distributed within and between countries (Lee, 1995). There is also an ideology surrounding globalisation that is linked to neoliberal economic policies that promote free trade and encourage deregulation whilst being unsympathetic towards organised labour, labour regulations and social safety nets (Debrah and Smith, 2001). However, as Stiglitz (2003) points out, the East Asian experience of high growth rates over the past three decades has been based on extensive government intervention and regulation of the economy intended to develop community and business infrastructures.

THE KEY QUESTIONS

The chapters included in this volume all adopt a different focus in terms of countries, issues and level of analysis. However, in most analyses of work in Asia (Rowley and Benson, 2000; Debrah and Smith, 2001) there are a number of issues that tend to dominate. These surround new patterns of work, new demands for skills and mobility, new forms of exclusion and inequality, and new challenges for policy makers. In this volume similar issues emerge which resulted from the following key research questions.

1   What are the costs and benefits of globalisation in terms of workforce development and opportunities? Economies are being transformed and becoming more closely integrated into the international and regional economies. Questions concern whether these changes are leading to more jobs, more transitions from unemployment into jobs, increasing real wages and improved working conditions? Or, are there new forms of inequality and exclusion taking place? Within the region it is clear that many countries embrace foreign investment as one manifestation of internationalisation, yet export and trade zones supporting foreign investment can be enclaves that are removed from the rest of the country. In chapter two Lee and Wood consider what this fundamental question means for the region.

2   *How is the workforce changing in terms of where people work (occupation,
industry, location) and what skills they need?* Some chapters in this book consider the
classic sectoral transformation of the occupational and industrial characteristics of the
workforce from agriculture to manufacturing, and the opportunities and tensions
associated with industrial transformation. Also discussed are the massive labour flows
within China from rural to metropolitan areas and similar population shifts that are
occurring in Thailand and Bangladesh.

3   *Does economic growth bring with it an improvement in access to jobs, job
quality and careers, or do the patterns of exclusion and inequality that are present in
the labour market remain?* In tandem with economic transformation a number of
authors consider whether or not there are more opportunities for careers, job security
and quality jobs? Or, does the current industrial transformation require employers to
draw upon the region's plentiful and relatively cheap labour supplies and low skilled
labour power? Several chapters provide an overview of employment transformation,
documenting changes that have occurred in terms of job opportunities, wages and the
sectoral location of labour (see Thailand, Bangladesh, Malaysia and the Phillipines).

4   *Does economic growth generate opportunities for those previously excluded
or segregated – those people living in rural areas, working in the informal sector and
women?* In many Asian countries there are informal labour markets that are outside of
industrial, labour and taxation regulation, where employment conditions are harsh and
incomes are low and irregular. Under these conditions it is important to consider what
opportunities exist for women in the newly emerging sectors? This issue is explored
in the chapters on Malaysia, Bangladesh, the Phillipines and Thailand. The chapter on
Indonesia has a particular focus on women as it examines the situation for skilled
women workers in the communications sector.

5   *What employment opportunities exist in the "new economy" that are linked to
the IT, communications and business services sectors within developing countries?* A
massive shift has occurred in the procurement of business services from the richer
countries and there are major offshore developments taking place in the call centre
and business services sectors, especially with regard to India (Taylor and Bain, 2006;
Srivastata and Theodore, 2006). Questions concern whether the jobs and workplaces

in those developing countries replicate those found in advanced countries. For example, in the call centre sector do strict controls and the monitoring of work lead to high labour turnover as is the case in the more developed countries? The chapter on India considers these issues in the context of the business process sectors.

6   Does growth generate new patterns in intra and inter country labour flows? There are traditional flows of surplus labour that occur within the region, for example, from Indonesia, Thailand and the Philippines to Malaysia and Singapore; from Myinmar and Cambodia to Thailand. Bangladesh and the Philippines have also provided surplus labour to other regions, especially the Middle East. It would be wrong to suggest that labour migration involved unskilled labour, as in some countries, such as Thailand, the emigration of skilled labour is an emerging issue that potentially limits development. Indeed, across many countries there continues to be major labour flows from rural to urban areas (see the chapters on Bangladesh and Thailand). In China, traditional controls over internal labour migration have been relaxed and, as a result, there has been a massive shift of labour to the rapidly growing industrialised cities.

7   Does growth generate new patterns of work and more insecure forms of employment that are associated with new labour use strategies surrounding labour flexibility? Globalisation is often associated with a neoliberal policy regime, and in many OECD economies flexible labour use patterns and numeric, functional and wage flexibility patterns have emerged (Standing, 1999). These flexible labour patterns include part-time work, casual work, at call work, self employment, home work and contracting. In both Japan and South Korea post industrial transformation has been associated with more irregular and insecure employment arrangements such as dispatch work (Goka and Sato, 2004). The overview chapter by Lee and Wood points to the emerging trend of flexibilisation in employment in Asia and the challenges this poses. The chapters on Singapore, South Korea and Japan all point to the development and emergence of non standard, precarious, forms of employment as a response to international competitive pressures. Furthermore, with this process new forms of exclusion and marginalisation are also emerging.

8   Are unions under pressure as in many Western countries due to structural changes occurring in the workforce and neoliberal policy regimes that are hostile to organised labour? (Verma and Kochan, 2004).   The chapters on South Korea, Bangladesh, Japan and the Phillipines consider the pressures and challenges facing unions in those countries.

9   What is happening to the regulatory regimes governing employment in the face of such apparent extensive structural change? Are they accommodating or obstructive and immovable? Are governments creating neo liberal environments that facilitate foreign investment but removing workers' rights and eroding safety nets? Or, is the process of economic development bringing about an improvement in labour conditions and labour standards? The issues surrounding the challenges to labour regulation in the context of rapid economic transformation, together with issues concerning workers' forms of exclusion and marginalization, are considered in the chapters on Malaysia, Bangladesh, the Phillipines and Thailand.

10   Are new forms of management practice and workplace organisation being implemented through foreign investment? Are workplaces in Asia becoming modernised and do the employment and management practices being utilized in them match those found in the source countries of foreign investment? These issues are considered in the chapter on Vietnam.

11.   What has been the impact of Asia's transformation and modernisation on the rest of the world? The rapid economic growth experienced by China has resulted in increasing demand for commodities, consumer goods and capital from the rest of the world. In turn, the expansion in Chinese exports is having a displacement effect on employment elsewhere. As a result, the chapter on China considers both the regional and international impact of Chinese growth on the rest of the world.

STRUCTURE OF THE BOOK

The book chapters are organised into five sections. In the first section, encompassing the chapter by Lee and Wood, an overview is presented of the developments in work and employment in the Asian region, together with an evaluation of the policy challenges that exist. The second section includes chapters on China and India. As they are the two most populous countries in Asia, their development and transformation will impact on both the region and the rest of the world. The third section of the book incorporates chapters that provide overviews of labour market and labour policy developments for the respective countries that are examined. These include chapters on Bangladesh, Thailand, the Phillipines and Malaysia. The fourth section examines specific sectoral issues that can be regarded as case studies. For example, the chapter on Indonesia examines the experience of women professional workers in the communications sector, while the chapter focusing on Vietnam examines the HR programs and practices with regard to Japanese and US multinationals that have located in Vietnam. Finally, the fifth section points to the emergence of non standard employment arrangements in those countries with the highest average living standards – Singapore, Japan and South Korea. The details of each chapter are as follows.

CHAPTER DETAILS

Chapter 2, by Lee and Wood from the ILO focuses on the dual factors of globalization and flexibilization and how these factors have influenced employment in Asia. The term globalization refers to economic integration through trade and foreign direct investment (FDI), while flexibilization refers to the labour market policy changes that have frequently occurred through coping with globalization. The authors point out that each element of employment conditions is not independent, but dependent, and as a result, employment conditions need to be understood as a *package*. For example, a recurring theme in this edited volume (particularly in the last three chapters that focus on various aspects of contingent work) is that there is a trend towards the informalization of employment in Asia which, in turn, is accompanied by inferior employment conditions. For instance, temporary employment is not simply about employment security (that is the length of a contract) but also tends to involve lower wages/fringe benefits, long working hours and high exposure to safety risks. Thus, the flexibilization of employment contracts implies a package of employment conditions that are quite different to traditional conditions. This means that when employment conditions are analyzed, the focus should be placed on how different elements of employment conditions are packaged for individual workers and what kinds of variations exist among different groups of workers (with regard to gender, age and so on). It is analysis such as this that will provide a better understanding of the way in which certain workers are marginalized while indicating the ways in which their conditions could be improved.

China is the focus of Chapter 3 by Zhang who points out that the reform and opening up of the Chinese economy has been accompanied by a process of globalization in the rest of the world. Indeed, these two forces have reinforced each other over the last three decades. Specifically, increasing exports have attracted more FDI inflows into the country exploiting the comparative advantage of China's labour force and the competitiveness of exports. As China possesses the world's largest labour force, comprising over 700 million workers, this means that any change in its labour market will affect the production, trade and employment patterns of many other countries throughout the world. For example, Zhang maintains that although labourers in the naturally resource abundant countries - such as Australia and New Zealand - will be more likely to benefit from the rapid economic growth and export boom in China, labourers in other countries, particularly those that are labour abundant in Asia, are more likely to be hurt. This, he states, is due to tougher international labour market competition and the processes of globalization, when goods produced by labour intensive countries are replaced in international markets by Chinese exports.

In Chapter 4 the topic of business process outsourcing (BPO) in India is explored by Thite and Russell. Four of India's largest BPO providers participated in the study. Here, the authors examine a sector which is heavily implicated in the current phase of globalisation - referred to as the IT/ITeS/BPO sector (information technology, information technology enabled services and business process outsourcing industries). The authors uphold that, at present, investment in this sector is powering the Indian economy. As a result, the knowledge and information based industries have very quickly attained prominence in the Indian economy. Most of the chapter concentrates on analysing emergent employment relations in the IT/ITeS/BPO sector. The authors argue that, despite the spectacular growth and visibility of the IT/ITES sector, it is still largely irrelevant to the vast majority of Indians. This means that while the Indian economy is moving ahead it is not yet known whether these changes will bring the societal standards that may be expected in the 21st century or new forms of economic dependence.

Chapter 5 by Hossain provides an overview of labour market developments that have occurred in Bangladesh since the mid-1980s – the period that the economy was deregulated and opened up for foreign trade and investment. Since that time the economy has been growing steadily at the rate of about 5 percent per annum. Foreign capital flows in the forms of overseas workers' remittances, foreign aid and loans, and foreign investment have all contributed to economic growth and caused a structural transformation of the economy in favour of the non-farm and service sectors. Consequently, labour markets have undergone some structural change in terms of employment and work patterns including a rise in the participation rate of women and changes in productivity and wage differentials across sectors. Lately, some of the global labour, trade and environmental issues, such as child labour, gender discrimination, trade union rights and unemployment have gained prominence in policy debates at both national and international levels. These issues are examined in this chapter with the author concluding that the imminent challenge for Bangladesh is to sustain a market-oriented, outward-looking development strategy where enough productive employment can be generated in the private sector that will absorb the growing labour force.

Chapter 6 by Ernesto identifies some of the major developments that have affected the labor market in the Philippines over the last two decades. The chapter takes a macro perspective of these developments, identifying the major issues that are seen to confront work and employment relations now and in the years ahead. Given the characteristics of the Philippine labor market and the economy over the last two decades, employment generation, maximizing the potential of the current labor force, and improving the quality of employment are proposed as the main challenges for the country. From a macro level, a basic problem is that the labor force is growing faster than the economy can generate jobs. Hence, there is a need to address the rapid population growth otherwise this will lead to chronic labor surpluses and the provision of limited access to quality education, training and other social services over time. This limited access will, in turn, weaken the country's transformative and absorptive capacity and slow down its push towards a modern economy. Accordingly, Ernesto contends that it is vital to improve labor productivity concluding that the role of the State will be important in terms of influencing the type of policy decisions that are taken. Such decisions will assist in shaping the pace, depth and extensiveness of change in the country's workplaces, as well as providing the opportunities that change will create for the Philippine economy.

Chapter 7 by Mahmood and Cheng evaluates the impact of the increasing globalization of the Malaysian economy on industrial reorientation and the resulting labour market outcomes. Over the past two decades, there has been a noticeable transformation of the Malaysian economy. Rapid and sustained economic growth has been accompanied by: falling poverty, falling unemployment, improved human development and low inflation. Specifically, an integration of the Malaysian economy with the rest of the world through inward Foreign Direct Investment (FDI) and trade has played a key role in transforming Malaysia from a resource-based economy to one that participates in high-skilled and technology-intensive sectors in the global markets. Recently however, the surge in Free Trade Agreements, regional economic integration, China's accession to the WTO, competitive trade and investment policies by regional competitors and the Doha Round of multilateral trade negotiations have all posed new challenges for Malaysia. The authors conclude that, in order for Malaysia to achieve its vision to become a developed country by the year 2020, it is imperative that an institutional environment is generated that provides optimum labour market outcomes for the country.

In Chapter 8 Thailand is in the spotlight where Chemsripong evaluates changes in the labour market that are linked to globalization, the labour market impact of recent internal and external crises in Thailand are examined and policy implications for the labour market are reviewed. Some of the factors affecting the Thai labour market have also occurred in other countries in Asia and beyond. For example, skill shortages, the ageing phenomena, changes from agricultural to non- agricultural work alongside the growth in the manufacturing and services sectors. Also in common with some Asian countries in sectors such as construction and housekeeping there has been an increase in casual in many cases constitutes both dirty and dangerous work. Despite the conditions of this type of casual work it has still attracted migrants to Thailand. To deal with these influxes of labour, the author argues that the Thai government needs to limit the registration of immigrant labour or set higher qualification standards for those who want to apply for work permits. Further, she maintains that if the labor situation in Thailand and globalisation continue on their current trajectories, and the government does not increase its policy to assist in filling labour gaps, it is predicted that the movement of a temporary and skilled labour force that is linked to investment activity will be higher than before.

Chapter 9 by Vo reports on the interaction between 'country-of-origin' and 'country-of-operation' effects in determining human resource management (HRM) policies and practices in multinationals (MNCs). The chapter is based on an empirical study whereby the focus concerns eight case studies comprising US and Japanese MNCs which are operating in Vietnam in the automotive and fast moving consumer goods (FMCG) industries. Based on an investigation of the reward systems and performance management of these companies the research confirms that the globalisation process does not simply sustain a single and homogenous pattern of firm behaviour. Moreover, it was found that greater economic efficiency in work systems within a country does not automatically lead to the dispersal of best practices to other countries. Vo explains that, in the cases studied, there were circumstances under which transfer was not attempted into the Vietnamese subsidiaries and other cases where it was transferred quite effectively depending on a number of factors which are explored in the chapter.

In Chapter 10 Nilan and Utari report on the situation for female workers in the media and communications industries in Indonesia. Currently in a period of slow growth, Indonesia has been one of the last countries in the region to begin recovering from the 1997 Asian currency crisis. That said, the ICT (Information and Communication Technology) sector is growing rapidly, having a direct effect on media and communications workplaces. Although women graduate from communications degrees in Indonesia in much larger numbers than men, they constitute only a small minority of media workers. Hence, the authors set out to discover why that might be by undertaking surveys and interviews with female communication studies undergraduates, their parents and lecturers in addition to media employees and managers. The findings supported the authors supposition that, due to gender-biased deficiencies in their professional ICT training, and the negative effects of traditional gender stereotyping in Indonesia, female media and communications workers were not empowered as workers and that, prior to even entering the workplace, the extremely scarce ICT resources in university departments were implicitly utilised for the training of male students. This was even though males constitute the minority of degree enrolments. Consequently, the authors conclude that, when global work trends such as the incorporation of advanced ICTs engage with resilient local discourses such as gender stereotypes, this may result in an increase rather than a decrease in existing labour force inequities.

Chapter 11 begins the first of three in this edited volume that focus on contingent work. The most advanced economies of the region are exhibiting a polarisation of employment arrangements and the development of contingent employment arrangements that can be found in many advanced economies (Felstead and Jewson, 1999). In Chapter 11 by Lee and Kwon they delineate the growing trends and employment conditions of the non-regular workforce in Korea. In addition to presenting overview statistics of the situation in Korea, the authors also present two industrial cases on the banking and automotive sectors which serve to illustrate the key issues. Compared to other industrialized economies, the growth of non-regular employment in Korea has been remarkable, particularly under the context of the 1997 economic crisis. For example, the share of non-regular workers in the waged labor population of the country exceeded that of regular (permanent and full-time) employees from 1999 onwards. In common with many other countries, the employment conditions of the former work group are quite inferior in comparison with the latter. Therefore, the authors call for the Korean government to protect non-regular workers and constrain employers' excessive use of non-regular labor, thereby limiting a situation which is currently damaging social integration in Korea to a large extent.

Chapter 12 by Hisano examines the changes that have occurred in the Japanese economy over the past two decades and the impact that these changes have had on the employment and occupational structure of the workforce. Changes include the rapid adoption and diffusion of microelectronic technologies in the machinery sector during the 1980s; and the appreciation of the yen. The technology revolution brought about a deskilling of the workforce in Japan and weakened the strength of trade unions. The appreciation of the yen, while it served to progress globalisation in Japan, resulted in the decline of labour-intensive industries and a weakening of worker's bargaining power. Currently, employment conditions in Japan are fragmenting with the growth of non-standard employees. This has meant an erosion of the employment practices which were once synonymous with employment in Japan – that is long-term employment, seniority based wage payments and enterprise unions. At present the Japanese enterprise unions intend to try and organise contingent employees into unions in a bid to improve overall working conditions for them. The author concludes that it remains to be seen just how successful such a move will prove to be.

Finally, Chapter 13 by Rosalind Chew and Chew Soon Beng analyzes the emergence of non-traditional employment in Singapore, a society that is characterized by a social safety net that is based on employment. Here, non-traditional employment is represented by part-time workers, employers, own account workers, family contributing workers and contingent workers. The chapter begins with an overview of the Singapore economy before discussing the extent to which firms can adopt various non-traditional employment methods instead of resorting to outsourcing and the use of foreign workers. The authors note the increasing trend for firms to employ part-time and contingent workers in Singapore because of increasing labour costs – including healthcare costs – and also because of the increasing intensity of competition due to globalization. Rosalind Chew and Chew Soon Beng also maintain that increases in healthcare cost will also discourage firms from employing part-time workers. In order to explore these issues they undertake statistical analysis based on data from the manufacturing and services sectors in Singapore.

CONCLUSION

Despite significant improvements in living standards and reductions in poverty the ILO (2006b) highlights an ongoing decent work deficit in Asia. The ILO points to falling real wages (in the Indian manufacturing sector); very long working hours (in Malaysia, South Korea and Bangladesh); an entrenched gender wage gap in Singapore, Malaysia, South Korea and Japan; and a high workplace fatality record across the Asian region (estimated at over 1m. per year). Hence, there remain challenges in Asia not only in terms of job generation, but also with regard to improvements in the quality of jobs and in community infrastructure to support living standards (Stiglitz, 2003).

In general, the book points to uneven economic development and transformation within the region, major changes in employment, the emergence of new job opportunities, massive labour migration and ongoing labour market challenges in the advanced economies of the region. Asia encompasses the traditional informal rural and urban labour markets that are found in Thailand, China, the Philippines, Bangladesh and Vietnam; the high tech robotic manufacturing sectors of Japan and South Korea; the high skill based information technology sectors of Singapore, Japan, Malaysia and South Korea; and the emerging business services sectors in India and China. Nevertheless, there are recurring issues that all of these countries have to address. These include: achieving reductions in extreme poverty; the emergence of significant inequalities associated with uneven economic development; the provision of access and opportunities for all to participate in the process of economic development; the need to modernise labour regulations to accommodate a globalised environment and a different economic structure; meeting core labour standards; and meeting new contours of exclusion and marginalisation.

Several authors have suggested changes in policies and strategies that may assist in meeting the challenges discussed here. However, as Lee and Wood point out in their chapter, analysis needs to take into account the context in which different policy measures are introduced as, to date, there have been a broad array of policy measures which frequently take different directions and have varying implications for workers. Moreover, Lee and Wood advocate the need for an examination into whether changes have addressed labour market failures and/or reflected the specific concerns and needs of workers. Clearly, the impact of these policies on individual workers (both targeted groups and those indirectly affected) need to be evaluated overall before any further action can be taken.

REFERENCES

Debrah, Y. and Smith, I. (2001), *Work and Employment in a Globalized Era: An Asia Pacific Focus*. Frank Cass, London. 1-20

Dicken, P. (1998), *Global Shift*. 3rd edition. Paul Chapman Publishing, London.

Felstead, A. & Jewson, N. (Eds), *Global Trends in Flexible Labour*, Macmillan: London

Goka, K. and Sato, A. (2004), 'Agency Temporary Work and Government Policy in Contemporary Japan', in J. Burgess and J. Connell (eds), *International Perspectives on Temporary Agency Work*. Routledge, London, 112- 28.

International Labour Office (ILO, 2006a), *Workers on the Move in Asia*. Press Release, August 24th.

International Labour Office (ILO, 2006b*), Asia Pacific Region Faces a Massive Job Gap*. Press Release, August 28th.

Lee, E. (1995), 'Globalisation and Employment: Is the Anxiety Justified?' *International Labour Review*. 135, 5, 485-497.

Munck, R. (2004), 'Introduction: Globalisation and Labour Transnationalism', in R. Munck (ed*), Labour and Globalisation: Results and Prospects*. Liverpool University Press, Liverpool.

Rowley, C. and Benson, J. (2000), 'Global Labour? Issues and Themes', in C. Rowley and J. Benson (eds) *Globalisation and Labour in the Asia Pacific Region*. Frank Cass, London, 1-15.

Sassen, S. (2001), *The Global City: New York, London and Tokyo*. Princeton University Press, Princeton.

Sengenberger, W. (2002), *Globalisation and Social Progress: The Role and Impact of International Labour Standards*. Friedrich Eberet Stiftung, Bonn.

Srivastata, S. and Theodore, N. (2006), 'Offshoring Call Centres: the View from Wall Street', in J, Burgess and J. Connell (eds), *Developments in the Call Centre Industry*. Routledge, London, 19-35.

Standing, G. (1999), *Global Labour Flexibility*. Macmillan, Basingstoke.

Stiglitz, J. (2003), 'Towards a New Paradigm of Development', in J. Dunning (ed), *Making Globalisation Good*. Oxford University Press, Oxford, 76-107.

Taylor, P. and Bain, P. (2006), 'Work Organisation and Employee Relations in Indian Call Centres', in J, Burgess and J. Connell (eds) *Developments in the Call Centre Industry*. Routledge, London, 36-57.

Verma, A. and Kochan, T. (2004), *Unions in the Twenty First Century*. Palgrave Macmillan, Basingstoke.

Chapter 2

CHANGING PATTERNS IN THE WORLD OF WORK IN ASIA:
AN OVERVIEW

Sangheon Lee and Alan Wood

INTRODUCTION

Globalization and flexibilization are probably the two most significant contributing factors which have changed the way many workers are working in Asia. Obviously these two phenomena are often closely interlinked, but conceptually they are different. In this chapter, globalization refers to further economic integration, notably through trade and foreign direct investment (FDI), while flexibilization is intended to capture the overall direction of labour market policy changes, often in coping with globalization.

The effects of these two phenomena have been subject to intense debates, but insofar as developing countries (and even some industrialized countries) are concerned, they tend to be limited to macro developments such as GDP growth, employment rates and average wages. Yet the extent to which these macro pictures can explain the changes *individual* workers have experienced in their workplace is not clear. This issue is increasingly important, as both globalization and flexibilization mean diverging (not similar) impacts on individual workers such that the analysis based on *national average* changes are insufficient and, in some cases, even misleading.

As is well known, views on the effects of globalization are divided. Optimistic views often come from economists who predict that increased trade based on comparative advantages will benefit the countries involved. Such optimism is in contrast with the negative public view echoed in public opinion surveys and anti-globalization campaigns. These conflicting views appear to be related to the fact that people experience and evaluate globalization in more concrete terms, through changes in their work and employment. It is important to stress the common (but often forgotten) wisdom that 'people see the world through the optic of their workplace' (ILO, 2004a: 64). This means that the globalization debates need to go beyond net employment volume (job destruction and creation) to address changes in employment conditions such as wages, employment status, working time, and work organization.

Some interesting studies on employment conditions in the context of globalization and flexibilization have been undertaken for Latin American countries, which tend to be preoccupied with the need for flexibilization in the region (see Edwards and Lustig eds., 1997; Heckman and Pagés eds., 2004). However, similar studies are particularly lacking for Asia and the Pacific, although this region has often been praised for it successful integration in the world market (Krumm and Kharas, 2004). At the same time, the risk relating to globalization has been dramatically revealed by a sequence of financial crises in this region in 1997. It is also noteworthy that the region has been witnessing the increasing popularity of the pessimistic view that 'the Asian crisis has transformed the region's perspective of globalization from a 'tide that lifts all boats' into a 'tsunami', increasing poverty and misery' (ILO, 2004b: 25).

Against this background, this chapter is intended to provide an overview of changes in employment conditions in Asia. As this region covers a great number of countries with different social economic experiences, this chapter concentrates on those countries where the changes appear to be considerable and even dramatic. The focus will be placed on two transition economies (China and Viet Nam), four South Tigers (Indonesia, Malaysia, Philippines, and Thailand) and industrialized countries in the region (Japan and Korea). The rest of the chapter is structured as follows: first, international debates and evidence on the effects of globalization and flexibilization will be briefly reviewed. This chapter will then discuss the developments in economic integration in the region and link them to the overall employment performance. After examining labour market policies since the economic crisis in 1997, key aspects of employment conditions will be investigated. This chapter will conclude with a brief summary and future research issues.

GLOBALIZATION, FLEXIBILIZATION, AND THE LABOUR MARKET

Globalization and Employment: Unfulfilled Promise?

There appears to be a widely recognized view that globalization 'induces' economic growth and its overall gains are larger than its costs. However, the empirical evidence is not clear and is in fact rather thin. A recent review concludes that 'the attempts of a long literature looking at cross-country evidence have failed to provide a convincing answer' on the effect of trade on economic growth. Methodological problems remain unresolved, and the mechanism whereby economic openness is translated into economic growth is yet to be clarified (Hallak and Levinsohn, 2004; see also Winter, 2004). Despite this, the size of these effects is often exaggerated in debates (Freeman, 2003).

Not surprisingly, evidence on the effects of globalization on workers in terms of employment volume, wages, income inequality and poverty is inconclusive and often conflicting (for a recent overview, see Gunter and van der Hoeven, 2004; Rama, 2003a). For example, does globalization create more employment than it destroys? Does job creation exceed job destruction? A positive answer is conceivable if we can safely assume a positive correlation between globalization and economic growth. As mentioned, this assumption is hard to justify. In addition, theoretical models do not help either, as most economic models assume full employment and are only able to predict how the given volume of labour supply will be reallocated to correspond to trade adjustments (see Davidson and Matusz, 2004). Thus, the employment effects of globalization are largely empirical questions and, indeed, empirical evidence varies (Freeman, 2003; Klein, Schuh & Triest 2003; Rama, 2003a).

The reallocation of employment in the process of economic integration implies changes in wages. While again the evidence is still inconclusive, the repeated finding is that skilled workers (or those with high educational attainments) are more likely to benefit from economic openness, while unskilled and older workers (and the less educated) are less likely to benefit from it (Arbache, Dickerson & Green 2004; Rama, 2003b). Some other studies indicate that in developing countries the wage effects of openness could be negative in the short-term but gradually become positive, presumably through economic growth (Majid 2004). This study also notes that there is no guarantee that such long-term positive effects will benefit all workers.

To the extent that employment adjustments are associated with different wage outcomes for individual workers, wage/income inequality has attracted much interest and concern. In fact, there appears to be genuine public concern about income inequality, which is reflected in numerous surveys (see Luebker, 2004). Two sets of indicators have been developed to analyze developments in income inequality: global and national Gini coefficients. As for global Gini coefficients, which appear to reflect the idea of a 'global citizen' in a globalized world, both negative and positive developments have been reported depending on data sources and methods of income conversion (see Aisbett, 2005: Table 2). In the case of national Gini coefficients, an increasing wage equality trend is found for many industrialized and developing countries. It is noteworthy here that good news in income inequality often comes from the Asian region (Dollar and Kraay, 2004).

Wages are just one important element of employment conditions, and in the process of globalization, the adjustment of employment tends to involve changes in other aspects of employment conditions as well. For example, a study on the impact of trade reform in Morocco shows that some affected firms increased employment mostly by hiring low-paid temporary workers (Currie and Harrison, 1997). While this implies potential links between trade liberalization and job/employment status, it is plausible that such links can be applied to other aspects of employment conditions such as working time, work organization, work intensity and health and safety (see Vaughan-Whitehead, 2005). By examining this link, we can recognize more explicitly the adjustment costs that individual workers have to bear in the process of economic change.

Labour Market Institutions: Obstacles to Employment?

The investigation of changes in employment conditions inevitably requires examining labour market institutions for at least two reasons. First, in the light of the existing evidence concerning the differing effects of globalization in different countries, it should be noted that this is, to a varying degree, related to considerable variations in labour market institutions, which filter 'external' shocks such as trade liberalization. Secondly, these institutions have undergone a series of changes in many countries, which can be characterized as 'flexibilization'.

There is a growing recognition of the positive (or at the very least, neutral) role of the ILO core labour standards such as freedom of association which is increasingly being recognized (Kucera, 2002: World Bank, 2004). Yet, when it comes to institutions that determine substantive aspects of employment, many economic studies concentrate on their 'rigidity' in developing countries, even identifying it as the main obstacle to economic growth. In doing so, the arguments made about industrialized countries such as those in the OECD are increasingly being applied to developing countries (see Heckman and Pagés, 2004; World Bank, 2004). The upshot of these debates is the conflicts between insiders and outsiders: insiders develop policies and institutions in their favor and at the expense of outsiders. With employment guarantees, for example, insiders can demand higher wages without considering their effects on the other part of the labour market, thereby creating involuntary unemployment. In other words, labour market institutions are 'captured' by insiders.

It is indeed tempting to apply such conflicts among workers to developing countries, as the major outsider group is easily recognizable in the informal sector. It also implies a scene change in labour market research for developing countries. For example, a recent World Bank report argues that '[I]t has been common to portray the tension as primarily between the interests of firms and workers. But this ignores the broader range of interests involved. Workers in the informal economy and the unemployed can have very different interests from those currently employed in the formal economy.' (World Bank, 2004: 141) From this perspective, it is suggested that 'strict regulations in developed countries, where compliance is high, tend to promote job stability for prime-age males but reduce job opportunities and lengthen unemployment spells for youths, women lacking work experience, and those with low skills' (World Bank 2004: 149). Heckman and Pagés (2004) argue that this finding holds for developing countries such as Latin America.

This approach can be questioned in two ways, among others: First, studies of labour market institutions, particularly those that focus on their negative impacts, often fail to recognize why they came to exist in the first place. With regard to employment protection, for instance, Pissarides (2001: 133) rightly pointed out that 'the analysis of employment protection has been mostly conducted within a framework that does not justify its existence'. In short, the perspective that labour market institutions have developed in response to market failures (not just the result of insiders' rent-seeking) is often lacking.[i] Indeed, employment protection can be 'the insurance of workers against income risk' in the imperfect labour market where workers are exposed to various income risks without any effective safeguard (Pissarides, 2001; see also Agell, 1999). If, as is widely agreed, globalization tends to increase workers' vulnerability to income risks, this implies that there is an increasing need for employment protection and more generally 'solid' labour market institutions (Agell 1999 and 2002).

Table 1. World Bank Employment Rigidity Index

Region/economy	Difficulty of Hiring Index	Rigidity of Hours Index	Difficulty of Firing Index	Rigidity of Employment Index	Firing Costs (weeks)
East Asia & Pacific	20	30	22	24	52
Europe & Central Asia	31	51	42	41	38
Latin America & Caribbean	44	53	34	44	70
Middle East & North Africa	22	52	40	38	74
OECD: High income	26	50	26	34	40
South Asia	37	36	53	42	84
Sub-Saharan Africa	53	64	50	56	59
Australia	0	40	10	17	17
China	11	40	40	30	90
Indonesia	61	40	70	57	157
Japan	33	40	0	24	21
Korea, Rep.	11	60	30	34	90
Malaysia	0	0	10	3	74
New Zealand	11	0	10	7	0
Philippines	22	60	40	41	90
Thailand	67	40	20	42	47
Vietnam	44	40	70	51	98

Source: World Bank database

Second, if labour market institutions are associated with different labour market performances across countries, how can labour market institutions be measured and compared? In this regard, it is interesting to see that the World Bank proposed the rigidity of employment index, which is derived from a simple average of three indexes concerning difficulty of hiring, rigidity of hours and difficulty of firing, each obtained by coding relevant legal provisions (World Bank 2004). The key results concerning East Asia and the Pacific are presented in Table 1.

It is clear from this table that developing countries tend to have relatively rigid employment regulation compared to industrialized countries (OECD countries): Sub-Saharan Africa, the poorest region, has the most rigid employment regulations, while East Asia and the Pacific provides the most flexible employment system. If the focus is narrowed down to East Asia and the Pacific, the pattern remains the same: the indexes are negatively correlated with national incomes.

However, the way these indexes are constructed is problematic. For example, the Rigidity of Hours index is derived from five components: (i) whether night work is restricted; (ii) whether weekend work is allowed; (iii) whether the working week consists of five-and-a-half days or more; (iv) whether the workday can extend to 12 hours or more (including overtime); and (v) whether the annual paid vacation days are 21 days or less. If the answer is no to any of these questions, the country is assigned a score of 1, otherwise a score of 0 is assigned. From the outset, it should be noted that it is highly controversial whether these five components are criterion for 'rigidity' or for 'decency', especially given the fact that all of them, except the third component, have relevant international labour standards (see Lee and McCann, forthcoming). A similar problem is found in the 'difficulty of hiring' index which basically assumes that a labour market which discriminates against part-time employment and offers unconditional use of temporary employment as 'ideal'.

It should also be noted that the legal framework, unless carefully analyzed, could prove misleading for an evaluation of the 'rigidity' of the labour market. The degree of enforcement is important in this regard. To show that the 'rigid' regulation of employment conditions is responsible for creating informal employment, the enforcement of such regulation in the formal sector should be assured, which makes it necessary to analyze *actual* employment conditions. In other words, the question is whether or not the (legal) regulation of employment conditions, which is easily observable, can be a good indicator for the actual situation of workers in the formal sector (see Lee and McCann, 2006). As is well known, this may not be the case in developing countries. Yet, empirical evidence is so scant that it is almost impossible to reach any tentative conclusion.

REGIONAL ECONOMIC INTEGRATION AND LABOUR MARKET OUTCOMES IN ASIA

Greater Economic Integration Without a 'Social Dimension'?

Before looking at the labour market situation in the region, it would be useful to review very briefly the progress made in economic integration. Due to its increasing share of international trade, the economic position of East Asia and the Pacific has greatly improved. In particular, economic integration in the region is also under way. Of course, the Association of Southeast Asian Nations (ASEAN) was initiated in 1992 to bring national economies closer through establishing a free trade zone (the ASEAN Free Trade Area), but such regional cooperation gained momentum as China, Japan and Korea joined free-trade discussions with ASEAN countries (ASEAN plus three). In addition, another powerful economic bloc – of Australia and New Zealand – also joined the bandwagon of free trade. Such a move towards greater economic integration is, to a large extent, attributed to the recognition of its economic benefits, especially in the context of remarkable economic growth in China.

The extent of economic integration can be gauged by the increasing share of intra-regional trade. As Table 2 shows, Asian countries account for an increasing share of imports, and in 2003 in most of the East Asian countries more than half of total imports came from their Asian neighbors. The importance of Asian countries in exports is mixed, due to the heavy exports to North American and European countries. Yet, a lion's share of exports is directed to the same region.

This process was accompanied by the experience of financial crisis which hit the region very severely in 1997. Some countries, such as Korea, recovered rather quickly but some other countries such as Thailand and Indonesia have yet to fully recover. The financial crisis was a painful reminder that national economies in the region were already closely linked and a regional mechanism should be in place to mitigate financial contagion and to ensure a reasonable level of exchange-rate stability. Very recently, significant progress was made in the Chiang Mai initiative of 2000 (Krumm and Kharas eds., 2004), which generated swap agreements between national central banks to handle short-term liquidity shortfalls.

Table 2. Trade Integration in Asia (2004)

	Total trade (% of GNP)		% of imports from Asia		% of exports to Asia	
	1990	2003	1990	2003	1990	2003
China, People's Rep. of	29.7	60.6	52.7	56.4	68.8	47.3
Korea, Rep. of	53.4	61.5	35.2	50.7	35.4	51.2
Indonesia	43.5	…	49.6	60.3	67.7	59.8
Malaysia	139.2	194.0	56.2	69.3	59.8	58.5
Philippines	48.2	85.4	46.3	60.2	37.5	59.4
Thailand	66.5	110.9	58.4	59.9	39.2	54.7
Viet Nam	79.7	116.3	35.5	76.3	40.3	38.6

Sources: ADB Key Indicators 2004

Such efforts towards regional economic integration are not unique to East Asia and the Pacific, although their potential importance on the global economy may be greater than those of other regional integrations due to the sheer economic size of East Asia and the Pacific. What distinguishes this region, however, is that integration has been driven largely by economic factors without paying much consideration to the social aspects of economic integration. The lack of regional initiatives in the social dimensions of economic integration contrasts dramatically with other regional integrations, most obviously the EU (Vaughan-Whitehead, 2005)

Changes in Employment Volume: Meeting Expectations?

With the advances in economic integration in the region, it has been widely believed that it would boost employment, particularly for the unemployed and the underemployed (Krumm and Kharas, 2004). One way of evaluating this is to look at the changes that have occurred in open unemployment in the region, although it is rather well known that unemployment data in developing countries are often unreliable (Kucera and Chataigner, 2005), particularly due to the presence of massive underemployment (see below). With these caveats, Table 3 presents the trends in employment rates in the region. One notable point is that, thanks to a high level of female employment, two transition economies (China and Viet Nam) tend to have high employment rates (70 per cent or over) while the figure is typically less than 60 per cent in other countries, except for Thailand. Second, developing countries have witnessed a decreasing trend in employment rates, partly reflecting the fact that they have yet to recover from the financial crisis of 1997-8. However, this trend should not necessarily be seen as a problem, as it is partly because more young people are at school and not in the workforce. Finally, with regard to the effects of the financial crisis, the impact is mixed, with longer term adjustment problems being experienced

Table 3. Employment rates (1990-2003)

		1990	1991	1992	1993	1994	1995	1996	1997	1998	1999	2000	2001	2002	2003	avg 99-03
China	All	77.9	77.7	77.5	77.7	77.3	76.8	76.9	76.9	76.9	76.8	76.6	76.4	76.0	...	76.4
	Male	...	...	...	...	...	...	...	...	...	...	...	...	...	...	...
	Female	...	...	...	...	...	...	...	...	...	...	...	...	...	...	...
Korea	All	56.9	57.8	57.9	57.8	58.5	59.1	59.4	59.5	55.6	55.7	57.4	58.0	59.0	58.4	57.7
	Male	67.7	69.2	69.5	69.5	70.2	70.8	70.9	70.5	66.7	66.3	67.7	68.1	69.4	69.2	68.1
	Female	46.1	46.5	46.4	46.2	47.0	47.5	48.1	48.7	44.7	45.3	47.2	48.0	48.8	47.7	47.4
Indonesia	All	66.5	65.4	65.3	64.6	63.8	63.8	65.2	63.6	63.9	63.4	62.7	62.3	61.7	...	62.5
	Male	81.7	81.2	79.9	79.8	80.4	80.7	81.1	80.9	79.0	79.1	...	...	79.7	...	79.4
	Female	51.4	49.8	50.7	49.5	45.1	49.2	49.6	49.0	48.9	47.9	...	...	44.1	...	46.0
Malaysia	All	57.8	...	57.8	59.0	...	57.9	61.7	61.1	59.5	59.3	60.7	59.5	59.2	59.8	59.7
	Male	74.0	...	74.1	77.0	...	76.1	80.5	80.2	78.6	78.1	78.8	76.6	75.9	76.3	77.1
	Female	41.4	...	41.2	40.7	...	39.5	42.7	41.9	40.1	40.3	42.4	42.2	42.4	43.2	42.1
Philippines	All	62.4	61.9	62.7	62.4	62.5	62.1	64.4	63.5	62.5	59.6	57.9	61.1	...	...	59.5
	Male	79.6	79.1	79.6	79.1	79.5	78.4	81.3	79.6	78.2	73.6	72.0	74.4	...	...	73.4
	Female	45.3	44.9	45.9	45.7	45.5	45.9	47.5	47.6	46.9	45.6	43.8	47.7	...	...	45.7
Thailand	All	81.4	80.6	82.2	80.0	78.3	77.9	75.6	76.3	72.5	71.0	71.5	71.8	72.6	72.6	71.9
	Male	88.2	88.5	90.1	88.2	86.0	86.4	84.8	85.2	81.6	80.5	81.0	81.5	82.3	82.2	81.5
	Female	74.9	72.9	74.5	72.0	70.8	69.6	66.7	67.8	63.8	62.0	62.6	62.6	63.4	63.5	62.8
Vietnam	All	...	...	...	...	...	...	74.9	73.4	74.3	74.6	73.2	72.8	73.1	73.2	73.4
	Male	...	...	...	...	...	...	74.9	74.3	75.7	76.7	76.0	75.8	76.2	76.5	76.2
	Female	...	...	...	...	...	...	74.9	72.6	72.9	72.7	70.5	69.6	70.1	70.0	70.6
Australia	All	58.8	56.8	55.7	55.3	56.4	58.0	57.9	57.5	57.9	58.0	58.7	58.7	59.1	59.7	58.9
	Male	69.4	66.5	64.9	64.3	65.5	66.8	66.6	65.9	66.2	66.1	66.3	65.8	66.3	66.6	66.2
	Female	48.4	47.3	46.7	46.4	47.6	49.3	49.3	49.2	49.8	50.1	51.3	51.7	52.1	53.0	51.6
Japan	All	62.0	62.6	62.8	62.3	61.8	61.2	61.2	61.6	60.8	60.0	59.5	59.1	58.2	58.0	58.9
	Male	75.8	76.4	76.5	76.3	75.6	75.0	74.9	75.2	74.2	73.3	72.7	71.9	70.9	70.4	71.8
	Female	49.0	49.6	49.7	49.1	48.7	48.3	48.2	48.6	48.2	47.4	47.1	47.0	46.3	46.3	46.8

Sources: Employment: Laborsta, KILM and Population 15+: WDI; adapted from Kucera (2006).

in some countries such as Thailand, while in some other countries (such as the Philippines) the employment effects are relatively small.

In relation to the debates on globalization and employment, it is interesting to note that economic growth does not always translate into more employment. In fact, the relationship between economic growth and employment volume is not clear. As Table 4 shows, the sign of elasticity is not necessarily positive. In Indonesia, for example, the employment elasticity was negative during the financial crisis, which means that despite the severe economic downturn, the employment volume increased. This phenomenon can, to a large extent, be explained by the fact that workers tend to resort to informal employment as a coping strategy for survival during periods of economic

Table 4. Employment elasticity by gender (1996-2003)

		1996	1997	1998	1999	2000	2001	2002	2003
Australia		0.34	0.18	0.41	0.46	1.3	0.32	0.74	0.6
	Male	0.32	0.11	0.35	0.39	0.88	0.15	0.71	0.48
	Female	0.38	0.27	0.48	0.55	1.84	0.54	0.76	0.76
China*		-0.04	-0.14	-3.79	1.96	na	na	na	na
	Male	-0.06	-0.15	-4.74	3.74	na	na	na	na
	Female	-0.02	-0.11	-2.27	-0.19	na	na	na	na
Indonesia		0.91	0.33	-0.05	1.65	0.23	0.31	0.25	na
	Male	0.33	0.39	0.01	2.36	0.2	0.88	0.69	na
	Female	1.97	0.24	-0.16	0.51	0.29	-0.61	-0.49	na
Japan		0.13	0.6	0.58	-13.74	-0.08	-1.29	3.62	-0.08
	Male	0.11	0.48	0.77	-12.28	-0.12	-2.11	3.52	-0.17
	Female	0.15	0.78	0.3	-15.85	-0.03	-0.09	3.77	0.04
Korea		0.24	0.24	0.71	0.12	0.47	0.47	0.4	0.05
	Male	0.27	0.3	0.77	0.15	0.51	0.51	0.4	-0.04
	Female	0.2	0.13	0.6	0.06	0.4	0.41	0.41	0.22
Malaysia		0.99	0.29	-0.03	0.45	0.62	1.19	0.48	0.65
	Male	0.9	0.36	-0.15	0.38	0.45	-1.57	0.34	0.56
	Female	1.15	0.18	0.19	0.6	0.94	6.37	0.73	0.8
Philippines		1.16	0.31	-2.33	-0.52	0.01	2.82	na	na
	Male	1.18	0.14	-2.16	-0.87	0.12	2.11	na	na
	Female	1.13	0.6	-2.6	0.06	-0.18	3.97	na	na
Thailand		-0.18	-2.1	0.29	-0.04	0.6	0.68	0.44	0.18
	Male	-0.03	-1.55	0.24	0.07	0.53	0.78	0.41	0.16
	Female	-0.35	-2.79	0.36	-0.16	0.69	0.55	0.47	0.19
Vietnam		0.77	0.08	0.66	0.66	0.1	0.24	0.42	0.35
	Male	na	0.18	0.71	0.75	0.2	0.34	0.44	0.41
	Female	na	-0.02	0.6	0.57	-0.01	0.14	0.41	0.29

Employees only.

Source: Employment figures are from LABORSTA and GDP growth figures are from WDI 2004.

Note: Employment figures represent those aged 15 years+ (except for Thailand which covers those aged 13 years+)

hardship. The increase in employment in Indonesia between 1997 and 1998 was accompanied by an increase in self-employment, the size of which was comparable to that of the reduction in employees. There also appeared to be a significant increase (roughly 4 percentage points) in underemployment during this period. Similar observations can be made concerning Thailand and the Philippines.

Another important factor is the gender variations in labour force experience. As Table 4 shows, there are notable gender differences in employment elasticity, not only in size but also in direction, and therefore, it is hard to identify a common pattern. Nonetheless, it is interesting to note that the employment increase that occurred during the economic crisis mentioned above can be largely attributed to the increase in female employment, especially in Indonesia, Thailand and the Philippines. This points to the possibility that at the household level, women may play a buffer role in periods of economic difficulty, increasing their participation in response to declining household income and reducing their participation as the economy picks up.

While the discussion so far suggests that women's active participation in the labour market is a common coping strategy to protect household living standards, women already in employment, especially in the private sector, are more adversely affected by economic downturn. In the industrialization process in the region, women workers provide the major source of 'competitiveness' or 'flexibility' in the workforce (lower wages, more tractable, easiness in layoff (after marriage or childbirth), lower probability of joining unions). Yet, 'the very features which have made women workers more attractive to employers ... are precisely those which are likely to make them the first to lose their jobs in any recession' (UNESCAP, 2002: 95).

LABOUR MARKET REFORMS AND FLEXIBILIZATION

The experience of East Asian countries over the last 10 years suggests that policymakers have attached renewed importance to laws, regulations and programmes relating to labour and employment flexibilisation. The following is a tentative assessment of labour market policy changes in East Asia and asserts whether or not government intervention in the social protection of workers and a shift in the quality (and beneficiaries) of regulations 'on paper' constitutes a general trend towards or away from greater labour market flexibility.

Economic Crisis and Labour Market Policies

Striking a balance between promoting job creation and job protection was particularly contentious in the aftermath of the Asian crisis as long-term benefits of increased employment and wages competed with short-term concerns for the job and wage security of those affected during the contraction. The application of a mix of active and passive labour market measures demonstrated the necessity of a holistic labour market response to the Asian crisis. Indonesia, for example, which was one of the countries most affected by the crisis, employed active labour market programmes (ALMPs) such as extensive public works. Job creation, rather than job protection was their policy priority. Burgeoning unemployment in Indonesia in 1997 forced the reinstatement of the public works programme, Padat Karya which was used as early as the 70s and 80s to provide income support through 'cash for manual work' welfare programmes to the unemployed and the poor to create production benefits in the form of lasting social capital, including people's skills and enterprise.

Job creation was also the priority in Malaysia whereby the government sought to increase employment opportunities through public works and privatisation projects with the private sector. Major public works programmes included infrastructure projects, agricultural and rural development projects (In-Situ and the New Land Development Programme) designed to help boost employment among the most vulnerable of informal sector workers such as indigenous people and women. Arguably the single most important labour market policy response was the use of another ALMP which was wage subsidies. Wage subsidies for employers were offered to encourage employers to use pay cuts, temporary lay offs, flexible work hours and part time work rather than retrenchment.

Of all the ALMPs, the emphasis on public employment services and training were key to addressing unemployment in the Philippines. Under the Public Employment Service Act 1999, a public employment service office (PESO) was placed in every province and key city in the Philippines (there were 146 new PESOs by 1998).

PESO's were designed to facilitate the exchange of labour market information between job seekers and employers and establish a manpower skill registry and information centre on job placement and promotion (Betcherman and Islam, 2001: 44).

With regard to key employment legislation developments, the introduction of the very first labour laws in 1994/95, legitimating the rights of labourers, the role of the state in promoting employment, training, labour standards and the role of trade unions, marks the beginning of labour 'commodification' in China and Vietnam. In China the new labour contract system (core provision of the Labour Law of 1995) replaced the lifetime employment system and introduces flexibility in wages through wage decentralisation. It extends the concept of labour contracts to all employees and opens the possibility of different forms of labour contract – fixed term, open-ended contracts and temporary contracts whereby individuals are able to terminate contracts immediately under certain circumstances (Zhu, 2004: 49). This also provides the freedom to choose to work for a specific work unit (or *danwei*) – a major change over past administrative restrictions.

Arguably the most significant labour market development in Japan was the 2003 amendment to the Labour Standards Law, which for the first time, explicitly requires employers to have just cause when dismissing employees. Previously, there was no legal provision preventing employers' decisions to dismiss employees at any moment. This amendment restricts the employer's right to dismissal reflecting the power of unions and the vested interests of 'insiders'.

Flexibilisation as a Common Trend?

Given the primary concern of flexibility in addressing unemployment, the trend of labour market developments represents a move towards greater structural labour market flexibility. The net effect of changes in labour policy and law in all countries examined is that intentional policy directives have liberalised/restructured/diversified industrial relations and human resource practices to alleviate unemployment. Therefore, it is not so much a question of whether or not policy is heading towards greater flexibility but rather what kind of flexibility and for whom?

In Indonesia labour market policies have not targeted informal workers, which constitute the vast majority of workers. The Trade Union Act of 2000 and Manpower Protection Act of 2003 strengthens workers' bargaining power, minimum standards for working conditions and rules for generous severance – but this only applies to formal sector workers which constitute a minority of the workforce (for instance, the share of employees is less than 30%). Functional flexibility is enhanced by the Manpower Protection Act 2003, which sets out the terms and conditions of contract work and outsourcing, yet numerical flexibility is hampered by the stringent restrictions on firing. Yet again, this does not apply to informal sector workers who, whilst operating outside the law, provide vast resources of flexible forms of employment such as temporary work, contractors, home workers and so on for the Indonesian economy.

Since 1995 Chinese workers have been able to enjoy occupational mobility with the freedom to choose to work or not to work for a specific work unit (or *danwei*), yet geographical mobility is highly restricted under the system of official registration in China. Registration restricts rural to urban migration since households are required to have a registration (*hukou*) card to legally reside in any given place. 'Floating workers', without a registration card, who have very limited access to housing and education in urban areas, are estimated at about 90 million, or 19% of the total rural labour force (ADB, 2005: 62).

In Japan there seems to have been a more subtle change in the way working conditions have been regulated under the new Labour Standards Law. The general direction of the 2003 revisions is towards deregulation and increased numerical flexibility via relaxing restrictions on fixed term contracts, introducing more provisions for labour contracts, allowing employees and employers more leeway in adopting various employment patterns and working regimes. Nevertheless, active labour market policy remains underdeveloped and employment protection is weak for young workers, female part-time workers and unemployed persons (Genda, 2004: 299).

In Korea, numerical flexibility gains have been in the form of provisions for easier hiring and firing, whilst labour market policies have been designed to enable greater functional flexibility through heavy reliance on training subsidies and upgrading the skill level of the workforce. Despite veritable efforts to avoid dismissals, the government allows for lay-offs enabling greater flexibility for small, medium and large firms. Meanwhile most workers (including non-regular and vulnerable workers) are provided with the security and capacity they need to envisage job turnover and to re-enter the labour market via extensive vocational education and training. This has enabled advanced industrial transformation where people have become flexible enough to change jobs to a more modern sector where education and skills are imperative. Yet the clear beneficiaries are firms with 5 employees or more, since firms with 4 or fewer employees represent loopholes for employers to evade legal obligations, since some provisions (relating to employment contracts, restrictions on dismissal, working hours, leave, etc.) are not applicable to the latter group.

The Philippine government has taken logical steps to cope with the side effects of the crisis including the lifting of prohibitions on flexible forms of employment such as contracting. This may be indicative of a country trying to achieve greater numerical flexibility, yet the market for non-regular workers resembles a form of 'protected' flexibility whereby contracting is conditional, permitted under protective conditions such as joint liability between principal employers and subcontractors for labour standards violations and the upholding of labour rights for the employee carrying out precarious forms of work. In sum, employers are in a better bargaining position as they have the ease to hire and fire and set wages flexibly, which fits in with the government's economic development strategy that is based on the competitive advantage of low (labour) costs.

A Balance Between Security and Flexibility?

The Asian crisis created a cyclical fluctuation too great to ignore and, as a result, these countries loosened controls on wages and employment arrangements and levels in order to respond to the threat of massive unemployment. Yet, these countries did not leave jobs entirely in the invisible hands of the market. Instead, governments engaged themselves in a balancing act of flexibilising the labour market by decentralising wages, easing the hiring and firing of workers, officially accepting more informal types/and status of employment, whilst securing (or compensating) those affected through reforms and extending social protection measures such as retraining programmes and social safety nets. For instance, a plethora of legal commitments were made in each country to combat the increasing dualism between regular and non-regular workers. For the first time provisions were made for part time or temporary workers. These include: the formalisation of precarious employment in Vietnam (Decree 44, 2003 Labour Code) and Malaysia; Worker Dispatching[ii] Laws in Japan and Korea, which encourages the hiring of temporary workers into permanent employment and lifts past restrictions that were placed on various job types for temporary workers; legislation of labour contracting in Indonesia and the Philippines to the general liberalisation of legal restraints for hiring irregular/temporary workers in China.

Optimal combinations of security and flexibility are most closely associated with the 'flexicurity' model evident in countries such as Denmark and the Netherlands. Flexicurity strategies, which in the Netherlands and Denmark appear to focus on enhancing both numerical flexibility and income security, seem to have favourable effects on labour market participation (Auer and Cazes eds., 2003).

Judging from the experience of Nordic countries, it can be argued that attaining an optimal balance between flexibility and security for most of the countries examined will become increasingly difficult given the relatively weak social safety nets and trends towards the decentralisation of wages and policymaking. The pattern of decentralisation evidenced in labour market developments in the Asian countries is more in tune with the Anglo-Saxon model where wages and working conditions depend heavily on employer-worker negotiation. This may be consistent with high flexibility, yet may also lead to greater wage inequality and weak social insurance coverage, creating further imbalances with regards to flexibility and security. Traditionally, the Nordic countries have had unions advocating openness and competition, in line with a highly coordinated and centralised approach to wage setting and decision making which allows all parties to internalise the consequences of their actions. Nevertheless, achievement of the 'right' contextual balance of flexibility and security will ultimately be determined by country-specific characteristics such as the labour market structure, institutional will and the capacity of social partners.

CHANGING PATTERNS OF WORK

We have seen a broad range of policy changes since the mid-1990s in the region, which are expected to affect actual employment conditions and, more broadly, the quality of working life. However, the effects of policy changes on individual workers and their working lives have hardly been analyzed to date, and therefore empirical evidence is lacking. Given such constraints, this section is intended to provide some preliminary analysis concerning development in employment conditions in the region. Based on the policy review in the previous section, the focus will be placed on those areas where policy interventions are commonly found across the countries. They include the introduction of 'non-standard' employment, wage moderations (and income inequality), new working time standards (or deregulation). There are other important issues which deserve special attention, such as work organization, work-family balance and health and safety, but the paucity of available information makes it almost impossible to conduct a proper analysis. As a result, only the issue of work organization will be briefly touched upon.

Employment Status: More Flexible?

We have already seen the role of informal employment in stabilizing employment volume in developing countries. Flexible wage adjustments in response to business cycles have also been discussed. It has been argued that such flexibility 'acted as an important source of social protection, partly in the absence of other formal sector forms of support in all countries, and especially in Thailand and Indonesia' (Manning 2003: 174). What this argument implies is the superiority of labour market flexibility over social safety nets is a more effective form of 'protection' in the East Asian context. However, what actually happened in the policy area appears to be that while efforts have been made to introduce a social safety net, new types of non-standard employment (such as temporary and part-time employment and contracting-out) are legalized. Indeed, a close examination of employment status in these countries indicates that employment flexibility is so extensive that the overall stability of the labour market could be questioned.[iii]

The Philippine case would be useful in this regard. First, almost half of total paid employment is carried out without any oral agreement or written contract. A recent ILO survey shows that, in 2004, 48 per cent of employees did not have any contract, while only 24 % had a written contract (Mehran, 2005) and about 25 % had an oral agreement (or 'contract'). This means that employment conditions are not specified for the majority in paid employment. Even among those with some kind of contractual arrangements, more than 60 per cent of them were not entitled to be paid sick leave or paid annual leave. Only 12 per cent of employees were reported to be able to take both annual/sick leave and social security benefits. Another survey, which concentrates on 'formal employment' (in establishments with 20 or more workers) shows that non-standard employment is widespread in the Philippines. When regular employees are defined as full-time employees with open-ended contracts, non-regular employment explains about 22 per cent of total employment in 2003 (see Table 5). This does not include contractor and agency-hired workers which account for another 11 per cent of total employment (see also Bitonio, 2004).

Table 5. Structure of employment in non-agricultural establishments in the Philippines (establishment with 20 or more workers, 2003)

	Total employment	Working owner	Unpiad workers	Mangers/ executives	Supervisors / foremen	Regular employees	Non-regular employees	Contractor/ agency-hired workers
All	2919110	15974	4738	147991	220920	1561845	651219	316423
20-99 workers	945964	12675	1892	66684	68203	516565	171885	108060
100-199 workers	370521	1684	439	18416	30044	190303	75423	54212
200 workers or more	1602625	1615	2406	62891	122673	854977	403911	154152

Note: Regular employees refer to full-time workers with open-ended contracts

Source: Bureau of Labor and Employment Statistics, 2002/3 BLSE Intergrated Survey.

This evidence implies that changes to 'non-standard' employment in developing countries in the region are associated with poor employment conditions with a lower probability of benefiting from a social safety net. Although some countries such as Viet Nam have introduced legal measures to improve employment conditions for non-regular workers, workplace practice may be far from ideal and enshrined in these measures. If this is the case, an increasing use of non-standard employment means there is a shrinking proportion of workers who can benefit from legal regulation of employment conditions as well as social insurances (which have only recently begun to develop).

The increase in non-standard employment has been indeed a big social issue in industrialized countries in the region such as Japan and Korea. Japan has witnessed the diversification of employment patterns with an increasing share of 'non-standard' employment. In 2004, about 32 per cent of employees were 'non-regular' employees which included part-timers (15 per cent), *arubaito* (temporary workers: 7 per cent) and dispatched/contract workers etc (10 per cent). Concerns have been expressed not only about the increasing trends in non-standard employment but also about the poor quality of these employment patterns (Japan Labour Institute, 2003). In Korea, the issue of non-standard employment has been discussed as one of key social issues, as the evidence indicates that since the financial crisis of 1997, firms are increasingly resorting to non-regular employment, although its overall size is still being debated due to the different definitions employed (*e.g.,* see Cho and Keum, 2004).

Wage and Earning Trends: Higher and More Equal?

Another important dimension of employment conditions is wages. As pointed out earlier, the severe wage effects of the economic crisis between 1997 and 1998 are clearly revealed in wage trends in the region. As Table 6 shows, the countries hit by the crisis witnessed a considerable reduction in real manufacturing wages. With the exception of the Philippines, where a decreasing trend had already kicked in even before 1997, the crisis was accompanied by a sharp decrease in real wages. A slow recovery seems to be on course afterwards. Such substantial wage adjustments are often believed to contribute to improving 'international competitiveness' (see Manning, 2003). Real manufacturing wages increased only moderately in the 1990s in Japan, which is in stark contrast to China where real wages almost doubled during the same period.

Table 6. Real manufacturing wage indices

	1990	1991	1992	1993	1994	1995	1996	1997	1998	1999	2000	2001
China	100.0	105.4	112.6	122.2	125.1	129.2	130.3	133.3	159.9	179.0	200.7	...
Korea	100.0	106.9	116.4	123.2	133.9	140.8	150.7	151.6	136.7	155.6	165.2	168.6
Indonesia	100.0	105.7	121.8	121.1	117.5	172.4	171.6	...	175.4	160.9	...	...
Malaysia	100.0	104.4	110.1	113.5	119.8	125.1	134.5	142.1	...	...	148.4	161.4
Philippines	100.0	99.1	101.4	97.7	102.5	100.6	94.5	95.4	92.3	77.3	78.3	...
Thailand	100.0	103.9	107.9	108.4	105.4	117.7	122.5	125.2	124.6	114.9	...	...
Vietnam	...	...	...	...	...	...	...	...	...	...	...	...
Australia	100.0	100.6	102.1	103.1	104.1	102.3	102.7	105.6	107.7	107.8	108.0	108.3
Japan	100.0	103.2	105.2	106.9	108.3	111.9	112.7	114.5	116.7	116.5	116.5	117.9

Sources: KILM (2005)

As mentioned earlier, Asian countries have been praised for their relatively good record in income inequality. Yet, there is some indication that the situation has recently worsened in many countries. Table 7 presents a popular indicator for income inequality, the Gini coefficient. Due to different data sources and estimation methodologies, it is difficult to compare the coefficients across countries. Instead, we focus on changes in each country over two decades. In transition economies such as China and Viet Nam, income inequality has increased considerably. A similar upward trend is observed for the Philippines and Malaysia. (Indonesian data indicates a high degree of fluctuation, which might be due to measurement errors.) Probably the most notable development in this regard has occurred in Korea which has been perceived as a good example for the coexistence of high-income equality combined with high economic growth (see Figure 1). The downward trend in the 1990s was reversed with the outbreak of the financial crisis in 1997, and the Gini efficient was increased to exceed the 1986 level. Recently, there is a sign of improvement, but it is not clear if this is a temporary phenomenon.

Finally, national statistical sources, as well as World Bank data, show that the incidence of poverty, either in national definition or in the 'one dollar' threshold, has decreased in the region (see Kucera and Chataignier, 2005). At the same time, minimum wages have gained importance in the region, which are thought to affect a group of workers in various ways (see Eyraud and Saget, 2005). Unfortunately, however, few studies have examined these effects in the region.

Table 7. Income Gini coefficients (1990-2002)

	China-Rural	China-Urban	Indonesia	Indonesia-Rural	Indonesia-Urban	Malaysia	Philippines	Thailand	Vietnam
1980	25.0	...	...	...	...	...	...	...	...
1981	...	18.5	...	...	...	...	...	45.2	...
1984	26.7	...	...	29.2	33.3	48.6	...	...	...
1985	27.1	17.1	...	...	...	...	41.0	...	...
1987	29.5	17.1	33.1	...	...	47.0	...	...	...
1988	...	...	...	...	...	...	40.6	43.8	...
1989	...	...	...	...	...	46.2	...	...	...
1990	30.6	...	...	26.4	34.7	...	...	...	...
1991	...	24.8	...	...	...	...	43.8	...	...
1992	32.0	24.2	...	...	...	47.7	...	46.2	...
1993	32.1	28.5	34.4	...	...	...	...	...	35.7
1994	34.0	29.2	...	...	...	...	42.9	...	...
1995	34.0	28.3	...	...	...	48.5	...	...	...
1996	33.6	29.1	36.5	...	...	...	...	43.4	...
1997	33.1	29.4	...	...	...	49.2	46.2	...	...
1998	33.1	29.9	38.4	...	...	...	...	41.4	35.5
1999	35.4	31.6	31.7	...	...	...	...	43.5	...
2000	...	...	30.3	...	...	...	46.1	43.2	...
2001	36.3	33.3	...	...	...	...	...	...	...
2002	...	...	34.3	...	...	...	...	...	37.1

Sources: PovcalNet (http://iresearch.worldbank.org/PovcalNet/jsp/index.jsp)

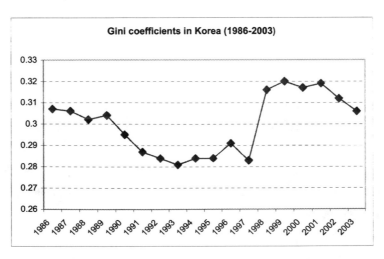

Figure 1. Gini coefficients in Korea (1988-2003)

Working Time: Working Longer?

The policy review of the previous section has shown that working time regulation has been intensively examined, which has often led to significant changes in legal standards. At the same time, from a comparative perspective, working time in this region is probably the most problematic issue affecting the quality of work. While there is no comparable data set on working hours which allows for regional comparison, there are good reasons to believe that working hours in East Asia and the Pacific are higher than in other regions. As Table 8 demonstrates, excessive hours (defined as more than 48 or 49 hours per week: see Lee, 2004) are widespread not only in developing and transition countries but also in industrialized countries. This means that legal working time standards in these countries (typically 48 hours in developing countries and 40 hours in industrialized countries) do not serve as a norm. In Thailand, for example, about 47 per cent of workers were working more than 50 hours in 2000. No exact figure is available for Indonesia, but it appears to be slightly lower. In Malaysia, more than 30 per cent of workers were working excessive hours in 2000, and the ratio was particularly high among sales workers (about 46 per cent: see Nagaraj, 2004). In the case of transition economies in the region, the situation is largely similar. In Viet Nam, long hours are widespread, and in fact, overtime wages constitute an important source for wage earnings. A survey indicates that in 2000, overtime payment accounted for about 14 per cent of total wage income (ILO, 2003: table 15). It was also found that many workers 'did not agree with a 40 hour weekly working time. The reasons given were that they receive piece rates and 40 hours is insufficient working time for them to produce enough to earn a sufficient livelihood to support themselves and their family' (ILO 2003: 81). While the information on working time is scarce for China, a recent study indicates a similar situation where overtime work is prevalent (often unpaid) but is often preferred by workers (see Zeng, Lu & Idris 2005). However, the overall incidence of excessive hours tends to decrease, especially in Thailand and Viet Nam.

Table 8. Changes in the distribution of working hours (% of total employment)

Thailand			*Viet Nam*			*Indonesia*		
Weekly Hours	1995	2000	*Weekly Hours*	1996	2003	*Weekly Hours*	1996	2003
1-19	1.5	2.5	1-19	1.5	0.7	1-19	6.8	4.3
20-29	4.2	4.7	20-29	4.9	3.5	20-24	5.0	4.5
30-34	2.1	2.4	30-34	1.9	3.6	25-34	12.9	11.4
35-39	10.3	10.6	35-39	3.6	2.9	35-44	28.4	28.8
40-49	30.1	33.1	40-49	45.7	56.9	45-54	26.9	31.9
50+	51.8	46.7	50+	42.4	32.4	55+	20.0	19.1
	100.0	100.0		100.0	100.0		100.0	100.0

Japan			*Korea*			*Australia*	(August)	
Weekly Hours	1995	2004	*Weekly Hours*	2000	2004	*Weekly Hours*	1990	2004
<15	3.7	4.9	<15	1.9	2.2	1-15	11.7	12.8
15-34	16.4	20.0	15-34	7.3	8.5	16-34	18.4	23.2
35-42	28.0	28.5	35-40	11.1	15.0	35-44	43.8	36.5
43-48	22.2	16.6	41-47	23.4	24.8	45-49	8.1	8.4
49-59	16.7	16.5	49-59	28.2	24.0	50-59	9.2	10.2
60+	13.0	13.5	60+	28.1	25.5	60+	8.8	8.9
	100.0	100.0		100.0	100.0		100.0	100.0

Note: (1) Thailand: 15 years old or more; (2) Viet Nam; urban sector; (3) Indonesia: 15 years old or more; (4) Japan: 25 years old or more; (5) Korea: 25 years old or more.

Sources: National labour force survey data

Working time developments have particularly concerned industrialized countries in the region. As mentioned earlier, both Japan and Korea have introduced shorter statutory working hours (*i.e.* 40 hours per week). In Japan, 30 per cent of workers were working excessive hours in 2004, a moderate increase compared to 1995. This means that the reduction of statutory working hours has had virtually no effect on excessive hours. By contrast, part-time employment increased considerably during the period. Korea, which has the highest annual working hours among OECD countries, has witnessed the reduction of excessive hours, but almost 50 % of workers were still working more than 48 hours per week in 2004. This figure is even higher than those for developing and transition countries as shown in Table 8.

And Shorter Hours: Under-employment

Table 8 also shows a significant presence of short working hours (less than 35 hours) in developing and transition countries, and much higher proportions in Japan. Two important policy issues concern these workers. First, the very fact that they are working shorter hours can also mean poorer employment conditions such as lower *hourly* wages, reduced access to fringe benefits and social insurances, and lower level of employment protection. The relatively poor employment conditions under which part-time workers are working is rather well documented for industrialized countries (see Lee, 2004), but empirical evidence is lacking for developing countries in the region. It is also not clear whether the policy measures towards better treatment of part-time workers in some of these countries have been effective in achieving their intended aims. Secondly, in developing countries, workers with shorter hours are by and large under-employed in that they would like to work more hours and are available to do so (Lee *et al.*, forthcoming). In other words, they cannot afford to be unemployed. This is why in some national statistics (*e.g.* Indonesia); the proportion of these part-time workers is presented along with official unemployment figures.

Work Organization and Work Intensity

With regard to changes in work organization, information is very limited for transition and developing countries in the region. Some studies indicate that, while these countries are gradually integrating into the 'global production system', these integrated manufacturing sectors rely on the traditional mass production and do not show any clear sign of the so-called high performing work organization (Gamble, Morris & Wilkinson 2004). Nonetheless, changes are under way and their scale appears to be considerable. For example, the 2000 Philippine Labour Flexibility Survey showed that about 46 per cent of companies had introduced new technologies, especially computer-related ones (Bitonio, 2004). One good example for further integration into the 'global production system' and its impact on work organization is the growing interest in call centers in developing countries in the region, such as Malaysia and the Philippines. The call centers in these countries have brought substantial job creation, but the way work is organized is unprecedented, sometimes demanding changes in the regulation of employment conditions, as has happened in the expanding Indian call centre industry (see Taylor and Bain, 2006). A Philippine study, for example, shows that, as call centers require 24-hour operation and shift works, those workers who accept these conditions (thus, normally young workers) are recruited primarily on a non-regular status. Different types of working time (*e.g.,* compressed workweek) have been introduced, and workers are willing to accept frequent changes in work schedule insofar as they bring premium payments. While many women are required to undertake night work in call centers, the current labour code prohibits women from doing night work, which led many call centers to call for an amendment to the article in question (Philippine Institute for Labor Studies, 2004). One important question in relation to work organization (also working time as discussed above) is whether or not there is any trend towards work intensification. There is some anecdotal evidence which points to work intensification, but more rigorous empirical evidence is lacking.

CONCLUDING REMARKS

This chapter began with asking why we need to look at employment conditions in Asia and the Pacific. It has been argued that the effects of globalization need to be evaluated in terms of changes in employment conditions for individual workers. In addition, the increasing pressure towards 'flexible' labour market through policy interventions (often combined with strong skepticism about labour market institutions) has made it more important to examine *actual* employment conditions. It has also been argued that while rhetoric is abundant, e current knowledge is very limited both conceptually and empirically. We believe that this gap is particularly serious for Asia and the Pacific where globalization has proceeded at an unprecedented scale. There is some evidence that 'flexible' employment patterns are, to a varying degree, spreading and that employment conditions are often problematic. Numerous policy measures have been taken to improve employment conditions for these workers, but their actual impacts are not well understood.

Therefore, there is an urgent need for research into changes in employment conditions. First, a comprehensive review of actual employment conditions in the region is urgently required, especially for developing and transition countries. Various aspects of employment conditions should be examined, including wages, employment status, working time, and work organization.

Second, in many cases, each element of employment conditions is not independent, but dependent. In a sense, employment conditions should be understood as a *package*. Such effect is commonly understood to apply to the distinction between formal and informal employment. However, as discussed, there is a trend towards the informalization of formal employment in the region which is accompanied by inferior employment conditions. For example, temporary employment is not simply about employment security (*i.e.* length of contract) but also tends to involve lower wages/fringe benefits, long working hours and high exposure to safety risks. Thus, the flexibilization of employment contracts should be understood to imply a different package of employment conditions. This means that when employment conditions are analyzed, the focus should be placed on how different elements of employment conditions are packaged for individual workers and what kinds of variations exist among different groups of workers (e.g., gender, age, etc). Such analysis will give a better understanding of the way in which certain workers are marginalized.

Finally, analysis needs to take into account the context in which different policy measures are introduced. We have already seen a broad array of policy measures which often have different directions, if properly implemented, with varying implications for workers. It is important to examine if these changes can be seen as simply the result of either: 'rent-seeking' by outsiders, 'exogenous shock', the outcome of addressing certain labour market failures or indeed whether they reflect the specific concerns or needs of workers for the overall stability of the labour market. In addition, whenever necessary, the impact of these policies on individual workers (both targeted groups and those indirectly affected) also needs to be evaluated.

REFERENCES

ADB (2005) *Key Indicators 2005: Labor Markets in Asia: Promoting Full, Productive, and Decent Employment.* ADB, Manila.

Agell, J. (1999) 'On the benefits from rigid labour markets: norms, market failures, and social insurance', *Economic Journal,* 109 (Feb): F143-F164.

Agell, J. (2002) 'On the determinants of labour market institutions: rent seeking versus social insurance', *German Economic Review,* 3(2): 107-35.

Aisbett, E. (2005) *Why Are the Critics So Convinced that Globalization Is Bad for the Poor?,* NBER Working Paper No. 11066, Cambridge, MA: NBER.

Arbache, J., Dickerson, A. and Green, F. (2004) 'Trade liberalization and wages in developing countries', *Economic Journal,* 114: F73-F96.

Auer, P. and Cazes, S. eds. (2003) *Employment Stability in an Age of Flexibility: Evidence from Industrialized Countries.* Geneva: ILO.

Betcherman, G. and Islam, R. (eds.). (2001) *East Asian Labor Markets and the Economic Crisis. Impacts, Responses and Lessons.* World Bank, Washington D.C.

Bitonio, B.E. (2004) *Workers Representation Amidst Labor Flexibility: Insight From the Philippine Experience,* Presented at the IIRA 5th Asian Regional Congress, June 2004, Seoul.

Cho, J. and Keum, J. (2004) 'Job stability in the Korean labour market: estimating the effects of the 1997 financial crisis', *International Labour Review,* 143(4): 373-92.

Currie, J. and Harrison, A. (1997) 'Sharing the costs: the impact of trade reform on capital and labor in Morocco', *Journal of Labor Economics,* 15(3): S44-S71.

Davidson, C. and Matusz, S. (2004) *International Trade and Labor Markets: Theory, Evidence and Policy Implications.* Kalamazoo: W.E. Upjohn Institute for Employment Research.

Dollar, D. and Kraay, A. (2004) 'Trade, growth, and poverty', *Economic Journal,* 114 (February): F22-F49.

Edwards, S. and Lustig, N.C. eds. (1997) *Labor Markets in Latin America: Combining Social Protection With Market Flexibility.* Washington, D.C.: Brookings Institution Press.

Eyraud, F. and Saget. C. (2005) *The Fundamentals of Minimum Wage Fixing.* Geneva: ILO.

Freeman, R. (2003) *Trade Wars: The Exaggerated Impact of Trade In Economic Debate,* NBER Working Paper No. 10000, Cambridge, MA: NBER.

Gamble, J., Morris, J. and Wilkinson B. (2004) 'Mass production is alive and well: the future of work and organization in East Asia', *International Journal of Human Resource Management*, 15(2): 397-409.

Gasparini, L. and Bertranou, F. (2005) 'Social protection and the labour market in Latin America: what can be learned from household surveys?', *International Social Security Review*, 58(2-3): 15-42.

Genda, Y. (2004) 'Employment Stability in an Age of Flexibility: Evidence from Industrialized Countries'. Book Review. *Journal of Japanese International Economics 18, pp. 298-300.*

Gunter, B. G. and van der Hoeven, R. (2004) 'The social dimension of globalization: a review of literature', *International Labour Review*, 143 (1-2): 7-43.

Hallak, J.C. and Levinsohn, J. (2004) *Fooling Ourselves: Evaluating the Globalization and Growth Debate*, NBER Working Paper No. 10244, Cambridge, MA: NBER.

Hasan, R. and Mitra, D. eds. (2003) *The Impact of Trade on Labor: Issues, Perspectives, and Experiences from Developing Asia.* Amsterdam: Elsevier.

Heckman, J. and Pagés, C. eds. (2004) *Law and Employment: Lessons from Latin American and the Caribbean.* Chicago: University of Chicago Press.

ILO (2003) *Equality, Labour and Social Protection for Women and Men in the Formal and Informal Economy in Viet Nam: Issues for Advocacy and Policy Development.* Hanoi: ILO.

ILO (2004a) *A Fair Globalization: Creating Opportunities for All.* ILO World Commission on the Social Dimension of Globalization. Geneva: ILO.

ILO (2004b) *Dialogues in Asia*, World Commission on the Social Dimension of Globalization, Bangkok: ILO.

Japan Labour Institute (2003) *The Diverse Working Situation Among Workers of Non-Standard Employment Type*, Survey Report No. 158, Tokyo: Japan Labour Institute.

Klein, M., Schuh, S. and Triest, R. (2003) *Job Creation, Job Destruction, and International Competition.* Kalamazoo: W.E. Upjohn Institute.

Krumm, K. and Kharas, H. eds (2004) *East Asia Integrates: A Trade Policy Agenda for Shared Growth.* Washington, DC: World Bank.

Kucera, D. (2002) 'Core labour standards and foreign direct investment' *International Labour Review*, 141(91-2): 31-69.

Kucera, D. and Chataignier, A. (2005) *Labour Developments in Dynamic Asia: What Do the Data Show?*, Policy Integration Department Working Paper No. 61, Geneva: ILO.

Lee, S. (2004) 'Working-hour gaps: trends and issues', in J. Messenger ed. *Working Time and Workers' Preferences in Industrialized Countries: Finding the Balance*. London: Routledge.

Lee, S. (2005) 'Working conditions and satisfaction at work: determinants and interactions in new EU member states and candidate countries', in D. Vaughan-Whitehead (ed).

Lee, S. and McCann, D. (forthcoming) 'Measuring Labour Market Institutions?: Conceptual and methodological questions on working hours rigidity' in *Labour Market Institutions in Developing Countries*, Geneva: ILO.

Lee, S., McCann, D. and Messenger, J. (forthcoming) *Working Time around the World*. Geneva: ILO.

Luebker, M. (2004) 'Globalization and perceptions of social inequality' *International Labour Review*, 143(1-2): 91-128.

Majid, N. (2004) *What Is the Effect of Trade Openness on Wages?* ILO Employment Strategy Papers 2004/18, Geneva: ILO.

Manning, C. (2003) 'Globalization, economic crisis, and labor market policy: lessons from East Asia" in Hasan and Mitra (eds).

Mehran, F. (2005) *Measuring Excessive Hours of Work, Low Hourly Pay, and Informal Employment through a Labour Force Survey: A Pilot Survey in the Philippines*. Presented at UNECE/ILO/Eurostat Seminar on the Quality of Work, Geneva, May 2005.

Nagaraj, S. (2004) *Working Time in Malaysia*, Unpublished ILO report, Geneva.

Philippine Institute for Labor Studies (2004) *Information and Communication Technology and Decent Work: Lessons from the Garments, Call centers, and Business Process Outsourcing Establishments*. Presented at the Meeting on Joint Investigative Studies for Determining the Impact of Information and Communications Technology on Decent Work in the Asia and the Pacific Region, Bangkok.

Pissarides, C. (2001) 'Employment protection', *Labour Economics*, 8: 131-59.

Rama, M. (2003a) *Globalization and Workers in Developing Countries*. World Bank Policy Research Working Paper No. 2958, Washington DC: World Bank.

Rama, M. (2003b) 'Globalization and the labor market', *World Bank Research Observer,* 18(2): 159-86.

Rodrik, D. (2005) 'Why we learn nothing from regressing economic growth on policies' mimeo.

Taylor, P. and Bain, P. (2006) 'Work Organisation and Employee Relations in Indian Call Centres' in Connell, J. and Burgess, J. (eds), *Developments in the Call Centre Industry: Analysis, Changes and Challenges*, Routledge, London.

UNESCAP (2002) *Economic and Social Survey of Asia and the Pacific 2002.* New York: UN.

Vaughan-Whitehead, D. ed. (2005) *Working and Employment Conditions in New EU Member States: Convergence or diversity?* Geneva: ILO

Winter, A. (2004) 'Trade liberalization and economic performance: an overview', *Economic Journal,* 114 (Feb): F4-F21.

World Bank (2004) *World Development Report2005: A Better Investment Climate for Everyone.* Washington DC: World Bank.

Zeng, X., Lu, L. and Idris, S. (2005) *Working Time in Transition: The Dual Task of Standardization and Flexibilization in China,* ILO Conditions of Work and Employment Series No. 11. Geneva: ILO.

Zhu, Y. (2004) 'Labour Law and Industrial Relations in China'. *Labour Relations in the Asia Pacific Countries* pp.37-63.

---

[i] See Agell (2002) for an elaboration of this point. More generally, once we recognize 'policy endogeneity', the existing empirical tests, which assume policy interventions as exogenous or random, are problematic. See Rodrik (2005).

[ii] This allows an employer to lease its employees to another firm, but the dispatching firm retains an employment relationship with its leased employer.

[iii] As regards the relationship between employment status/conditions and social protection, Gasparini and Bertranou (2005) provide an excellent analysis for Latin America. For the role of employment status in determining working conditions in new EU member states, see Lee (2005).

Chapter 3

THE IMPACT OF GLOBALISATION AND LABOUR MARKET
REFORMS IN CHINA

Zhang Xiaohe

INTRODUCTION

To understand the rapid growth of the Chinese GDP and its impact on the world economy, one must firstly have a close look at its labour market. As the most populous country in the world, the Chinese labour market has several distinctive characteristics that other countries do not share. Primarily, as China possesses the world's largest labour force, comprising over 700 million workers, this means that any change in its labour market will subsequently affect the production, trade and employment patterns of many other countries throughout the world.

One of the characteristics of the Chinese labour market is the expansion in employment in non-state owned enterprises (NSEs) which emerged following the economic reforms which were begun in the early 1980s. The NSEs increased even more dramatically when the reforms deepened moving towards to a fully fledged market economy in the 1990s. In 1999, the NSEs accounted for more than 70% of total industrial employment and output, about one third of government tax revenue and over two thirds of manufacturing exports. The rapid development of NSEs has, therefore, been widely regarded as one of the major successes of the country's transformation from a centrally planned economy into a market oriented one.

In spite of the remarkable success of the NSEs, questions are raised as to how, and to what extent, the development of NSEs has eroded the dominance of state-owned enterprises (SOEs), particularly with regard to industrial production, employment and international trade. Also, questions regarding how the reforms in China's labour market have affected the world economy, particularly in the labour intensive industries, remain unresolved. Answering these questions will not only shed light on the key determinants of China's evolutionary reforms, but will also generate valuable policy implications for the rest of the world. Given the significance of these issues on the one hand, and the lack of a comprehensive survey and analyses of the situation on the other, this chapter attempts to fill a gap by identifying the main driving forces of the rapid development of NSEs while elaborating on the impact of their development in terms of long term development in China.

Based on the dramatic development of the NSEs, this chapter further explores the impact of labour market reforms characterized by the abolishment of the household registration system that has prohibited permanent migration from rural to urban areas for more than 50 years. It is expected that free mobility of rural surplus labour into China's urban industrial sector will have a significant impact on production, employment and trade patterns both in China and in the rest of the world, particularly in the labour-intensive industries. This will result in large-scale restructuring of the world economy in line with regional specialization and patterns of comparative advantage.

This chapter is organized as follows. The first section provides a brief overview of the distortion and reforms of the labour market and the dramatic increase of NSEs, in contrast with the shrinkage of SOEs in China. This overview provides some insight into issues concerning how the ownership structure has been changed during processes of de-facto privatization. The next section, in turn, identifies the causes behind this change by surveying the most recently released statistical data and literature. Next, the discussion is extended to include the likely consequence of the rapid growth of NSEs and estimates the economic impact of the abolition of the household registration regime on the world economy. Finally, conclusions and policy implications are summarized in the final section.

LABOUR MARKET DISTORTION AND REFORMS

As one of the most populous developing countries, China is, and will remain, a surplus-labour economy. Following Lewis (1954) Ranis and Fei, (1961) and Sen (1984), this means that the withdrawal of a substantial number of workers from the labour force would have little or no effect on the productivity of existing labourers. In such an economy, factor rewards will not equal either their marginal productivity or their opportunity cost, and factor price differential exists for the same factors used in different sectors. What makes the Chinese labour market distinctive is that the dual nature of the labour market is not only a consequence of its relative underdevelopment, but is also the result of a policy used to quarantine the urban labour force from competition and to accumulate capital for heavy industry oriented industrialization in the pre-reform era.

The labour market in China has been seriously distorted since the late 1950s when the restriction on rural-urban migration was implemented. China is one of the few countries in the world that uses a household registration (*hukou*) regime to prohibit internal migration, not only from rural to urban areas, but also from one province to another. Starting in 1955, the *hukou* regime virtually prohibited inter-sector migration (Cheng and Selden, 1994). Chinese citizens were thus broadly divided into two groups: rural residents and urban residents. Since the *hukou* regime differentiated not only rural and urban residents, but also urban residents in different provincial administrative units, the mobility among different provincial units was also prohibited. The *hukou* regime, in conjunction with an elaborate rationing mechanism that restricted food and housing supply to urban dwellers, froze and formalized each individual's job position and eliminated possibilities of changes in residential status. A hierarchic economic structure was thereafter created in China with big cities at the apex, provincial and smaller cities in the middle, and the poorest rural areas at the base.

According to the *hukou* system, a mere 30.4% of the population is classified as "non-agricultural" and the corresponding percentage of the labour force designated as urban was 29.6% (SSB, 1999:111:133) in 1998. The 206 million people in the urban labour force can be further divided into employees in SOEs of 90 million, in urban collective owned enterprises (UCEs) of 20 million and in all other forms of enterprises including foreign owned enterprises (FFEs) of 96 million.

THE STRUCTURE OF ENTERPRISE OWNERSHIP

The number of NSEs in mainland China increased dramatically since the 1980s when the *hukou* regime was partially eroded through the abolition of state subsidies for the food and accommodation of urban dwellers. As a result, the proportions of NSEs in total employment increased over the last two decades. To date, the economic pillar of the country has been shifted from SOEs to their non-state counterparts. According to the nature of their ownership structure, NSEs in China can be classified into five components. They are urban collective enterprises (UCEs), township and village enterprises (TVEs), foreign funded enterprises (FFEs), private and individual enterprises (PIEs), and a set of diversified joint ventures (JVEs), with or without the involvement of the SOEs. Although there is no such unified item of NSEs in China's official statistics, an approximation can be derived from summing up all of these five components.

Before China's economic reforms began in 1978, virtually all NSEs were "collectively owned". Among these NSEs, UCEs fell into three categories with different historical backgrounds and somewhat different characteristics. The largest category was formed during the 1950s through the forced participation of handicraft workers. These firms were called "big collectives" since they were owned by local authorities at different levels. Big collective enterprises could retain a significant proportion of their profits, though this occurred with regard to a group of enterprises rather than individual ones. Before the reform for successful collective enterprises was introduced there had been a strong tendency for them to be converted into state ownership, thus reinforcing concentration of ownership in the state sector. By 1978, these large collectives accounted for slightly over half of all employees and 56% of the industrial output of all UCEs (Naughton, 1995:163).

The second category consisted of collectives created by neighbourhood committees during the Great Leap Forward Period (1958-62), hence they were called "street industries". They were usually small in size and their employees were mostly housewives and middle school graduates. The third category was collective firms that were established and managed by large SOEs. They were primarily established to provide employment for dependents of workers employed by the SOEs. The second and third categories were also called "small collectives" not only because they were usually small in size but also due to the fact that they had to be responsible for their profits and losses.

Another category of the "collectively owned" firms is the TVEs. In spite of the "collective' label, residents of local communities possess no right of membership in TVEs, nor do TVE workers possess any rights to participate in management. Rather, they are economic entities established and run by various levels of township and village government in the countryside. Sharing some common features of public ownership characteristics, there are some distinctions between the TVEs and SOEs or UCEs. One is that the local officials in their official capacity possess all the key components of property rights: control of residual income; the right to dispose of assets; and the right to appoint and dismiss managers and assume direct control if necessary (Naughton, 1994:267). Another is that they have a hard budget in the sense that they receive no allowance from governments so if they cannot cover their production costs, they have to go bankrupt (Putterman, 1994).

FFEs are enterprises that are owned, wholly or partially, by foreigners. They can be classified into three categories: wholly foreign owned, equity joint ventures and cooperative joint ventures. The last two categories include some joint operations not only between the foreigners and SOEs, but also between foreigners and UCEs or TVEs. Among these three categories the equity joint ventures have become the most important with a share of more than 50% over all FFEs since the late 1980s.

PIEs consist of two statistical entities: privately owned and individually owned. Private enterprises are, therefore, defined as those firms that hire eight or more employees, and that are run by individuals, partnerships, or up to 30 shareholders. Conversely, individually owned enterprises are those in which workers hired comprise less than eight and they are run by individuals or households. Small private enterprises were initially developed in the early 1980s, with the larger ones, only formally being recognized and regulated after 1988. Since both individual and private enterprises are privately owned as per western convention, they are categorized as one entity in this chapter.

JVEs can consist of any combination among domestic firms, including share-holding enterprises that have emerged in recent years. JVEs were relatively insignificant until the 1990s, when a cross ownership and cross sector integration was encouraged. Except for the item of investment in fixed assets, JVEs' share in most of the economic indicators was still the smallest by 1996.

EMPLOYMENT

Table 1 highlights the change in China's ownership structure in total non-agricultural employment in the post reform era.

Table 1 reveals several interesting points. Firstly, the growth in employment in the SOEs and UCEs has fallen since the late1990s, not only in relative terms of employment shares but also in the numbers of employees.. Secondly, with the exception of the UCEs, all other NSEs have achieved sustainable growth, particularly in these FFEs and PIEs. In other words, a clear path of privatization, indicated by the fall of public enterprises, and an increase in the FEEs, PIEs and JVEs has emerged. By 2002, more than one fourth of the total urban labour force worked in a variety of privately owned firms. Although the TVEs, as a semi-privately owned entity, have maintained a growth trend, they have stabilised with regard to the total number of employees.

Table 1. Change in Ownership Structure of Total Non-agricultural Employment

	Total Non-agricultural Employment (million)							
	Total	SOEs	NSEs	Of Which:				
				UCEs	TVEs	FFEs	PIEs	JVEs
1980	134.44	80.19	54.25	24.25	30.00			
1985	193.31	89.90	103.41	33.24	69.79			0.38
1990	256.15	103.46	152.69	35.49	92.65	0.66	22.93	0.96
1995	337.52	112.61	224.91	31.47	128.62	5.13	55.88	3.81
1996	349.26	112.44	236.82	30.16	135.08	5.40	61.97	4.21
1997	348.61	110.44	238.17	28.83	130.50	5.81	67.91	5.12
1998	330.63	95.58	235.05	19.63	125.37	5.87	78.24	5.94
2000	318.70	81.00	237.70	15.00	128.20	6.40	74.70	13.40
2001	316.90	76.40	240.50	12.90	130.90	6.70	74.80	15.20
2002	221.20	75.10	146.10	12.50	133.60			
	Shares (%)							
1980	100	59.65	40.35	18.04	0	0	0	0
1985	100	46.51	53.49	17.2	36.1	0	0	0.2
1990	100	40.39	59.61	13.86	36.17	0.26	8.95	0.37
1995	100	33.36	66.64	9.32	38.11	1.52	16.56	1.13
1996	100	32.19	67.81	8.64	38.68	1.55	17.74	1.21
1997	100	31.68	68.32	8.27	37.43	1.67	19.48	1.47
1998	100	28.91	71.09	5.94	37.92	1.78	23.66	1.8
2000	100	25.42	74.58	4.71	40.23	2.01	23.44	17.94
2001	100	24.11	75.89	4.07	41.31	2.11	23.60	20.32

Sources: SSB, various issues from 1999 to 2005.

Notes: Non-agricultural employment is derived from the difference between total employment and the employees worked on farming, forestry, animal husbandry and fishery activities.

THE FACTORS BEHIND THE CHANGES

The fading out of SOEs and the expansion of NSEs has been explained by a wide range of determinants. These include: the encouragement policies formed by different levels of authorities; the existence of an effective incentive and motivation mechanism and economic efficiency created through relatively low real labour costs in the NSEs. This has transpired as a result of their low social status, lack of social welfare, such as a guaranteed life-long employment scheme and free medical care, and a relatively light social burden compared with those in SOEs (Selden and You, 1997:1661-2). These differences dampen the ability of raising productivity in SOEs and endowed the NSEs with a comparative cost advantage in producing labour intensive products.

Before the reform, China's labour allocation was characterized by restrictions on labour mobility between different sectors, especially between rural and urban areas. The rural economy was limited to producing farming products while the urban state sector monopolized manufacturing production. After the reform, the restrictions on rural manufacturing activities were partially relaxed by permitting the development of rural industries and by allowing temporary employment of the rural residents in the urban areas. However, the real wage differential and different treatments in many welfare programs between the two sectors have remained. These programs include: various benefits such as accommodation, medical care, transportation, employment, pension, labour protection, entertainment, child care, education and the like, in the urban sector. However, in the rural sector these programs are either absent or of low quality (Zhang, 1992, Selden and You, 1997).

Welfare programs in the urban areas have largely been provided by enterprises, a system that not only limits inter-enterprise labour mobility because of the non transferability of benefits between enterprises, but also tends to place unequal burdens on older enterprises, especially those SOEs with large pension bills. It is estimated that pension bills accounted for about 21% of total wage bills in SOEs in 1995. Already, by the mid-1980s, in some old factories the number of retirees exceeded the number of active workers (Selden and You, 1997:1661-2). These heavy social burdens prevent the ability of raising productivity in SOEs.

In the rural sector, the existence of cheap labour and access to urban capital accounted for the most important impetus for the rapid growth of TVEs (Zhang, Findlay and Watson 1995). This is because the isolation and segmentation of labour and capital markets between rural and urban areas created gaps in the marginal productivity of each factor in different sectors before the reform. When the marginal productivity of capital is higher, and the marginal productivity of labour is lower in the rural sector than that found in the urban sector, capital moves into the rural sector to earn high profits, which boosts the development of rural manufacturing activities.

In terms of initial income and social status, the entrepreneurs and workers of PIEs in the urban sector resemble their counterparts of TVEs in the rural sector, except that they hold a non-agricultural household registration (*feinongye hukou*). Hence, they are allowed to stay in the urban areas permanently. It is also true that the entrepreneurs and workers in NSEs are willing to work harder and for a longer time than their counterparts in SOEs. This is because they will have lived in poverty for many years. Therefore, they have high elasticity to commit their labour, and a high tendency to save more when their income increases. This provides advantages to NSEs in hiring labour as well as in accumulating capital.

The average firm size of SOEs is much greater than that of NSEs. In 1995, the average number of employees hired in SOEs was about 25 times greater than that of NSEs, while their average fixed asset per worker was two-and-half-times greater. The relatively small size of NSEs, especially the TVEs and PIEs, enables them to adjust the scale of production and change the scope of a product quickly. For instance, after the economic austerity in 1989, the numbers of TVEs were reduced and several millions of workers were dismissed. However, more firms were started up and employment soared within two years, especially after Deng's inspection tour of the South in 1992.

THE IMPACT OF GLOBALISATION

The reforms and the opening up of the Chinese economy have been accompanied by a process of globalization in the rest of the world. In fact, these two forces have reinforced each other over the last three decades. For example, the Chinese export of labour intensive goods has boomed, particularly in the coastal areas. In turn, this has attracted more FDI inflows into the country which has assisted in exploiting the comparative advantage of China's labour force and increasing the competitiveness of Chinese exports.

When compared with the SOEs, the NSEs are more labour intensive and more efficient. As a result, NSE's products are developed towards a strong export orientation. The share of FFE export on total national exports was below 1% in 1985, 13% in 1990, and 41% in 1996. The share of TVE exports also increased dramatically from about 5% in 1985 to an inconceivable 43% in 1995. While China's foreign trade sector is moving toward a more liberalized stage, FFEs and TVEs have been overtaking the state sector to play a dominant role in exporting manufacturing goods.

The values and shares of exports in TVEs and FFEs during the period 1985-96 are shown in Table 2. It can be seen that the average annual growth rate of export value in these two sectors was higher than the nation as a whole. This resulted in an increase in the shares of TVEs and FFEs in total national exports. Since there is a certain degree of overlap between TVEs and FFEs in export data, it is difficult to identify exactly what proportions they account for in terms of total exports. Nevertheless, Perkins (1997:501) has estimated that NSEs produced more than two thirds of China's total exports.

The critical role played by the NSEs in international trade has led to some significant changes in the institutions and structure of the Chinese economy, particularly in its labour market. For example, employees working in a foreign funded firm can enjoy superior social status and relatively higher incomes, in addition to greater prospects for future promotion than can those who work for domestic firms. Nonetheless, these workers may also be more stressed, and feel insecure since the possibility of being dismissed is high. As a result, the rate of employee turnover is also relatively high in FFEs and PIEs.

Table 2. Export Growth of in TVEs and FFEs, 1980-96

Year	Total Exports [1] million Y	Exports of The TVEs [2] million Y	Exports of The FFEs [3] US$ million	[2]/[1] %	[3]/[1] %	Exchange Rate RMB/US$
1980	18119		8.24		0.05	1.7050
1985	80890	3900	296.7	4.82	0.37	2.9367
1986	108210	9949	582.03	9.19	0.54	3.4528
1987	147000	16196	1220.00	11.02	3.09	3.7221
1988	176670	29871	2460.00	16.91	5.18	3.7221
1989	195600	37144	4920.00	18.99	9.47	3.7659
1990	298580	46230	7810.00	15.48	12.51	4.7838
1991	382710	95884	12050.00	25.05	16.76	5.3227
1992	467630	119279	17356.79	25.51	20.47	5.5149
1993	528480	219300	25237.17	41.50	27.52	5.7619
1994	1042180	339831	34712.97	32.61	28.71	8.6187
1995	1245100	539500	46875.87	43.33	31.44	8.3507
1996	1257640		61506.36		40.66	8.3142
Annual Growth	**24.94**	**49.30**	**55.74**			

Sources: SSB, 1991:65:97:10. 1992:627. 1995:537. 1997. ZGXZQYNJ, 1990:174. 1993:148, 1994:202. 1995:100. ZGDWJJTJDQ (1979-91):200.

In comparison, workers employed in the SOEs tend to be more comfortable and secure, though there are still employee lay-offs. According to Brook and Tao (2003:15), about 25 million employees in SOE and UCEs were laid-off in 1998-2002 as part of a reemployment program that provided laid-off workers with a safety net. Such laid-off employees could stay in Reemployment Centres which are organised by the government until they found a job or for a period of up to three years, but they had to receive lower monthly benefits than the wage they had received previously.

The number of these laid-off workers declined from 9.5 million in 1999 to 6.4 million by 2002, as many have found jobs, transferred to the registered unemployed or dropped out of the workforce altogether (Brook and Tao, 2003:16).

The institutional setting of the TVEs, and PIEs are somewhere in between the FFEs and the SOEs, yet they are diversified among different firms. For the large firms, particularly those publicly listed ones, employees are well paid, and they also receive standard payment for a variety of social insurances, while in the smaller ones, particularly those family based firms, these social and medical insurances are either set at a relatively low level, or completely absent. In addition, some of the migrant workers have to work overtime without appropriate compensation, and sometimes their pay has been delayed or even cancelled.

A QUANTITATIVE ESTIMATION OF THE LABOUR MARKET REFORM ON THE WORLD ECONOMY

Labour market liberalization, characterized by the relaxing of rural to urban migration control, has led to several significant changes in China's labour market. Although the household registration regime is still effective in the major capital cities at the provincial level, the restrictions on rural to urban migration have been relaxed in most of the smaller and middle-sized cities. This may indicate that labour market segmentation between the rural and urban sectors has begun to diminish. Even in the large cities, rural migrants are now able to stay as long as they can finance their own living expenses. At the same time, the lifetime employment which has been maintained for the privileged urban workers in the SOEs for more than 40 years is being replaced by some temporary, casual and fixed-term working contracts. In some provincial cities in the South, residential status plays no role in worker's recruitment, compensation and promotion prospects. In addition, a special phenomenon known as *rural industrialisation*, which is partially created by the segmentation of the rural and urban labour market in the early period, continues to develop. These rural enterprises as a whole have overtaken the state-owned enterprises to become the largest employer of non-farming workers since 1996 (Zhang, 1999, 2000b).

The changes in the landscape of the labour market in China seem irreversible. According to Cai (2003) there were about 77 million rural migrants working temporarily in the cities in 2000. In addition to this, there were 151.6 million rural labourers working in manufacturing and service activities in the rural areas. In total, there were about 230 million rural workers, which accounted for about one third of the entire labour force working on non-farming activities.

Another event accompanying labour market liberalization was the dramatic increase in FDI in the 1990s. By 2003, China used US$54 billion of FDI, setting a record in China's history and ranking the first place in the world. These FDIs are mainly used in urban manufacturing activities. Two particular areas, the high-tech industry and industries with a strong export-orientation are particularly encouraged by the governments through several preferential treatment measures such as tax concessions and subsidized land use fees (Zhang, 2000a).

Zhang (2005) incorporated all these factors into a theoretical model to show that the liberalisation in labour and capital markets in China will have a significant worldwide impact on production and international trade, particularly in the labour intensive industries. The world economy is divided into ten regions. The changes in GDP in the ten regions are presented in Table 3.

It is clearly shown in the table that when the GDP increases significantly in China, it declines in almost all the other regions, with the exception of Australia and New Zealand (ANZ) and the region classified as the rest of the world (ROW).

The third column of the table shows an indicator of the economic welfare that can be disaggregated into a group of components. These components include allocative efficiency, technical efficiency, the terms of trade and investment-saving balance effect.

The equivalent variation which shows the change in utility measured by real income change is used as an indicator of the changes in economic welfare.

Table 3. Changes in Regional GDP (%) and Economic Welfare (US$ Million)

	An Exogenous Growth of Labour and FDI in China on Regional GDP	Economic Welfare Measured by Equivalent Variation
NAFTA	-0.28	3306
China	6.97	117689
ANZ	0.13	619
East Asia	-0.41	-846
Japan	-0.56	-2076
EU15	-0.45	-1216
ASEAN	-0.2	266
South Asia	-0.45	-285
Non-EU Europe	-0.34	339
ROW	0	3968
World		121763

Source: Zhang (1995)

In terms of the change in EV, Table 3 shows that a combination of labour and capital augmenting technology in China could generate the largest welfare gain. This result seems to suggest that the two productive factors of labour and capital are cooperative. In other words, the increase of one factor will significantly increase the productivity of the other, and vice versa. For China, the welfare gains are mainly created by the improvements in its allocation efficiency and technical efficiency. For the other beneficiaries, the gains are created by the improvement in their terms of trade.

Despite the huge welfare gains to the world as a whole that are generated by labour market liberalization in China, these gains are not evenly distributed among different regions. As expected, China gains the most, followed by NAFTA, ANZ, ASEAN, non-EU members in Europe and the ROW countries, whereas Japan, the EU15, the East Asian and South Asian countries are the losers. This seems to indicate that a *complementary* relationship exists between China and its Australasian, ASEAN, non-EU and American trading partners, whereas a *competitive* relationship exists between China and its East and South East Asian neighbors, as well as the EU15.

CONCLUSION

Based on a brief review of the dualistic nature of the Chinese labour market and a discussion concerning the development of NSEs in China, this chapter has examined the origins and consequences of labour market reforms in China and their likely impact on the world economy. Firstly, it verifies that the market oriented reforms in China have indeed led to a structural change in its labour market, characterized by the shrinkage of the SOEs and the expansion of the NSEs. Secondly, it shows how and why the NSEs are more labour intensive and economically efficient, and therefore more internationally oriented. These factors are partially revealed through an analysis of the specificities of China's dualistic labour market. While the workers in the SOEs are privileged with a group of welfare programs, the migrant workers and workers in the PIEs and TVEs are less rewarded, and hence, are more economically attractive in helping the FFEs and TVEs to export their labour intensive products.

In terms of the impact of the labour market reforms in China on the world economy, this chapter has shown that the net impact on economic welfare is positive for the rest of the world in general and for the Chinese economy in particular. Furthermore, the welfare gains are magnified when labour market liberalization is accompanied by foreign capital inflows in China. Nevertheless, it also shows that these gains are not evenly distributed across different countries and across different industries.[i] While China, the NAFTA and Australasian countries seem to benefit from labour market reform in China, the EU15 and the rest of Asia, perhaps with the exception of the ASEAN countries, are more likely to face fiercer competition and a possibility of their exporting market in the advanced countries.

The findings of this chapter seem to support the view that tremendous potential economic gains exist in China and these gains can be captured should the labour market reforms be continued and deepened over time. Moreover, these economic gains will be greater if labour market liberalization is accompanied by a continuing rapid growth in FDI inflows. To the rest of the world, it may imply that the labour market has almost been integrated worldwide during the process of globalization. Meanwhile it should be noted that, although labourers in the naturally resource abundant countries like Australia and New Zealand, are more likely to benefit from the rapid economic growth and export boom in China, labourers in other countries, particularly those that are labour abundant in Asia, are more likely to be hurt. This is due to tougher international labour market competition, when some of their labour intensive goods in international markets are replaced by Chinese exports during the process of globalization.

REFERENCES

Brook Ray and Ran Tao. (2003) 'China's labour market performance and challenges', *IMF Working Paper*, WP/03/210.

Cai, F. (2003) "Removing the barriers to labour mobility: labour market development and its attendant reforms", paper presented at the World Bank Workshop on national market integration in Beijing, China.

Cheng, T. and Selden, M. (1994) 'The origins and social consequences of China's hukou system', *The China Quarterly*, September, 139:644-68.

Lewis W. A. (1954) 'Economic development with unlimited supplies of labour', *The Manchester School*, May, pp.139-91.

Naughton, Barry, (1994) "Chinese institutional innovation and privatization from below", *American Economic Review*, AEA Papers and Proceedings, 84(2):266-70.

Naughton, Barry, (1995) *Growing Out of the Plan: Chinese Economic Reform, 1978-1993.* Cambridge University Press, Cambridge.

Perkins, F.C. (1997) "Export performance and enterprise reform in China's coastal provinces", *Economic Development and Cultural Change*, 45(3):501-40.

Putterman, Louis, (1994) "On the past and future of China's township and village-owned enterprises", *World Development*, 25(10):1639-55.

Putterman, L. (1992) 'Dualism and reform in China', *Economic Development and Cultural Change*, 40(3):467-94.

Ranis G. and J. C. H. Fei (1961) 'A theory of economic development', *American Economic Review*, 51(4), September, pp533-65.

Selden, Mark and You Laiyin, (1997) "The reform of social welfare in China". *World Development*, 25(10):1657-68.

Sen. A. K. (1984) "Peasants and dualism with or without surplus labour". In A.K. Sen *Resources, Values and Development*, Oxford:Blackwell.

SSB (State Statistical Bureau), (1999-2005) China Statistical Yearbook, China Statistics Press, Beijing.

ZGXZQYNJ, *Zhongguo Xiangzhen Qiye Nianjian* (1990-1995) (Yearbook of China's Rural Enterprises), various issues.

Zhang, X. (1992) 'Urban-rural isolation and its impact on China's production and trade Pattern', *China Economic Review*, (USA) 3(1): 85-105.

Zhang, X.. (1995) 'Classification and the dualism of China's industries in the 1980s', *Industry and Development*, United Nations Industry and Development Organisation (Austria), 34:.61-91.

Zhang, X. (1999) 'Growth of township and village enterprises and change in China's export pattern', *Advances in Chinese Industrial Studies*, 6: 89-102.

Zhang, X.. (2000a) 'Motivations, objectives, locations and partner selections of foreign invested enterprises in China', *Journal of Asia-Pacific Economies*, 5(3):190-203.

Zhang, X. (2000b) 'The tale of two sectors: a comparison between state-owned and non-state-owned enterprises in China', *Asian Thought and Society: An International Review*, 25(74):200-18.

Zhang, X. (2005) "Labour Market Liberalization in China and Its Economic Impact on the World Economy". Paper presented in the international conference "Globalization, migration and labour mobility in India and China", Monash University, Melbourne, Australia 29-30 September 2005.

Zhang X, C. Findlay and A. Watson. (1995) "Growth of China's rural enterprises: impacts on urban-rural relations", *The Journal of Development Studies* (UK), Volume 31, No. 4. pp.567-584.

APPENDIX: THE AGGREGATION OF REGIONS

Table A1. The Aggregation of the Ten Regions

No.	Region code	Comprising economies	Description
1	NAFTA	USA, Canada, Mexico	North American Free Trade Area
2	China	China	China
3	ANZ	Australia, New Zealand	Australia, New Zealand
4	East Asia	Korea, Hong Kong, Taiwan	Korea, Hong Kong, Taiwan
5	Japan	Japan	Japan
6	EU15	Austria, Belgium, Netherlands, Luxembourg, France, Italy, Germany, UK, Ireland, Denmark, Greece, Spain, Portugal, Sweden, Finland	The 15 member countries of European Union in 1997
7	ASEAN	Singapore, Malaysia, Indonesia, Philippines, Thailand, Vietnam	ASEAN members in 1997
8	South Asia	India, Pakistan, Bangladesh	India, Pakistan, Bangladesh
9	Non-EU Europe	Hungry, Poland, the rest of Central European Association, former Soviet Union, Turkey	Non EU member countries in Europe
10	ROW	Rest of the World	All other countries that are not included in the other 9 groups

---

[i] See the Appendix for the aggregation of the ten regions of the world economy. A detailed report on the output changes at industrial level is available upon request.

Chapter 4

INDIA AND BUSINESS PROCESS OUTSOURCING

Mohan Thite and Bob Russell

INTRODUCTION

Employment and work relations in India are as complex as Indian society itself, which, more than ever, is characterized by extreme forms of uneven development. In this chapter we largely focus on one sector of the economy, which is heavily implicated in the current phase of globalisation – referred to as the IT/ITeS/BPO sector. This acronym stands for information technology, information technology enabled services and business process outsourcing industries. At the moment, it is investment in this sector which is powering the Indian economy and which has drawn attention from around the world. It is sometimes said in India that the country largely missed out on the opportunities and benefits of the industrial revolution. However, the IT revolution is seen as means of redressing this situation in the context of a developing knowledge economy. It is certainly the case that up until the recent parliamentary elections of 2004, governments dedicated much of their policy emphasis towards attracting both foreign and domestic IT/ITeS/BPO investment. In short, knowledge and information based industries have very quickly attained a place of prominence in the Indian economy and are centrally implicated with the processes of globalisation that are so hotly contested. For these reasons, the bulk of the chapter concentrates on analysing emergent employment relations in the IT/ITeS/BPO sector.

This chapter is based upon a month of field work which the authors carried out jointly in India in 2005 as well as earlier field work conducted by Thite. In preparation for this work the authors designed two open-ended, qualitative interview protocols, one for the operations manager(s) and another for the human resources manager(s) at each organisational case study site. Four of India's large BPO providers participated in the study. The average number of employees in these firms was 5500 and their call centres were spread across all the major cities in India. Detailed information was sought in these interviews on topics such as employee costs, business profiles, recruitment and labour market challenges, relationships with clients, and work design. Interviews were conducted at each company's headquarters. In total eight managerial interviews were conducted, although in a number of cases, these included sessions with part or all of the whole managerial team in charge of operations or HR. Observer triangulation was practiced in each case. That is, both authors took notes, entered them into computer files and then exchanged the files with each other in order to add additional material that might have been missed.

This primary data is supplemented by other material that is referred to in the chapter. Company, industry (such as National Association of Software and Service Companies – NASSCOM) and consultant reports were accessed while in India. National and state level Government documents pertaining to industrial relations statutes in general, and to the IT/ITES/BPO sector specifically were collected. As were local Shops and Establishment Acts and Rules, which establish local employment conditions. Other material that was used includes census data and Bureau of Labour data, that were collected during the field trip to India.

Unfortunately, it was not possible to engage in direct field observation during this project. Each of the four Indian companies included in the study were strictly outsourcing providers to overseas (mainly American) clients. Concerns over principle/ provider confidentiality, especially in the wake of damaging international press stories concerning data privacy, proved to be too large a hurdle to overcome. Each of the companies did, however, agree to administer an employee survey that the authors had designed as a counterpart to the management interviews. Results from this work are referred to only *en passant* in this chapter, which is intended to provide an overview of Indian employment relations in the context of globalisation.

Before focusing on the Indian outsourcing phenomena, a general overview of the Indian economy is provided in the next section. This is then followed by three sections that examine: the growth and current state of the IT/ITeS/BPO sector in the Indian economy; labour and employment relations in this sector; and the challenges and contradictions that are emerging from the unique mix of a knowledge intensive industry set in the context of marginal social conditions. A short concluding section draws the main themes and issues of the chapter together.

THE INDIAN ECONOMY IN THE NEW MILLENIUM

With a land mass less than 25 percent larger than the state of Western Australia, and an economy that is ranked as the twelfth largest in the world, India passed the one billion population mark early in the new millennium and is predicted to become the most populous country on the planet within the next 20 years. It is necessary to keep in mind that the overwhelming majority of this population, around three-quarters, remains on the land or lives outside of the major cities. Just under 60 percent (58.2 percent) of the country's labour force is to be found in agricultural production, listed either as cultivators (31.7 percent), or agricultural labourers (26.5 percent). Another four percent of the total workforce is included within the category of household industry, while just over one-third of the labour force, (37.6 percent), lumped together in the residual 'other' category, which would include both manufacturing industry and service provision (Census of India, 2001). Women are over-represented in the agrarian labour category (39 percent of all recorded female workers, compared with 21 percent of male workers) and have less than half the representation in the industry and service categories (21.7 percent) that are recorded by men.

Official data also makes the distinction between the organised sector of the economy and the unorganised. The former refers to public and private enterprises, which pay wages and salaries, are covered by federal and state laws and maintain annual accounts. This sector accounts for approximately 10 percent of the total labour force, with the remainder falling outside of the official sector in small, informal undertakings that are often characterised by underemployment and casualisation. Within the organised sector community, social and personal service labour constitutes the largest element – 42 percent of all workers in this category. This includes workers in both the expanding private sector and public sector employment (Director General of Employment and Training, various years). Workers in manufacturing employment account for 24.7 percent of the total, transportation another 11.3 percent, while employees in finance, insurance, real estate and associated business services compose 6 percent of total employment in this sphere. The bulk of IT/ITeS/BPO employment is located in this latter category.

All up, the combined IT/ITeS/BPO sector employs under 1 million workers out of a total workforce (waged, salaried and other) that is approaching half a billion workers! It is difficult to fathom a large new middle class being thrown up by these developments, and indeed it is still the case that 35% of all Indians live on less than $1 US per day (Economist, March 5, 2005). Rather, we suggest that the importance of this sector is to be found elsewhere, specifically in the changes wrought to trade patterns, as they affect India as an exporter and her new found trading partners. In 1995, the top five exports (by value and in order of importance) from India were gems and jewellery, garments, textiles, marine products and leather ware (not including footwear). Ten years later the list reads as follows: software; engineering goods; gems and jewellery; chemicals and related products; and textiles. Software design chalked up $US 17.2 billion in exports in 2005, compared with 13.7 billion for gems/jewellery (Gupta and Kumarkaushalam, 2005). India's largest export market and overall trading partner is the US, which accounted for 20% of exports, many in the IT/ITeS field, followed by China (8.3%), UAE (8%) and UK (5%) (Economist, 2006). Even though India's share of global trade remains at under 1 percent, ($250 billion US in 2004), it is these shifting trade patterns that have become synonymous with globalisation and, in the process, have attracted considerable attention in both India and overseas (Sheshabalaya, 2005; Kripalani and Engardio, 2005). Notably, IT/ITeS/BPO activity has been associated with surpassing what had become known in the 1970-80s as the 'Hindu rate of growth'. This refers to economic growth rates, which although positive, lagged behind population growth. In the first years of the new millennium (2001-2005) real economic growth ran at 6.5%, still well behind China's, but against population growth of 1.5% per annum (Economist, 2005).

THE INDIAN IT/ITES/BPO SECTOR

Off-shoring, as part of global business realignment, is considered the third wave in global expansion by companies, after global export and global production. IT services include systems integration and information systems consulting, application development and support as well as IT training services. IT-enabled Services (ITeS) cover a wide range of services, depending on the nature of expertise, from:

- back-office data entry and processing, to
- customer contact services (such as complaints, tele-marketing, collections support), to
- corporate support functions (such as HR, finance, procurement, IT services), to
- knowledge services and decision-support (such as customer analytics, claims and risk management and consultancy), and to
- research and development services (such as engineering design, content development and new product design). (KPMG, 2004).

The global IT/ITeS market was estimated to be worth US$1,322 billion in 2003 and is expected to grow to US$3,391 billion by 2012 at a compounded annual growth of 11%, while the size of the ITeS market will continue to be around twice that of the IT services market (Taskforce, 2003). India is quickly emerging as "the services-hub of the world" with a 24% share of the off-shored IT/ITeS market in 2002; however, India's share of the global IT/ITeS market was still low at 0.8% in 2002. (KPMG, 2004). The Indian IT/ITeS sector is expected to earn a revenue of US$28 billion in 2004-05 (Nasscom-a, 2005). This is expected to grow to $148 billion by 2012, accounting for about 4.4% of the global market (Taskforce, 2003).

India's bid for off-shore IT/ITeS business is driven by a number of factors. Most notably there is the availability of an appropriately skilled human resource base that is estimated to include 14 million tertiary educated graduates. Moreover, by international standards, even highly skilled labour remains cheap. Salary levels although escalating (see below) still range between one-tenth and one-fifth of that of equivalent jobs in the US. Finally, and more controversially, according to some, the ability to generate better quality work, more efficiently (with improved service levels of 5-10% across different parameters such as customer satisfaction, response time, accuracy and speed) (KPMG, 2004) is a feature of out-sourcing. However, it needs to be noted that it is difficult to measure efficiency levels at the macro level in the absence of hard, empirical data. In particular, it is necessary to distinguish between more productive work and more intense work. With regard to the latter topic, it remains the case that the legal work week in India is still 8 to 12 hours longer per week (48 hours) than is the norm in Western economies.

The spectacular growth of the Indian software industry, which first took India global, in the early 1990s has been mostly export led. The industry started its journey in the USA with the on-site model, where it cheaply rented out Indian software programmers to work at client sites under client supervision in the US. Thanks to factors such as Y2K projects and a shortage of IT personnel in the USA, the on-site model worked so well that, by the close of the1990s, Indians accounted for nearly half of the H-1B work permits, which are employer-sponsored non-immigrant visas for temporary workers, issued by the US Department of Immigration for IT-related occupations (Mittal and Goel, 2004).

Over the years, Indian software companies built a reputation for supplying large numbers of cheap, but high quality IT personnel, pushing IT companies in the USA to continue to lobby the US government to relax work permit regulations. With Euro conversion projects coming on stream in the late 1990s, European companies followed the US example in hiring Indian IT personnel, pushing up their demand as well as the profit margins of the Indian companies that employed them. As the confidence in the service delivery capability of Indian companies increased, part of the outsourced work (mainly coding) was shifted to India. In this way the off-shore model of export led informationalism gathered steam.

By early 2000, the Indian software industry had firmly established its capability and credibility as a strategic IT business partner using both on-shore and off-shore models. With the crash of the dot.com bubble, overseas companies started cutting their IT budgets and in the process, put pressure for increased efficiency at reduced cost on both their internal IT departments as well as outsourcing providers. This coincided with multinational firms' revaluation of their business processes, including back-office support functions, customer contact and care and corporate support functions through such initiatives as business process re-engineering. That is when business process outsourcing (BPO) came into being.

To most Indian software companies, BPO was an accidental opportunity and in many cases was initiated by their overseas clients. They had to quickly set up subsidiaries to exploit this new found opportunity which came in handy in the face of the downturn in the IT industry. Another stroke of luck for the industry was the cheap availability of abundant and under-utilised fibre optic cables laid under the sea by western companies during the e-commerce hype generated in the 1990s and their increasing bandwidth capacity (Friedman, 2005). While the Indian software industry took more than 10 years to mature and climb up the value chain, the Indian ITeS/BPO industry has taken just 5 years (between 2000 and 2005) to do just that. Many of the top Indian software companies, namely, Infosys, Wipro and Satyam, have now set up subsidiary companies such as Progeon, Wipro BPO, and Nipuana, which are their ITES arms.

According to NASSCOM, the premier trade body and the chamber of commerce of the IT software and services industry in India, the Indian IT/ITeS industry earned an estimated USD 28.2 billion in 2004-05, of which IT services and software accounted for 58.6%, the ITeS-BPO, 20% and hardware 21% (Nasscom-b, 2005). Today, there are around 3000 IT companies in India currently exporting to over 150 countries with an employee base of around 700,000. The top 5 Indian IT software & service exporters are Tata Consultancy Services, Infosys, Wipro, Satyam and HCL (Nasscom-c, 2005).

There are over 400 ITeS/BPO companies in India that include a mix of captive units (wholly dedicated set ups of both Multi National Companies and Indian companies accounting for 65% of the market) and third-party services providers with a total employee base of around 350,000 (Nasscom-d, 2005). In 2004-05, the ITeS-BPO segment witnessed a growth of 45% to reach USD 5.2 billion that constituted 30% of the total IT-ITeS exports from India. The top 5 third-party (call centre & BPO) players are WNS Global Services, Wipro BPO, HCL Technologies BPO, IBM-Daksh and ICICI OneSource. Reflecting complementary strengths between IT and ITeS, the integration of IT-BPO contracts is becoming more common. Nasscom also reports that "the ITES-BPO companies are gaining significant traction in transaction processing; with more and more firms balancing voice and non-voice business portfolios to diversify revenue and raise seat utilisation" (Nasscom-e, 2005).

The Indian ITeS/BPO industry is maturing very quickly. Today it includes, high-end business services, such as knowledge services and decision-support (that is customer analytics, claims, risk management and consultancy) and research and development services (eg. engineering design, content development and new product design). These high-end services are part of what is now called Knowledge Process Outsourcing (KPO) and they are expected to provide over 40% of total Indian BPO revenues in 2010 (The Hindu, 2005a). In line with this growth, the ITeS/BPO/KPO industry now employs not only generic graduates as Customer Service Representatives (CSRs) but also MBAs, doctors, engineers and chartered accountants as process executives. Even at the CSR level, the data collected by the authors in four Indian companies suggests that more than 85% of employees are university graduates. This compares with a figure of about 20% of their counterparts in Australia that was turned up in comparative research conducted by Russell at twenty Australian customer contact centres. Another interesting point of comparison is to be found in the age demographics of the industry. Over 90% of employees in the Indian ITeS/BPO industry are under 30 years of age (DQ-IDC, 2004). In our survey at the four Indian BPO centres, 92% of the respondents (N=638) were under the age of 30. This compares with 40% of Russell's Australian call centre sample (N=1232) that were under 30 years of age.

The IT/ITeS sector has inserted itself at various levels of the value chain from low level, low value services (such as code-writing and call centres) to complex and more profitable functions such as data management, market analysis, consulting, and computer-aided design (Chandler, 2005). However, this has not been a linear development progressing from low end to high value activities over time. Rather, it is better stylised as a set of ad hoc opportunities that began with IT, and then moved down the ladder into ITeS. It is now entering into KPO with the outsourcing of medical diagnostic, legal, financial and other forms of professional work from western economies. The growth of Indian IT/ITeS firms has been stellar, occurring via mergers and acquisitions, through the expansion of operations overseas (investments by Indian BPOs in such countries as the Philippines, China, Czechoslovakia and Australia), and through strategic alliances with multinational companies. This form of globalisation has entailed obtaining internationally recognised quality accreditation certificates, adopting world-class HR best practices, and benchmarking with leading firms from across the globe (ibid). Quality certification is a hallmark of the Indian IT/ITeS sector. For example, 90% of ITeS/BPO companies have a dedicated quality department with 50% having implemented various levels of ISO and 45% having Six Sigma and other certifications (Nasscom-f, 2005).

Leveraging on human capital to overcome deficiencies in physical capital figures largely in these processes and lies at the heart of current economic developments (Mittal and Goel, 2004). To date, this represents a unique, if untested, strategy for overcoming decades of lagging performance. The absence of adequate infrastructure in India poses real problems for development. For example, the nation's patchy highway network includes just 124,000 miles of road compared to China's 870,000 (Chandler, 2005). Urban congestion on the roads and in the skies is notorious. Rather than denigrating the importance of physical infrastructure, many 'new economy' theorists (Reich, 1991; Florida, 2002) stress the importance of not only physical infrastructure but also cultural amenities as a key to successful transition/prosperity in the knowledge economy. Whether infrastructural inadequacies prove to be an insurmountable obstacle to development, or whether the new economy of export led service provision has peculiarities that render such infrastructure less important remains to be seen.

Meanwhile, many western firms are now looking at different ways of leveraging both domestic and offshore markets. In the US, "leading-edge providers are upskilling US-based agents to take on revenue generating as well as customer retention activities and offshoring the support and service enquiries" (Datamonitor, 2005: 65). In Australia, the ANZ bank is similarly increasing its operations roles in Bangalore and, at the same time, creating new jobs and opportunities in customer facing areas in Australia (Jones, 2005). The implications of this are considered later in this chapter.

EMPLOYMENT REGULATION

This section examines the relevance of the Indian industrial relations system, specifically the existing political/legal framework to the IT/ITES/BPO industries. Unsurprisingly, we come to the conclusion that the national regulatory regime and the global BPO industry mainly exist in different 'worlds'. IT/ITES/BPO is largely regulated by the interaction of global capital flows and local labour market dynamics while existing forms of regulation have been marginalised. We begin by describing what those forms of regulation are. Next, we describe the current HR-Employment Relations scene in the ITES/BPO sector. These dynamics have important implications for both workers and other organisations in the IR system, such as trade unions. The implications of this are also analysed.

Employment relations in India are regulated by a number of legal instruments, commencing with the Trade Union Act of 1926. This Act, initially provided for the registration of trade unions and, in the process, provided specific immunities from conspiracies in restraint of trade and civil actions for breach of contract (Krishnamurthi, 2002). The legislation still specifies a minimum membership of only seven workers for registration. This, in turn, has given rise to a huge number of registered unions (64,817 in 1999), with a very small average base (786 members) (India Labour Bureau, 2004).

The Trade Union legislation was silent on the question of union recognition by employers and this remained the case until 1958, when the Standing Labour Committee of the Federal Government devised protocols for representation and collective bargaining rights that were agreed to by representatives of industry and labour. These were appended to the Voluntary Code of Discipline, wherein management agreed to recognise the union which had the largest membership constituency for any given establishment or industry. This could be determined by either an examination conducted by the Ministry of Labour of the financial records/membership of the contending unions or, where all parties, including the employer agree, by way of a secret ballot conducted by the Ministry. To trigger recognition, the actual union membership threshold is quite low – minimally 2 percent of the workforce in question. In exchange for this, unions agreed to subscribe to a code of discipline of their own. This includes such provisions as no strikes without notification, a renunciation of coercion, work to rule tactics and sit-down strikes and a willingness to discipline officials and members who act in disregard of the code, (Krishnamurthi, 2002, ch.6).

With respect to all of these undertakings it is important to keep two essential points in the foreground. First, these protocols represented a *voluntary* undertaking on the part of business and labour leaders. They may or may not be respected in any specific case. Union recognition is not a statutory requirement of Indian employment relations law. As one commentator reminds us, such "codes are virtually buried for all practical purposes and have become part of industrial relations history" (Ratnam, 2001 :42). In part, inter-union rivalry, (see below) has militated against finding agreement on principles for union recognition. Secondly, under the 1926 Act, union membership also remains voluntary. There are no legal provisions for closed or union shop rules, or for the automatic check-off of membership dues.

Union recognition is also referred to in the 1947 Industrial Disputes Act. This omnibus bill was designed to foster orderly industrial relations on the sub-continent (Sodhi and Plowman, 2001). Appended to the bill (Schedule Five) is a lengthy list of unfair labour practices, which includes proscriptions against interference in union organising, including discrimination against union members, the use of threats or coercion, including threats to shut down operations, the creation of company or company dominated unions, or the refusal to bargain in good faith with the recognised union. Employers are also forbidden from recruiting replacement workers during legal strikes or employing casual or temporary workers on a long term basis, although penalties for transgressions of such rules seem to be minimal.

The 1947 Act also establishes rules for the settlement of disputes involving wages, working hours, occupational classifications, layoffs, retrenchments and technological change. Depending upon the issue, a Labour Court may be established to deal with cases of dismissals, the legality of strikes/lockouts, or the withdrawal of existing conditions while an Industrial Tribunal may be created to process disputes over compensation, hours of work, job classification, technological change or reductions in employment. Awards are made by the Labour Courts, Industrial Tribunals or National Tribunals that have been established for that purpose and are binding upon the parties unless vetoed or modified by the relevant state or Federal government. From the available, if dated evidence, it appears as though settlements through adjudication rather than collective bargaining have been the most pervasive form of interest based settlement (Sodhi and Plowman, 2001 :59). Recognised unions are given statutory rights to represent workers in any disputes which come before a conciliation officer, board, labour court or tribunal that is established under the Act.

In addition to specifying a host of unfair labour practices, the Industrial Disputes Act is immediately relevant to two other areas of employment relations. First, it provides detailed rules with respect to employer initiated changes (such as layoffs and retrenchments), which first must receive approval from the appropriate court or tribunal and second, it criminalises certain categories of industrial action. With respect to the former, in establishments of 100 or more employees who have at least one year of service, workers are entitled to half their normal pay for a period of 45 days in the event of a layoff being approved. One month's notice must be provided for any retrenchments and workers are again entitled to 15 days of their normal pay for each year of service. The same provision also applies to permanent closures, except here, the employer is required to provide 60 days advance notification. Any other changes in the terms or conditions of employment must be preceded by a 21 day notification.

On the union's side, notice of strike action must be provided to employers two weeks before such action is taken, while strikes and lockouts are outlawed during, and seven days after, any conciliation hearings or for the two months following any Labour Court or Tribunal hearings. Additionally, strikes are not permitted during the term of any conciliation award, which may be for a period of up to three years. Existing strikes can also be prohibited once reference has been made to the Act, with fines and jail terms imposed upon transgressors. All provisions in the Act cover establishments and industries that have been declared a public service, but the definition of such, contained in Schedule One of the Act, is very elastic. Governments can rule that just about any activity is temporarily a public service, including manufacturing and financial pursuits in the private sector. Thus, governments may choose to include or to exclude various activities from the provisions of the Disputes Act as they see fit.

The laws regulating strike and lockout activity seem to be 'honoured in the breach'. By no stretch of the imagination has such activity ceased to occur in Indian employment relations. The numbers of recorded strikes has declined dramatically since the early 1980s, falling by more than 80 percent, although strikes and lockouts have become larger in the sense of involving many more workers. Overall, the number of person days lost on account of disputes has declined somewhat since 1981, but nowhere near as dramatically as the actual number of disputes (India Labour Bureau, 2004). It would be incorrect to attribute any of these trends to statutes that have been on the books for over 50 years. Rather, the foreign exchange crisis of 1990-91, the turn towards the IMF and the subsequent adoption of neo-liberal remedies, as elsewhere, had a chilling effect on employment security, which made its effects known in the number of recorded industrial disputes.

Overall, and given the ambit of the Industrial Disputes Act, it can be seen that it is weighted in terms of the status quo (Chibber, 2003). Proposed changes for shutdowns, labour force reductions, or other significant alterations can quickly be removed from the realm of managerial prerogative and become the subject of an award. The whole tenor of the Indian system is *control through protection*, a logic that is largely at odds with the market rationality of globalisation. And although this is frequently an object of complaint, in truth requirements such as those contained in the Industrial Disputes Act, have had little impact on the IT/ITES/BPO sector. There are several reasons for this.

First, existing legislation was mainly intended to apply to and protect low wage manual workers. Those earning more than 1,600R per month ($US 35) and/or exercising supervisory, administrative or managerial tasks are exempt from the Industrial Disputes legislation. This would include most of the IT/ITES/BPO sector, where for example, average starting salaries in call centres are many times that amount. In other words, salaries in ITES are at a level which exempts workers in the sector from essential features of the system, but still renders them hugely inexpensive by western standards. Second, to date, the main issue for Indian IT/ITES/BPO providers has been recruiting and retaining labour, not shedding it, (see next section).

Given this mix of conditions, or what might be best described as a highly unstable 'equilibrium', it is still the case that despite reports of spontaneous job actions at individual call centres, the IT/ITES/BPO sector remains completely union free. To understand why this is the case, and to appreciate the challenges that union organising in the IT/ITES/BPO sector face, it is necessary to revert back to the IR context once again.

As part of this legacy, trade unions have been described as a "frail but enduring part of India's labour relations" (Ratnam, 2001). As we have seen, statutes governing unions have been permissive of the creation of very small entities. As a result, only 2 percent of registered unions have a membership exceeding 5000, while 40 percent have less than 100 members (Sodhi and Ploughman, 2001:140-156). Historically, this has gone along with excessive fragmentation. Thus, there are no less than a dozen central labour organizations operating in India, each with its own political affiliations, to which only 20 percent of registered unions are affiliated (Ratnam, 2001). As a result, specific enterprise unions also proliferate. Multiple plant/office unionism has added immensely to the complexity and divisiveness of the situation. It has resulted in a situation described by one analyst where "the arduous task of organizing a trade union from scratch has suddenly lost is relevance: the easier path to ascendance as a leader is to take over existing organizations." (Ramaswamy, 1988). This has gone along with an intense politicization that has left unions beholden to specific political parties, as well as dependent upon state patronage and reliant upon professional outside leaders (Chibber, 2005). None of these traits are favourable to an organising model (Bronfenbrenner, Friedman, Hurd, Oswald and Seeber, 1998) of union growth into information and knowledge based industries. As result, overall union densities in India are estimated to be about one-third of the organized sector of the economy or about 1 percent of the total societal labour force (Ratnam, 2001 :32).

On top of the historical legacy and peculiarities of trade unionism in India, more recently, various state governments have announced several special promotional schemes that encompass a comprehensive package of incentives and policies for the IT/ITES/BPO industries and further add to the uniqueness that is encountered in this sector. Most of the states in India have Software Technology Parks (STPs) and Export Processing Zones (EPZs) that offer first world infrastructure within the STP gates. With respect to changes in existing labour codes, a majority of the states have either promulgated a government order or notification permitting all establishments in the respective jurisdictions engaged in IT-enabled services (including call centres) to: work on national holidays; allow women to work through night shifts; and permit offices to function 24 hours a day, all through the year (Nasscom-g, 2005), although such practices have traditionally been banned through urban Shops and Establishment Acts (Confederation of Indian Industry, 2004).

For example, the 2003 IT and ITES Policy (Nasscom-h, 2005) of the state of Maharashtra (of which Mumbai, the commercial hub of the country, is the capital) and which accounts for 20% of the country's exports, aims to "create hassle-free and industry friendly, 24x7x365 working environment" for the sector by amongst other things:

o Relaxing working hours, work shifts and employment of women under Shops and Establishments Act,

o Applying all relaxations under the Industrial Disputes Act and Contract Labour Act to all IT and ITES units in the state on par with Special Economic Zones,

o Notifying IT & ITES units as continuous process units

o Issuing special passes to vehicles transporting women workers of IT & ITES units during night times,

o Declaring IT & ITES units as public utility services and essential services (Nasscom-h, 2005).

Similarly, the state of Andhra Pradesh's "AP Policy on Information Technology Enabled Services" dated 29th January, 2002 also commits to providing a supportive environment by amending the AP Shops and Establishments Act to allow ITES companies to:

o Employ women and young persons (between the age group 18-21) during night shifts, subject to provision of adequate security and transport

o Have "flex-timing" by asking an employee to work for more than 8 hours a day, without exerting an additional financial burden on the companies, in terms of overtime payments, as long as the statutory requirement on the maximum weekly working hours of 48 hours is respected

o Operate 24 hours a day and 365 days in the year, and

o Reduce the procedure involved in retrenching employees, if certain conditions are satisfied (Nasscom-i, 2005).

Currently, the IT/ITeS sector is devoid of the presence of trade unions. Existing unions appear to be unprepared to enter the new economy, but there is also a growing sense, as one manager put it "it's not a question of if, but of when" a trade union presence will develop. Considering the massive increase in employment in the ITeS industry and work environments characterised by round the clock work shifts, monotony, burnout and performance based employment, the question of whether trade unions will enter this new age industry raises heated discussion amongst politicians, trade unionists, industry analysts and employers. The employers' view is that there is no need for an external entity to represent employee voice because the IT/ITeS sector needs more people than it can get due to its phenomenal growth rate. This fact is said to promote best practices in people management and according to Bhargava, the former CEO of Progeon, "there is more that is good here than it has ever been in any single economic sector of India". Attrition rates in the industry, however, testify to alternative realities. More than likely, should the manager's prognosis cited above come to pass it will be at individual worksites, generated by specific grievances, and will assume the form of enterprise unionism. In the meantime, internal employment relations are largely regulated through HR practices, which are described in the next section.

HR ISSUES AND CHALLENGES

For an industry that is labour intensive and one that has experienced phenomenal growth in a short period of time, the implications for human resource management (HRM) of Indian ITES/BPO are enormous. Based on our research and secondary data, we conclude that the Indian IT/ITeS industry faces five important HR issues and challenges, namely, acute skill shortages, attrition, a leadership vacuum at the team level, escalating labour costs and a squeeze in profit margins. These are discussed in detail below.

Skill Shortages

Offset against the huge pools of surplus labour that define the Indian economy in general, are the employability demands of the BPO sector. Each component of the sector requires tertiary level education in a society where literacy rates hover around 65 percent for the population as a whole and at 45% for females. Jobs in IT minimally require a tertiary degree in engineering, computer science or mathematics, while call centre and data processing operations insist upon a Bachelors' level degree and high levels of proficiency in spoken and written English. Paradoxical as it may seem, it is currently a sellers market for labour in this particular enclave economy. It is estimated that by 2012, the labour power requirements for the off-shore Indian IT/ITeS markets, as well as domestic and captive IT/ITeS support requirements, will add up to 4-6 million workers (KPMG, 2004). While India could be one of the few countries with a qualified surplus labour pool by 2020, there is a possibility of a shortage in terms of skilled personnel for IT/ITeS to the tune of about half million workers, even in the medium term, that is, by 2009. (KPMG, 2004: 19 & Taskforce, 2003: 6).

The employable labour shortage is already impacting on the performance of the Indian IT/ITeS industry today in terms of attrition levels and wage trends (see below). The question here is of quality, not quantity. While it is estimated that approximately 17 million people will be available to the IT industry by 2008 (Nasscom-j, 2005), the problem relates to their employability and trainability. "The issue of manpower gap is not as much about institutional seat availability as about the nature of skills and training provided in these institutions" (Taskforce, 2003: 6).

According to one report, "Different categories of work at the agent level ... will require specific qualifications. These must be supported by some necessary delivery-related skills, such as language skills, analytical skills, computer proficiency, customer service orientation and behavioural traits" (KPMG, 2004: 34-36): While these are common requirements for CSRs anywhere in the world, in the context of India, staff need to be equipped with additional skills, such as language neutralisation, cross-cultural skills and familiarity with products that are not commonly used in India, such as credit cards. For high-end R&D work, Indian employers are constrained by the low base of available PhDs, the low enthusiasm of higher educated staff for R&D activities and the low growth in R&D staff (KPMG, 2004: 53; Saini and Budhwar, 2004).

To address the manpower requirements, the Ministry of Communications and Information Technology's Taskforce on meeting the HR Challenges in IT and ITES (2003: 12) recommends addressing the entire development lifecycle of human resources, from attracting the right people through to education, certification, deployment and retraining. This requires close cooperation and coordination between governments, education institutions, industry bodies and individual firms.

NASSCOM, the industry body, has already moved to establish a common certification system for some of the standard skills. For example, it recently launched the NASSCOM Assessment of Competence (NAC) for potential employees in the BPO industry as an industry standard assessment program with the aim of ensuring the transformation of a 'trainable' workforce into an 'employable' workforce (The Hindu, 2005b). Some states, such as Karnataka and Andhra Pradesh, have already moved to establish centralised testing and certification for potential employees in the industry (KPMG, 2004: 65-66). However, the breadth and depth of skills and competencies required for the industry are of such a nature that the scope for effective standardisation of skill testing and training will be quite limited. Therefore, KPMG (2004: 63) recommends a hybrid model with base-level common testing and certification supported by company-specific programs.

One of the leading BPO firms that we studied is engaged in educating the public and local colleges in enhancing the employment reputation of ITES work, tarnished by the social stigma of working unsocial hours and allegations of sweatshop like conditions. Other companies also following suit with open-days for the parents of young staff to see first hand what the ITES industry is all about. To spread employment networks beyond tier one cities, such as Bangalore, Delhi and Hyderabad, the ITeS companies are also moving to set up facilities in tier two cities as well. Additionally, some Indian ITeS companies have started attracting "non-employed" people, such as retiring army personnel, teachers and housewives (KPMG, 2004: 73)

Attrition

This currently seems to be the biggest challenge currently facing the ITES/BPO sector. The 'race for talent' as one HR manager described it between BPO suppliers is fierce, and with turnover rates that are cited to be between 90 and 120 percent per annum in the ITES sector (Datamonitor, 2005 and interviews), the poaching of workers has created much distrust among industry participants. Typical of these dynamics, is one firm of 2600 CSRs where the authors carried out field work. Just to keep the workforce on an even keel, 300 agents per month need to be recruited, while half of the centre's 100 percent quit rate occurs within the first three months of an agent commencing work. These figures mirror overall ITeS/BPO corporate experience where, particularly in voice based call centres, the average tenure of CSRs is less than 12 months. Of the four ITeS companies that the authors have first hand experience with, employee attrition was hovering at above 100% except in one where it was said to be 45%, possibly because the bulk of its operations are non-voice. Absenteeism ranges from 2-8% on a daily basis (Business Line, 2004). Some companies try to artificially bring down the attrition figures by excluding those who leave during the training/induction period or by omitting involuntary turnover, such as dismissals due to poor performance.

The reasons for attrition are manifold. One survey identified the following top five reasons for turnover in the industry: dissatisfaction with salaries (47%), lack of career opportunities (45%), leaving to pursue higher education (29%), illness (28%) and physical strain (22%) (DQ-IDC, 2004). The average working day in the organised sector of the economy, including ITES/BPO is nine hours, which includes an hour of break time, or over an hour per day longer than is typical of economies such as Australia's. To this can be added lengthy commuting times in company supplied vehicles to and from work on clogged infrastructure. However, according to the survey, the average employee satisfaction score remained high at 80.7% with bigger companies achieving higher satisfaction ratings. As jobs are not being seen as careers, significant numbers of people leave to pursue higher education (Datamonitor, 2005).

In the interviews that the authors conducted with the HR managers, marriage and pursuing higher education were frequently quoted as the main reasons for attrition. The night shift work that most of the employees are engaged in causes them, particularly, women, to leave this employment when they get married; hence, marriage is given as the reason for attrition. In addressing the issue of employees leaving to pursue higher education and greener pastures, some companies are beginning to explore the possibility of providing scholarships, tuition reimbursement and special arrangements with education institutions that would allow them to offer courses in the workplace – thereby enabling employees to pursue higher education. However, part-time employment and flexi-hours are rarely practiced. Internal promotion is another measure frequently taken to address attrition but its scope is limited. In companies that do undertake both IT work and ITES there is little movement from the latter to the more highly skilled work of IT support and development. Within the ITES sector there is little sense of opportunity for significant career development. Performance bonuses, which are very popular in Indian call centres, are also used to prevent job-hopping but the intense 'race for talent' temporizes the effects of such schemes. Most big companies provide various facilities, such as transport and subsidised meals and conduct frequent 'town-hall meetings' to ascertain and address grievances.

Escalating Wage Costs

Rising wage costs are an increasing worry for the industry and its peak organisation Nasscom. Although salaries are high by the standards set by the Industrial Disputes Act and regional minimum wage rates, there is still pressure to increase them further as occurred between 2000 and 2003 when salary costs increased from USD 200/month to USD 330/month. As a result of this, company operating profit margins decreased from 30-40% to 17-25%. This has made the industry as a whole in India less competitive on a global scale and less attractive for potential entrants (KPMG, 2004: 29).

An escalating wage bill is driven by a variety of factors including: fierce competition for skilled personnel, particularly for those with a year or more of experience; the increased emphasis on performance bonuses; and poaching via hefty salary increases especially on the part of the multinationals. Anecdotal evidence suggests that between 1995 and 1999, Indian software salaries increased by 45%, whereas in the USA, the increase was only 21% (Mittal and Goel, 2004). In 2005, India had the best average pay increase in the whole of Asia at 14.1% as against China at 8.1%. The pay hikes in the Indian IT and ITeS industry were even higher at 16% and 15.4%, respectively (Sify, 2006). The performance based variable pay in one IT company varies from 30-50% at higher levels and 7-15% at lower levels (Saha and Chatterjee, 2004). Add to this employee transport costs funded by the employer, which are peculiar to India due to the poor transportation infrastructure. One company where the authors undertook field work logged 60,000 kms per day in providing transportation to ferry the workforce between home and the office! Food vouchers, which are supplied for company canteens, are also a standard 'benefit' and they account for another 15% or so of total employee costs, according to the managers who were interviewed for this study. This is further compounded by the ever recurrent recruitment costs arising out of high attrition rates and training periods which may be prolonged through having to include extra modules in language and culture.

Thus, one can see the cost advantage of the IT/ITeS sector being eroded. However, according to some analysts, "as long as productivity and the value of work done are high", this should not pose a serious problem in the short to medium term (Mukherjee, 2005). Clearly, with basic wage costs (wages minus associated costs such as transportation and bonuses) in ITES being only about 10% of Australian wages there is still room for manoeuvre. Indeed, the model of employment we have been describing is mainly sustainable in the context of very low basic wages.

A Profit Squeeze

Clients on multi-year contracts with BPO providers expect costs to fall over the course of the tender as the provider becomes more experienced and familiar with the client's products and markets. These expectations are forwarded on to the supplier with multi-year contracts that reflect the expectation of declining costs being shared with the client. However, given the levels of turnover in the industry, and the associated costs of recruitment, training and wage/benefit competition, diminishing unit costs over time are anything but a foregone conclusion. Instead, training costs are more likely to remain constant, while both wage bills and associated costs such as workforce transportation are under pressure to rise, especially with rapidly escalating energy costs. BPOs can quickly find themselves being squeezed, while this pressure is passed on to the workforce in terms of work expectations and heightened levels of work intensity, which feed back into the attrition and related problems that we have already discussed. In this manner, what was a 'virtuous circuit' for the industry may be on the verge of turning into something quite different.

Supervisory Skill Vacuum

Leadership and supervisory skills shortages, particularly at the team/project level are another challenge to the IT/ITeS sector (Agrawal and Thite, 2003 and 2006). It is estimated that it takes about five years for a call centre market to establish its own middle management capabilities and India is still a couple of years behind before "all parts of the market are sufficiently staffed from within" (Datamonitor, 2005). NASSCOM, the industry's apex body, has moved to address this issue by instituting a "Certification Program for Building Frontline Managers" for quality analysts and team leaders (Nasscom-k, 2005).

CONCLUSION

In the 21st century, the world of work is changing rapidly both in manufacturing and services. In the last century, most of the blue and white-collar work was conducted in developed economies and in-house. Just as falling transportation costs have enabled the globalisation process to separate the geography of industrial production and consumption with countries, such as China, emerging as new manufacturing leaders, the spread of the internet, with cheap and abundant telecommunications bandwidth, has enabled businesses to outsource white-collar work to specialist outside suppliers, with countries, such as India emerging as important hubs for producing services for consumption at the other end of the fibre-optic cable (Edwards, 2004).

Apart from its sheer size, India currently constitutes an intriguing part of the globalization story for its pioneering of what can be termed an Export Led Services Provision (ELSP) model. Today, anybody who visits India will see that changes are everywhere and the country is well and truly on the move. It still remains a country of complete contrasts – five star hotels surrounded by slums, white collar workers rushing past unskilled labourers using primitive technologies, new globally branded cars navigating congested roads along with antiquated models, free ways and flyovers that suddenly lead to unpaved, snarled roads and so on.

Optimists such as Akshaya Bhargava, the former CEO of Progeon (the ITES arm of the globally reputed Indian IT multinational, Infosys), argue that what the IT industry did to India during the 1990s is akin to an "underwater earthquake" (The Business Standard, 2004). He asks a pointed question, "if half a million people (employed by the IT industry) can transform India in 10 years, imagine what 12 million (expected to be employed by the IT/ITeS sector by 2014) can do"? According to him, this

88

invisible, but real rising tide, will create a tectonic social shift, improving the lot of what is soon to be the most populous nation on earth. Its imprint on the world is already unmistakable. Yet this begs larger questions.

Currently, the BPO sector appears poised on an unstable knife edge. It involves a young, highly educated workforce conducting often routine work for which, in many cases, it is patently over qualified. As a result, the explosive growth of BPO in India has also given rise to startling attrition rates and working conditions that, although perhaps (temporarily) acceptable in urban India may well prove to be far short of employee aspirations.

Will India become the first successful case of Export Led Services Provision (ELSP) in the same way that the Asian Tigers have successfully pursued and brought to fruition a model of Export Led Industrialisation (ELI)? Or will the ELSP economy remain an enclave or 'island' economy as is currently the case? Can an ELSP model develop in the absence of political coordination and coherence, or without massive public investment in physical infrastructure, or will neo-liberal policies prove sufficient to launch a new era of socio-economic development on the sub-continent? Despite the spectacular growth and visibility of the IT/ITES sector, it is still largely irrelevant to the vast majority of Indians. Still, there is no mistaking the changes that IT/ITES/BPO have brought. While the Indian economic elephant is certainly stirring and moving, only time will tell whether its insertion into the global knowledge economy will bring with it societal standards befitting the 21st century, or new forms of economic dependence.

REFERENCES

Agrawal, N. M. & Thite, M. (2006) 'Nature & importance of soft skills in software project leaders'. *Asia Pacific Management Review*, 11(2), 405-413.

Agrawal, N. M. & Thite, M. (2003) 'HR issues, challenges & strategies in Indian software services industry'. *Intl. Journal of Human Resources Development and Management*, 3(3), pp. 249-264.

Bronfenbrenner, K., Friedman, S., Hurd, R., Oswald, R., and Seeber, R. (1998) *Organizing to Win: New Research on Union Strategies.* Ithaca: Cornell University Press.

Business Line. (2004) 'Attrition, absenteeism bug BPO cos'. April 22nd.

Census of India (2001) www.censusindia.net. T 00-009: Distribution of workers by category of workers.

Chandler, C. (2005) 'India on the move'. Fortune. October 31, 2005.

Chibber, V. (2003) *Locked in Place: State-Building and Late Industrialization in India.* Princeton: Princeton University Press.

Chibber, V. (2005) 'From Class Compromise to Class Accommodation: Labor's Incorporation into the Indian Political Economy' in Ray, R. and Katzenstein, M. (eds), *Social Movements In India: Poverty, Power and Politics.* Lanham MD: Rowman and Littlefield.

Confederation of Indian Industry, Northern Region. (2004) 'Driving Growth Through Reform: A comparative Analysis of Labour Practices in Select Northern Region States'.

Datamonitor. (2005) The future of contact centre outsourcing in India and the Philippines. February, 2005.

Director General of Employment and Training (various years) *Employment Review.* Delhi: Government of India

DQ-IDC. (2004) 'India BPO Employee Satisfaction Survey' http://www.bpo. nasscom.org/artdisplay.aspx?art_id=3709&cat_id=609   downloaded   9th December, 2005

The   Economist,   (2006)   http://www.economist.com/countries/india/profile.cfm? folder=Profile-FactSheet

Economist. (2005) http://www.economist.com/countries/India/index.cfm

Edwards, B. (2004) 'A world of work'. *The Economist.* November 11, 2004.

Florida, R. (2002) *The Rise of the Creative Class: and how it's transforming work, leisure, community and everyday life.* New York: Basic Books.

Friedman, T. L. (2005) 'The world is flat: A brief history of the twenty-first century'. New York: Farrar, Straus & Girou.

Gupta, A. and Kumarkaushalam. (2005) 'The Changing Face of Indian Exports', *Business Today*, November, 6th.

India, Labour Bureau (2004) *Indian Labour Yearbook.* Delhi: Ministry of Labour, Government of India.

Jones, C. (2005) 'ANZ jobs head to India', *The Courier Mail*, November, 29th.

KPMG. (2004) 'Strengthening the human resource foundation of the Indian IT enabled services industry'. Report by KPMG Advisory Services Private Limited in association with NASSCOM under the aegis of the Department of IT, Ministry of Information Technology and Communications, Government of India.

Kripalani, M. and Engardio, P. (2005) 'The rise of India'. *BusinessWeekOnline*. http://www.businessweek.com/magazine/content/03_49/b3861001_mz001.htm downloaded on 9th May, 2006.

Krishnamurthi, S. (2002) *Commercial's Commentary on Trade Unions Act, 1926 As Amended by Trade Unions (Amendment) Act 2001*. Delhi: Commercial Law Publishers.

Mittal, A. & Goel, S. (2004) 'Globalization and Indian IT industry: A strategic perspective'. In *Information technology: Issues and challenges of globalisation*. New Delhi: Indian Institute of Foreign Trade.

Mukherjee, A. (2005) 'India's software dream run is far from over'. *Bloomberg*. June 10th 2005

Nasscom-a. (2005) http://www.nasscom.org/strategic2005.asp downloaded on 9th May, 2006.

Nasscom-b. (2005) http://www.nasscom.org/articleprint.asp?art_id=4163 downloaded on 27th November, 2005.

Nasscom-c. (2005) http://www.nasscom.org/articleprint.asp?art_id=4413 downloaded on 29th November, 2005.

Nasscom-d. (2005) http://www.nasscom.org/articleprint.asp?art_id=4154 downloaded on 27th November, 2005.

Nasscom-e. (2005) http://www.nasscom.org/articleprint.asp?art_id=4400 downloaded on 29th November, 2005.

Nasscom-f. (2005) http://www.bpo.nasscom.org/artdisplay.aspx?cat_id=588 downloaded on 29th November, 2005.

Nasscom-g. (2005) (http://www.bpo.nasscom.org/artdisplay.aspx?cat_id=563 downloaded on 27th November 2005)

Nasscom-h. (2005) (http://www.bpo.nasscom.org/download/Maharashtra%20ITeS Policy2003.pdf downloaded 23rd December.

Nasscom-i. (2005) (http://www.bpo.nasscom.org/download/AP%20ITES%20Policy.pdf downloaded on 23rd December

Nasscom-j. (2005) http://www.nasscom.org/articleprint.asp?art_id=4728 downloaded on 29th November, 2005

Nasscom-k: (2005) http://www.nasscom.org/artdisplay.aspx?cat_id=869 downloaded on 29th November, 2005

Ramaswamy, E.A. (1988) *Worker Consciousness and Trade Union Response.* New Delhi: Oxford University Press.

Ratnam, V. (2001) *Globalization and Labour-Management Relations: Dynamics of Change.* New Delhi, Sage.

Reich, R. B. (1991) *The work of nations: Preparing ourselves for 21st century capitalism.* New York: A.A.Knopf.

Russell, B. 2006. 'Voice, Representation and Recognition: Unions and Call Centres', unpublished report conducted for the Queensland Council of Trade Unions.

Saha, A. & Chatterjee, S. (2004) 'Human resource and cultural dynamics of global IT companies'. In *Information technology: Issues and challenges of globalisation.* New Delhi: Indian Institute of Foreign Trade.

Saini, D. and Budhwar, P. (2004) 'HRM in India', in Budhwar, P. (ed), *Managing Human Resources in Asia-Pacific.* London: Routledge.

Sheshabalaya, A. (2005) Rising *Elephant: The Growing Clash with India over White-Collar Jobs and its Challenge to American and the World.* Delhi: Macmillan.

Sify. (2006) 'India Inc gave heftiest pay hikes in Asia'. http://headlines.sify.com/ news/fullstory.php?id=14136242 downloaded 3rd May, 2006

Sodhi, J.S. and Plowman, D. (2001) *Economic Change and Industrial Relations: India and Australia.* Nedlands WA: Scholastic Press Australia.

Taskforce. (2003) 'Taskforce on meeting the human resources challenge for IT & IT enabled services'. Government of India, Ministry of Communications and Information Technology. Department of Information Technology. 18th December 2003.

The Business Standard. (2004) 'Akshaya Bhargava: The underwater earthquake'. July 23rd, 2004. http://www.nasscom.org/artdisplay.asp?Art_id=3015 downloaded 9th May, 2006.

The Hindu. (2005a) Knowledge services: Leveraging Indian talent. The Hindu Survey of Indian Industry 2005. Chennai: The Hindu.

The Hindu. (2005b) 'NASSCOM programme for future BPO workers'. October, 14th.

Chapter 5

LABOUR MARKET DEVELOPMENTS IN BANGLADESH
SINCE THE MID-1980s

Akhtar Hossain

INTRODUCTION

This paper provides an overview of labour market developments and issues that have occurred in Bangladesh since the mid-1980s. It was during this period that the economy was deregulated and opened up for foreign trade and investment. Since that time the economy has been growing steadily at a rate of about 5 percent per annum. Foreign capital flows in the form of overseas workers' remittances, foreign aid, loans, and foreign investment have contributed to economic growth and caused a structural transformation of the economy in favour of the non-farm and service sectors. Consequently, labour markets have undergone some structural change in terms of employment and work patterns. This did not lead to the expected rush of workers to the urban areas. The significant improvement in the agricultural terms of trade since the beginning of economic deregulation in the mid-1980s, inherent rigidities in urban (formal) labour markets and the increasing urban pollution and environmental problems appear to have slowed the shift of labour from agriculture to manufacturing and services in the urban areas. Nevertheless the structural changes in labour and work patterns that have accompanied modern economic growth have been reflected in a number of different ways. These include: the associated labour mobility from the rural to the urban areas, between the farm and non-farm activities[1] within the rural areas, between the formal and informal activities within the urban areas and from both the rural and urban areas to overseas destinations for employment and migration. Additional changes in the labour markets have included the rise in the participation rate of women and the productivity and wage differentials across sectors. With such developments, the economy has recently moved to a higher growth path exhibiting some dynamism, although the Lewisian[2] turning point in the rural labour market, which would suggest a steady rise in the real wage rate, is yet to be witnessed in this otherwise 'labour surplus' country. Lately, with the increasing importance of the private-sector employment in the urban areas, some of the global labour, trade and environmental issues, such as child labour, gender discrimination, trade union rights, unemployment, sickness, disability pensions and benefits and wage disparities have gained prominence in policy debate at both national and international forums.

STRUCTURAL CHANGE IN EMPLOYMENT: HISTORICAL TRENDS

The distribution of employment in Bangladesh indicates that agriculture employed about 80 percent of the total labour force in the 1950s and 1960s. It has only been since the early-1980s that the share of agriculture in employment started to significantly decline. The corresponding increase in the share of employment was in the services sector. The share of employment in the industrial/manufacturing sector increased from merely four percent in 1950 to about 9 percent in the mid-1980s (Hossain, 1995).

Table 1 reports the *Labour Force Survey* data for the 1990s. It reveals that only about 10 percent of employment falls under the category of formal employment. The main characteristic feature of employment remains the overwhelming dominance of self-employed and daily wage-labourers.

Table 1. Types of Employment and Distribution by Economic Activity: 1991-2000

	1991	1996	2000
Total Labour Force (million)	51.0	56.0	58.0
Types of Employment (percent)	100.0	100.0	100.0
Formal	11.7	12.4	13.1
Non-formal	87.9	87.6	86.9
Family-based	47.2	40.1	37.0
Daily basis	13.9	17.9	17.6
Self-employed	26.8	29.6	32.3

Employment by Activity (percent)	100.0	100.0	100.0
Agriculture, forest, and fisheries	66.4	63.2	62.5
Mining and quarrying	...	...	0.7
Manufacturing	11.8	7.5	7.4
Electricity, gas and water	0.1	0.2	0.2
Construction	1.0	1.8	2.1
Trade services	8.5	11.2	12.0
Transport and communication	3.2	4.2	4.6
Finance and business service	0.6	0.4	0.5
Community and personal service	3.8	9.3	10.0
Others	4.5	2.2	0.0
Memorandum items:			
	1980-1990	1990-2000	2000-2002
Labour force growth rate (percent, per year)	2.35	3.15	2.26
	1981	1991	2001
Inter-censal population growth rate (percent, per year)	2.35	2.17	1.48

Sources: Author's compilation/computation based on *IMF Country Report No. 03/194, Bangladesh: Statistical Appendix*, June 2003; Government of Bangladesh (2003), *Bangladesh Economic Review (Bangla* version); and Bangladesh Bureau of Statistics, *Statistical Yearbook of Bangladesh 2001*. Note: *No Labour Force Survey* has been conducted since 2000.

The employment data suggest that there was no major structural change in employment in Bangladesh during the 1990s. Agriculture's share in employment has declined. And this trend is expected to continue with an improvement in agricultural productivity and the continuing rural to urban migration. In the urban areas the incremental labour force has been absorbed mostly in the services sector, especially retail trade, transport and communication services (Hossain, 1996). One area of concern is the apparent decline in the share of employment in the manufacturing sector. Instead of rising, it has sharply decreased from 12 percent in 1991 to 7 percent in 2000. There are a number of reasons for the lack of growth of employment in the manufacturing sector. Although the phenomenal growth of the ready-made garment industry over the past two decades created employment for (female) workers, the manufacturing sector as a whole did not show similar dynamism. It appears that, with the availability of cheap imported goods from India and China, domestic manufacturing industries have lost market shares for their products. At the same time the state-owned loss-making industries have retrenched large number of workers (Khan, 2005). During the first half of the 1990s the labour force also increased at a faster pace than the population growth rate primarily because of the growing labour force participation rate of women.

Therefore the structural transformation process in employment in Bangladesh over the past two decades was unique in the sense that it was the services sector, rather than large manufacturing, that absorbed the incremental labour force. The structural transformation process bypassed the stage where the manufacturing sector becomes dominant in terms of its contribution to output and employment. Inflexibility in the structure of production and employment was the reason why the manufacturing sector failed to take the lead in absorbing labour and raising output. In contrast, the flexible production and employment structure in the non-farm sector allowed it to respond quickly to rising demand for non-farm products and services by increasing output and employment. An important reason why the informal sector can respond better to labour utilisation is that it produces non-traded commodities and hence does not have to compete with imports. An increase in demand for non-traded goods has to be met by an increase in local production and formal industries comprising tradable goods cannot presuppose that will occur (Hossain, 1996).

CHANGES IN THE PATTERNS OF EMPLOYMENT IN THE 1990s

Until the mid-1980s most workers in the rural areas of Bangladesh worked in the farm sector, especially in the crop sector. There were only limited non-farm activities available as a source of employment or earnings. This situation has changed significantly since the mid-1980s. The agricultural sector is now diversified and workers are engaged in both farm and non-farm activities. Similar changes have taken place in the urban areas. Traditionally the urban labour market was male-dominated and not many women were in the labour force. The scope of employment in the informal sector was also limited. This has changed significantly, especially since opening up the economy in the early-1980s. An increasing number of female workers now work in the newly emerging industries in the private sector, such as the garment industry and various construction and retail trade activities. Many rural workers are therefore able to divide their time between the rural and urban sector activities, which include construction, petty trade and services. Such switch from rural to urban sector activities remains conditional on the relative availability of work in the rural and urban areas given that there are seasonalities in both the rural and urban activities. For example, rural farm activities are heavily concentrated during the plantation and harvesting seasons, while the urban construction activities rise sharply during the dry seasons. The entry, as well as exit, of rural workers into urban sector activities is relatively easy given the informal nature of job contracts and the availability of replacement with a short notice. This section provides an overview of such changes in work patterns in both the rural and urban labour markets.

Changes in Rural Employment and Work Patterns

Farm Mechanisation and Employment

Agriculture in Bangladesh is basically a small-scale family-based farming operation. The agricultural technology remains predominantly traditional and only since the mid-1970s the agricultural sector has undergone change by adopting the seed-fertilizer-irrigation technology. In traditional agriculture, land, labour and capital are complementary inputs, and, given that land and capital are limited in supply, employment cannot increase beyond a certain limit unless there is any technological change, which augments land and capital. Technological change alters factor proportions and creates scope for factor substitution (Hossain, 1995).

Although in an overpopulated country like Bangladesh farm mechanisation remains a contentious issue, since the late-1970s farmers have started small-scale mechanisation of activities in the areas of cultivation, plantation, processing and distribution (Hossain, 1988). The process accelerated in the 1990s. For most farm activities, small-scale mechanised tools and implements are now widely used. There are a number of interrelated factors behind the increasing demand for mechanised farm tools and implements, including the shortages of draught power, the availability of imported cheap tools, the availability of electricity in villages, the consideration of low time-requirement for cultivation and the utilisation of mechanised tools for alternative income-generating activities (Alam, Rahman and Mandal, 2004). Some farmers who need funds for the purchase of farm machineries are able to borrow subsidised loans from publicly owned agricultural banks. A large number of non-government organisations also provide small-scale loans to rural borrowers for investment purposes. Contrary to expectations, the increased farm mechanisation, along with infrastructural and technological developments, has created employment opportunities for otherwise low-skilled workers while the most enterprising and skilled farm workers have opted for relatively more remunerating non-farm activities in both the rural and urban areas. With increasing farm mechanisation the women labourers' involvement in both farm and non-farm activities has also increased significantly.

Expansion of Non-Farm Activities

According to a study by Hossain, Bose, Chowdhury and Meimzen-Dick (2002), the importance of agriculture as a source of employment for the rural workforce has decreased significantly over the past two decades. For example, only 14 percent of the rural land-poor households depended on agriculture for their employment in 2000 while this rate was 31 percent in 1988. Income from rural non-farm activities has also grown at a significantly faster rate than agricultural income during 1987-2000. About 40 percent of the rural labour force is presently engaged in rural non-farm activities. These include construction, retail trade and business, transportation and professional services (Ahmed and Sattar, 2004). The increasing importance and potential for rapid growth of the rural non-farm sector has lately been recognised by the World Bank (2003:p.46):

> *Domestic demand for processed food is likely to increase as personal incomes increase. An important precursor of this has been the rapid increase in recent years of the demand for snack food and fruit juices. Rural non-farm activities also offer considerable potential, such as in the manufacturing of small agricultural implements and agricultural machinery and spare parts, construction and construction material, and services activities related to transport operations. Moreover, Bangladesh is ahead of many comparator countries in the density of its network of rural roads and waterways, which is an essential infrastructure requirement for the expansion of rural industry.*

Livestock and Poultry Rearing

As indicated earlier, until the 1970s the crop sector dominated agriculture. It is only since the early 1990s the livestock sector has become important in terms of its contribution to output and employment. Presently this sector contributes about 10 percent of value added in agriculture and about 3 percent of GDP. Leather and leather products also contribute significantly to exports. This sub-sector remains labour-intensive and provides employment for about 20 percent of the population.

Export-Oriented Shrimp Sector

Since the economy opened up in the early-1980s, Bangladesh has developed an export-oriented fishing industry. This activity grew at a record pace in the 1990s, driven by the export-oriented shrimp production. Fisheries doubled its share in agriculture value added during the 1990s and accounted for nearly a quarter of total value added in agriculture in 2001 (World Bank, 2003). The favourable exchange rates, trade incentives and the liberalisation of imports (that allowed duty-free inputs for commercial fish farming) helped the rapid growth of this sector. In the coastal areas, shrimp farming has become the most profitable economic activity. In fact in the mid-1990s Bangladesh accounted for about 4.4 percent of the global production of commercial shrimps. After garments, the shrimp sector has now become the second largest export industry of the country. As shrimp-farming remains labour-intensive, this sector employs over half a million rural poor in various stages of processing and shrimp culture. This sector also employs a large number of female workers in both upstream and downstream activities, such as services, transport, catching of shrimp fries, and shrimp processing (Ahmed and Sattar, 2004).

Summing Up: This brief review suggests that the rural economy of Bangladesh has gradually become diversified and this has created employment opportunities for both skilled and unskilled workers in farming and non-farming activities. Given the informal nature of employment contracts, the switch from farm to non-farm activities remains relatively easy. The increase of employment opportunities in non-farm activities explains why there has been absorption of the incremental labour force in the rural economy. Given few wage-rigidities, employment increased while the real wage rate increased only at a slow pace (Table 5). This fits well with the Lewisian model (Lewis, 1954; Todaro and Smith, 2003) of the unlimited supply of labour in the rural sector. However it was not agriculture *per se* but the non-farm activities that provided most employment for the incremental labour force. The agricultural sector did not show much dynamism for various reasons, including controls over output pricing and marketing, less export orientation and the slowdown of demand for agricultural products, especially food crops that have a lower than one income elasticity of demand (Ahmed and Sattar, 2004; Abdullah and Shahabuddin, 1997).

Changes in Urban Employment and Work Patterns

Since the mid-1980s two major changes have taken place in the urban labour markets in Bangladesh. They are the rapid growth of the garment industry and the establishment of export promotion zones as part of export-oriented industrialisation strategy of development. This took place along with the privatisation of some state-owned enterprises and the greater emphasis the government has put on the private sector-led economic development.

Growth of the Garment Industry

The phenomenal growth of the ready-made garment industry has been a success story for Bangladesh. This is an export-oriented industry. Unlike other industries, the garment industry has experienced minimum trade-union activity and disruption. Within only one and a half decades the garment industry has changed the structure of manufacturing production, exports and employment in Bangladesh. The employment opportunities in both backward and forward linked activities have been considerable. For example, although approximately 1.8 million workers were employed directly in the garment industry in 2002, the Bangladesh Garment Manufacturers and Exporters Association (BGMEA) claimed that nearly 3 million workers were then directly or indirectly employed in garments and complementary industries or services, such as accessories, packaging, toiletries, courier, finance, transport, telecommunications services and so on (Ahmed and Satter, 2004).

This sector's emergence and expansion in Bangladesh has been the direct outcome of the global Multi-Fibre Agreement (MFA) regime. It started with a small share of about four percent of total exports in the early 1980s. Presently garments constitute about 75 percent of the country's exports. In 2002 they earned about US$5 billion of foreign exchange out of $7 billion of export earnings. The European Union and USA are Bangladesh's major export markets. Despite a myriad of domestic problems, such as politically-motivated general strikes, transport, port and infrastructure bottlenecks, disruption in electricity supply, lack of quality control and slowness in the delivery of ordered products, newly emerging entrepreneurs have been successful in gaining and maintaining significant shares of global garments markets. Importantly, contrary to expectations, the phasing out of the MFA in 2005 did not cause any setback to garment exports from Bangladesh. However the garment industry still relies heavily on imported fabrics, yarn and accessories. This is despite the fact that the domestic shares of these inputs have increased substantially over the past decade (Ahmed and Sattar, 2004).

Another important characteristic of the garment industry is the dominance of female workers. About 90 percent of workers in the garment industry, comprising approximately 4000 factories, are young women. Most of these female workers have come from the rural areas. This has made a major contribution to the well being of several million rural families, as well as advancing the cause of women's empowerment. Since garment wages are generally well above the poverty equivalent wages and most workers come from rural families, it is estimated that more than two million households (that is, about 15 percent of poor households) have moved out of poverty (Ahmed and Sattar, 2004). As Paul-Majumder (2002:p.144) points out, the employers' preference for female workers has arisen from both gender-specific and pragmatic reasons:

> *It could be argued that, aside from the fact that women's labour is relatively cheaper, employers are led to recruit more women in the export-oriented garment industry because of prevailing beliefs that women are more patient and nimble; more controllable than men; less mobile and less likely to join trade unions; and better at sewing, since this job resembles their traditional work.*

Such employers argue that meeting global demand requires an undisturbed, docile, sincere, and flexible labour force.

Until the 1970s women with low educational attainment and/or those coming from the rural areas were confined to the informal labour market while the female formal sector jobs were the preserve of the urban elite. With the rapid expansion of employment opportunities in the garment industry, the rural poor families have allowed their unmarried females to seek urban employment. The significance of this is that economically rewarding employment opportunities outweighed cultural and social inhibitions for participating in labour markets. The willingness of rural households to send their daughters to distant cities for work suggests that rural households remain ready to endure considerable social and economic sacrifices for the well being of their families. The employment opportunities of young women in the garment industry have decreased the prevalence of early marriages and contributed to the reduction of fertility and health-related problems, often caused by this (World Bank, 2004). With the rise in employment of women in the garment and associated industries, the societal perception of women's roles in the labour markets has also changed. Although it is still mildly positive, it has worked towards narrowing the gender gap in employment in other industries as well.

Nevertheless, there is considerable scope for improvement in the working condition and terms of employment for female workers. Female workers still have low bargaining power, low wages, job insecurity, no non-wage benefits, high occupational segregation, no trade union support or representation, poor work conditions and suffer from various occupational health hazards, especially dust and toxic hazards (Paul-Majumder, 2002). There are reports that about 90 percent of garment workers in the country suffer from respiratory problems, abdominal pain, runny noses and coughs. There are also reports that headache, fever, tuberculosis and jaundice are common among the garment sector workers (The Daily Star, August 17, 2005).

In response, the government has encouraged the factory owners to maintain a healthy environment at the workplace. The impetus to such response from the government has come from the fact that it intends to maintain the status of the garment industry as the highest foreign exchange earner of the country. During the past few years there were several incidents of fire and the collapse of low quality buildings where garment factories were housed that killed a large number of workers. Because of both domestic and international sensitivity of safety issues in the garment industry, the authorities have taken some remedial safety measures at the workplace, including compulsory installation of fire exits at all factories.

The Export Promotion Zone

Along with other developing countries, Bangladesh started to set up *Export Promotion Zones* (EPZs) in the early-1980s. These are special enclaves where 100 percent export-oriented firms are provided with favoured treatment with respect to custom regulations, the import of raw materials and intermediate goods, company taxation, the provision of infrastructure, and industrial regulations (Hossain, 2002). The first EPZ was established in Chittagong (CEPZ) in 1983 and the second one was established in Dhaka (DEPZ) in 1993. Four additional EPZs are under construction. Preparations are underway for two other private EPZs. Table 2 provides information on investment, exports and employment in the EPZs until 2000.

Table 2. Investment, Exports and Employment in EPZs in Bangladesh: 1984-2000

Year	Investment US$ million	Employment (Cumulative)	Exports (US$ million)	Share in Total Exports (%)
1984	9.8	624		
1990	42.1	7001		
1991	47.9	9364		
1992	23.7	14614	77.0	3.9
1993	22.1	17728	127.7	5.3
1994	37.4	26336	145.6	5.8
1995	35.9	32477	228.3	6.6
1996	30.6	42183	337.0	8.7
1997	53.9	55956	462.8	10.5
1998	68.6	70005	636.1	12.3
1999	71.6	84074	711.7	13.4
2000	35.0	94694	890.8	10.2

Source: Author's compilation based on Hossain (2002).

Although Bangladesh has liberalised its industrial policy since the early-1980s, it has not been successful in attracting large-scale foreign investment primarily because of political instability. Nevertheless the EPZs have been an important means of attracting foreign direct investment. As most trade unions remain affiliated with political parties and exhibit militancy concerning political issues, one of the attractions for foreign investors in EPZs has been the absence of trade union activities. Although the Bangladesh government has ratified the ILO conventions that guarantee workers their rights of association and collective bargaining, the EPZs remain exempt from trade union activities. Lately, this has become an issue, especially for the USA where Bangladesh's exports have preferential access under the Generalised System of Preferences (GSP). While the American Federation of Labour and the Congress of Industrial Organisations (AFL-CIO) has put pressure on the Bangladesh government to introduce the trade union rights at EPZs, South Korea and Japan, two major investors in EPZs, remain opposed to the provision of the trade union rights and have threatened withdrawal of their investments if such rights are granted. For Bangladesh, EPZs remain an important means of attracting foreign investment and employment creation. This would allow the country to reap the technological and managerial benefits of globalisation. Therefore the introduction of trade union rights would create a complicated situation for the country, as it may destroy this nascent but promising industrial sub-sector. It is to be noted that in the EPZs of Bangladesh most of the workers filling the low-skill, low-wage category jobs are female (Hossain, 2002). Working conditions in EPZs also remain much better than those in non-EPZ factories (Table 3).

FOREIGN EMPLOYMENT

Bangladesh has been a major labour exporting country since the mid-1980s. The initial impetus to labour export came from the Gulf during the OPEC oil shock of the early-1970s. Over the period 1976-2004 about 3.8 million workers went to the Middle East and recently to East Asia. During this period a significant number of professionals and skilled workers have also migrated to North America and Europe. About 48 percent of total expatriate workers over this period were unskilled. However the shares of professionals and skilled and semi-skilled workers have been rising. Their combined share increased from 42 percent in 2001 to 47 percent in 2003.

Table 3. Working Conditions and Terms of Employment in EPZ and non-EPZ Factories

Working Conditions and Terms of Employment	Factories outside DEPZ	Factories within DEPZ	All
Bad/very bad ventilation	35.5	5.0	26.7
Very congested	42.3	4.9	36.8
Not clean	52.6	-	41.6
Percentage of workers having smell from toilet	50.5	11.6	44.7
Mean work hours (in hours)	11.9	9.9	11.8
Wage rate (female, in *Taka*)	1285	1504	1321
Wage rate (male, in *Taka*)	2252	2299	2258
Female share in male earnings (%)	57.1	65.4	58.5
Factory size in terms of employment	559	1767	714
Share of female workers (%)	51	79.4	59.5
No of weekly holidays per factory	0.5	3.0	1.4
Share of paid leave in total leave (%)	20	48	24.1
Percentage of workers having transport facilities provided by factory	0	93	13.9
Percentage of workers having lunch in the lunch room	38.8	93.4	41.0
Percentage of workers having rest room	39.4	100.0	48.5
Percentage of sick workers having access to doctor provided by the factory	10.5	58.0	17.6
Percentage of workers having attendance card or identity card	90	100.0	92

Source: Author's compilation based on Hossain (2002).

Overseas workers' remittances remain the major contributor to the country's economic and social development. The level of workers remittances has been steadily rising, reaching 3.4 billions in 2004 which were equal to 6 percent of GDP (Table 4). Most of the remittances come from the Middle East. The Saudi Arabia remains the main source of foreign remittances. Recognising the increasing socio-economic importance of labour export, the Bangladesh government in recent years has taken various initiatives to boost manpower export and the easy transfer of funds from overseas given that many workers encounter difficulties in remitting money, especially from Europe and North America. In fact the introduction of the Money Laundering Act in Bangladesh in April 2002 has led to an increasing trend in reported inward remittances. This has improved the country's foreign exchange reserve position substantially (GOB, 2004).

Table 4. Bangladesh: Foreign Employment and Remittances, 1991-2004

Fiscal Year	Number of Expatriates (thousand)	Remittances	
		US$million	% of GDP
1991-92	185	848	2.7
1992-93	238	944.0	2.9
1993-94	192	1088.8	3.2
1994-95	200	1197.6	3.2
1995-96	181	1217.1	3.0
1996-97	228	1475.4	3.5
1997-98	243	1525.4	3.5
1998-99	270	1705.7	3.7
1999-00	248	1949.3	4.1
2000-01	213	1882.1	4.0
2001-02	195	2501.1	5.3
2002-03	241	3062.0	5.9
2003-04	273	3372.0	6.0

Source: Author's compilation based on GOB, *Bangladesh Economic Review* (various years).

TRENDS IN REAL WAGES

Table 5 reports data for real wages in different sectors of Bangladesh since the early 1970s. It shows that real wages in manufacturing have steadily increased from a very low level in the 1970s. Meanwhile those in agriculture increased from a low level in the 1970s until the 1980s and then increased only mildly throughout the 1990s. The real wages in construction and fisheries have increased at a pace higher than that found in agriculture but much lower than that in manufacturing. This explains why there has been an outflow of labour from agriculture to non-agricultural activities. Given that the manufacturing sector is yet to exhibit dynamism, the mobility of labour has so far been more to non-farm activities in both the rural and urban areas than towards the formal sector in the urban areas.

Table 5. Real Wages in Bangladesh: 1970-2004 (1969-70=100)

Year/Period (Average)	General	Manufacturing/ Industry	Construction	Agriculture	Fisheries
1969/70	80.6	79.8	83.8	81.7	73.5
1976-80	72.5	64.4	87.0	78.3	68.5
1981-85	87.2	85.0	95.7	81.5	89.7
1986-90	104.0	108.7	111.3	90.2	101.0
1991-95	110.3	117.7	105.4	101.5	109.5
1996-00	118.9	131.7	111.6	104.8	114.5
2001	124.5	141.7	117.9	107.1	114.7
2002	130.3	150.0	120.8	111.8	119.1
2003	141.5	169.3	126.9	118.1	123.9
2004	146.1	176.8	125.4	121.3	130.3

Sources: Author's compilation based on BBS, *Statistical Yearbook of Bangladesh* (various years) and GOB, *Bangladesh Economic Review* (various years).

If real wages are considered an indicator of economic well being, their increase over time suggests an improvement of workers' welfare in a general sense. Some groups who possess skills and efficiency in manufacturing appear to have made significant gains. Rashid (2002) however points out that the rapid increase in real wages in manufacturing was actually because of government interventions, causing a slow growth of employment in this sector. It has now been recognised by all concerned that rapidly rising real wages, without a corresponding rise in productivity, are not sustainable over a longer period. This would discourage labour absorption in the formal manufacturing sector and exacerbate the problem of unemployment and underemployment in both the rural and urban areas. However it is possible that a rising real wages in manufacturing reflects an increasing capital intensity of production. Otherwise, there would be an erosion of international competitiveness of manufacturing exports.

GLOBALISATION, LABOUR MARKET ISSUES AND POLICIES

As pointed out earlier, as part of globalisation and with the increasing importance of the private-sector employment in the urban areas, some of the global labour, trade and environmental issues, such as child labour, gender discrimination, trade union rights, unemployment, sickness, disability pensions and benefits, and wage disparities have gained prominence in policy debate at both national and international forums. This section provides an overview of some of these issues.

Trade Unions

Most trade unions in Bangladesh remain affiliated with political parties. Their programmes are usually motivated by political considerations rather than for promoting labour rights. Since the globalisation process started in the early 1980s, the main issue for trade unions was the privatisation of state-owed enterprises and the liberalisation of foreign trade that removed both tariff and non-tariff barriers. Almost all the trade unions opposed privatisation because it meant the retrenchment of workers and the loss of power of trade union leaders, who often misused their power for personal gain. The major impact of globalisation was the loss of jobs of many workers due to the privatisation of state-owned enterprises, as well as for the demise of many private enterprises that could not adjust and cope with foreign competition. For example, in the 1980s about half a million workers were employed in the nationalised sector. Because of privatisation, however, there was closure of many nationalised industries and the retrenchment of a large number of workers.

Throughout the 1980s and 1999s, the *Saramik Karmochari Ykko Parishad (SKOP)* (an apex body of diverse labour organisations) opposed privatisation and globalisation. In 1984, the SKOP made an agreement with the government that the latter would stop the privatisation of jute, textile and cotton, chemical, steel and engineering industries, as well as of the banking sector. The government did not implement this agreement and the process of privatisation proceeded, albeit at a slow pace. As most trade unions are linked to political parties and divided, the government finds it easier to co-opt them and weaken any labour movement. Therefore, so far there has been no effective movement against privatisation. In August 2003 an agreement was signed between the State Minister of Labour and Manpower and the SKOP, where it was agreed that there would be no 'massive privatisation' (Khan, 2005).

Bangladesh has become a focus for the US labour rights advocates because the EPZs do not allow trade union activities. In 1990 the AFL-CIO filed a petition with the US Trade Representative (USTR) and argued for the withdrawal of importers' rights to import duty-free products from Bangladesh into the United States under the GSP. As Bangladesh promised to introduce some remedial measures (such as the introduction of compulsory education law, the removal of prohibitions of trade union activity, the increase in minimum wage and the enforcement of labour standards) to ensure workers' rights, the USTR denied the petition. The AFL-CIO also targeted the garment industry, as there is only limited trade union activity in this industry. During the past few years the AFL-CIO has advised the garment workers of their rights, including overtime premiums, legally mandated days off and the enforcement of minimum wages, under Bangladesh's labour law and has encouraged trade union activity under the premise of the *Bangladesh Independent Garment Union (BIGU)*. The government has so far refused to recognise the trade union's right to engage in collective bargaining. The official reason is that only enterprise level unions, not industry-wide organisations, would be recognised for such purposes.

Lately, the garment industry has come to the limelight because of a series of clashes of workers with the factory owners and the law-enforcing agencies. The immediate issue was related to the workers' demand for higher wages and other benefits. This issue has been resolved at least temporarily through negotiations between the representatives of the workers and the owners and the government got involved in resolving the dispute as an intermediary. However it appears that the success of the garment industry in Bangladesh has damaged the interests of the country's international competitors. Some political provocateurs with international connections have infiltrated into the garment industry and influenced the ordinary workers to participate in destructive activities that in the long-run would go against their own interests. This suggests that although it may appear simple, the trade union rights issue has turned out to be more complex given its international dimension. Therefore, unless the issue is handled carefully, the workers' would suffer and the country's economic interests would be damaged.

Child Labour

Child labour has become a major global policy concern for a number of reasons. The immediate issue is the children's physical and emotional well being. The children's future well being is also at stake whereby any trade-off between work and school means a lower level of human capital investment. The future growth of an economy ultimately depends to a great extent on the level of human capital present in children. The presence of child labour can also depress wages in adult labour markets and this may make families more dependent on children's earnings, thus creating a vicious cycle of continued child labour (World Bank, 2004).

Bangladesh has a child labour problem and this has become a major economic and social policy issue. The World Bank (2004) reports that about 14 percent of children in the age group 5 to 14 years (20 percent boys and 9 percent girls) are in the labour force. Table 6 reports data for working children (aged between 5 and 10 and between 10 and 14) by status of employment, sex and residence for the years 1996 and 2000.

Most male child workers in the rural areas work in agriculture while female child workers operate as unpaid family helpers in both the rural and urban areas. Girls usually work outside the home only as a last resort. In families where adult females work outside the home, young girls often work at home as substitutes for their mothers (World Bank, 2004).

The efforts of the AFL-CIO have forced the BGMEA to sign a memorandum with UNICEF to end the employment of children under age 14. The agreement required each manufacturer to subsidise schools to be established by the UNICEF for workers who leave employment to attend such schools, and pay stipends for child workers who leave employment to such schools. The AFL-CIO was originally a formal party to the negotiations but withdrew because of political opposition to its interference in Bangladesh's internal affairs. The US Ambassador did however sponsor the negotiations. Following the AFL-CIO withdrawal, monitoring and informant provisions in the draft agreement were dropped. In order to escape liability for school subsidies and stipends, manufacturers began to fire children before the effective date of the agreement. Following these events, the AFL-CIO and BIGU established their own primary schools for child-members of the union who had been fired by their employers to evade subsidy payments.

Table 6. Working Children in Bangladesh: 1995, 2000

Employed children aged 5 to 14 by status of employment, sex and residence, 1995-1996					
	Total	Employed	Self-employed	Unpaid family helper	Paid apprentice	Day labour/ casual labour
	Thousand	Percentage Distribution				
Bangladesh	6304	14.6	3.5	63.2	1.5	17.1
Male	3771	13.0	4.5	59.1	2.3	21.2
Female	2533	17.2	6.0	69.5	3.8	10.9
Rural	5244	9.2	3.2	68.3	1.1	18.2
Male	3173	9.6	4.0	62.3	1.8	22.3
Female	2071	8.7	1.9	77.5	0.1	11.8
Urban	1060	41.3	5.4	38.2	3.5	11.6
Male	598	30.6	7.4	42.0	5.0	15.1
Female	462	55.2	2.6	33.3	1.5	7.6
Working children aged 10 to 14 years by industry, sex and residence, 1999-2000					
	Total	Agriculture	Manu-facturing	Transport/ Communi-cation	Other services	Household services
	Thousand	Percentage Distribution				
Bangladesh	6302	64.2	8.2	2.6	14.4	10.6
Male	3760	62.2	7.2	4.2	21.5	4.9
Female	2542	67.2	9.8	0.2	3.9	19.0
Rural	5161	7.3	5.2	2.1	12.2	7.6
Male	3111	71.1	4.6	3.3	17.8	3.2
Female	2050	75.7	6.0	0.2	13.6	4.6
Urban	1141	24.6	22.1	4.9	24.5	23.9
Male	649	19.4	19.3	8.5	39.8	13.1
Female	492	31.5	25.6	0.2	4.5	38.2

Source: Author's compilation based on BBS (2001), *Statistical Yearbook of Bangladesh.*

In the international arena the issue of linkage between trade and labour standards, such as child labour, and between trade and human rights has reached centre stage. Several non-governmental organisations have been demanding that the World Trade Organisation formally incorporate this linkage through a Social Clause on labour standards. Most developing countries, as well as international financial organisations, generally oppose such moves.

The issue of how to deal with labour standard issues in relation to trade policy is fairly difficult. It is not at all clear that trade policy is the most effective instrument for addressing labour and human rights issues. There is substantial risk that what starts out to be a well-intentioned exercise, where trade policy is used to address a value-laden objective, (even if one is not sure about the effectiveness of the instrument) it becomes captured by people who really want to use it for protecting certain industries. This would provide protectionism with a good public relations cloak rather than actually addressing the problem.

The issue of child labour in Bangladesh is yet to be resolved successfully. As indicated above, in the case of the garment industry, there has been some success in resolving the child labour issue. Some agreements have been reached that allow the use of child labour so long as employers provide them with a safe working environment and encourage education through on-site instruction or work schedules that enable children to attend school before or after work. There is also a view that factory work in the garment industry is somewhat benign because it enables girls to delay marriage and motherhood and reduces their reliance on alternatives or more risky activities, including working as housemaids and at construction sites.

In summing up, it would be virtually impossible to eradicate child labour in Bangladesh until the economy is adequately developed. In poor households, incomes from child labour supplement those of the adults. Ensuring work for adult members of such households remains important. Provision of some minimum income to poor households to compensate for any loss of a child's income could be one option. Sometimes a learn-and-earn methodology in non-hazardous occupations could also be considered for students of appropriate ages to whom full-time education is difficult because of extreme poverty. This may include mandated reduction of daily working hours to accommodate education for the children at the expense of the employer (World Bank, 2004).

RIGIDITIES IN BANGLADESH'S LABOUR MARKETS

One major labour market issue in South Asia is the higher degree of inflexibility that keeps the labour markets segmented and lowers employment growth, especially in the formal sector. In all South Asian countries there are myriad of Labour Laws that have been designed to protect workers from unfair labour practices and to create a productive workplace environment. Such Laws fall into four categories: (a) employment regulations, (b) social security provisions, (c) industrial relations, and (d) workplace safety. Table 7 reports summary measures of labour market rigidities in Bangladesh vis-à-vis other countries in Asia.

There are three distinct dimensions of labour market flexibility: (a) difficulty of hiring, (b) difficulty of firing, and (c) rigidity of working hours. These three indices can be used to define an index of *Rigidity of Employment* as a measure of labour market flexibility. Table 7 shows that labour markets in South Asia are very rigid compared with two comparators, Singapore and Hong Kong. Within South Asia, Bangladesh's labour markets are relatively flexible. However, as Bangladesh's formal labour markets are still rigid in terms of employment protection, this has a negative impact on employment. Lowering exit barriers and allowing for flexible working arrangements may create more jobs in the formal sector (World Bank, 2004).[3]

Table 7. Rigidities in Labour Markets in Selected Countries of Asia

	Bangladesh	India	Pakistan	Sri Lanka	Hong Kong	Singapore
Difficulty of Hiring						
Ratio of minimum to average wage	0.42	0.24	0.40	0.25	0.00	0.00
Fixed-term contracts are only allowed for fixed term tasks	No	Yes	Yes	No	No	No
Maximum duration of fixed-term contracts (in months)	No limit	No limit	9	12	No limit	No limit
Index of difficulty in hiring (max: 3, most difficult)	0.33	1	2.33	1	0	0
Rigidity of Working Hours						
Maximum no. of working	9	9	11	8	12	24
hours allowed in a day	6.5	6	5.5	6	6	6
Maximum no. of working days	No	No	No	Yes	No	No
per week	Yes	No	Yes	Yes	No	No
Restrictions on night work						
Restrictions on weekly holiday work	20	12	14	14	14	14
Days of annual leave with pay in manf. after 20 years continuous employment	2	1	2	2	0	0
Index of rigidity working hours (max: 5, most rigid)						
Procedural Difficulties in Firing Workers	No	Yes	No	Yes	No	No
The employer must notify a third party before dismissing one redundant employee	No	Yes	No	Yes	No	No
The employer needs the approval of a third party to dismiss one redundant workers	No	Yes	No	Yes	No	No
The employer needs the approval of a third party prior to a collective dismissal	No	No	Yes	No	No	No
The law mandates retraining or replacement prior to dismissal	Yes	Yes	Yes	Yes	No	No
There are priority rules applying to dismissal or layoffs	Yes	No	Yes	Yes	Yes	Yes
Is redundancy considered a fair ground for dismissal?	2	9	3	6	0	0
Index of procedural difficulty of firing (max: 10)						

Source: Author's compilation based on World Bank (2004).

DECENT WORK INDICATORS: FUTURE WORK AGENDA[4]

Bangladesh's labour markets remain somewhat dualistic. There is an entrenched segmentation between a relatively small, well-protected, inflexible formal sector and a large, unprotected, under-capitalised informal sector. The formal sector, comprising the public sector and large private enterprises, enjoys better working conditions, better pay (particularly in the public sector), has access to fringe benefits such as pension and health care, and benefits from job security. Workers in the larger informal sector consisting of self-employed, paid workers in informal enterprises, and unpaid family workers face hard and dangerous working conditions, are unprotected by labour legislation, and remain outside the realm of social insurance (World Bank, 2004).

The ILO has recently articulated a development paradigm that it calls the 'decent work' agenda. The objective of this is to promote opportunities for workers to obtain decent and productive work, in conditions of freedom, equity, security and human dignity. The agenda encompasses four inter-related strategic objectives: (a) promotion of *employment* as a central objective of economic and social policy making; (b) promotion and safeguarding of *fundamental rights* at work, emphasising the need to recognise that all those who work have rights; (c) *social protection*, and (d) the promotion of *social dialogue* to forge fair compromises and consensus on otherwise conflicting issues of distribution and conditions of work.

Table 8 reports changes in selected measures of decent work indicators for Bangladesh since the early 1980s.

Table 8. Decent Work Indicators for Bangladesh

Decent Work Indicators	1985-90	1995-2000	Level (change)
Employment Opportunities			
Labour force participation rate (%)	49.3	72.1	+
Employment population ratio (%)	45.7	63.2	+
Unemployment rate (%)	1.8	4.9	-
Underemployment rate (% of total labour force, working less than 35 hours in a reference week)		16.6-31.9	
Ratification of ILO's core labour standards	Ratified 7 out of 8 core conventions, except C138 (minimum age convention, 1973)		
Unacceptable Work			
Children in wage employment (%, by age)	12.2	12.9	-
Real manufacturing wage index (1969/70=100)	102	137	+
Decent Hours			
Excessive hours of work (% of employed)	36.4	39.0	+
Stability and Security at Work			
Temporary work (% of employees)	15.1	23.8	-
Fair Treatment in Employment and at Work/ Gender Equality			
Female labour force participation rate (%)	61.6	51.8	-
Female/male in major occupation (%)	16.7	25.4	+
Ratio of female/male average wage rate (day labourers)		58.46	+
Female employment in RMG industry (% of total employment)	85	90	
Female unemployment rate (% of total female labour force)			
Female/male in professional, technical occupation (%)	1.9	2.3	-
Ratio of female to male (%, primary school enrolment)	41.9	31.4	-
Ratio of female to male (%, secondary school enrolment)	86.7	96.0	+

Share of women in public service (%)			
Share of women in the total primary school teachers (%)	50.6	111.1	+
Share of female embers in the Parliament (MPs) (%)	6.3	9.1	+
Women participating in the national election (%)	12.9	27.5	+
Gender development index	10.3	11.2	+
Social Protection	1.7	1.9	+
Social security benefits expenditure (% of GDP)	0.34	0.47	+
Health expenditure, total (% of GDP)			
Public educational expenditure (% of total government expenditure)	2.1		
Total social sector allocation in annul development program (%)	2.8	3.6	+
Formal sector employment (% of total employment)	9.9	13.8	+
Self-employment (% of total employment)			
	11.0	24.1	+
	11.7	13.1	+
	26.8	32.3	+
Unemployment benefit (establishments under regulation)	Labour Act of 1965 provides ½ average basic wage for 120 days for monthly rated (permanent) workers; 60 days for causal workers; and 30 days for temporary workers		
Social dialogue and work place relations			
Union density rate	15.3	4.3	-
Number of strikes and lockouts	95.0	5.0	+
Workers involved in strikes and lockouts ('000)	198.0	6.0	+
Workdays not worked as a result of strikes and lockouts ('000)			
	285.0	3.0	+
Collective wage bargaining coverage rate	Trend in past 10 years, increase in both national/sectoral level. And company/plant level		
Economic and Social Context of Decent Work			
GDP growth rate (% annual change, real)	4.3	4.8	+
GDP per capita growth rate (% annual change)	1.7	3.0	+

Output per employed person	4265	4790	+
Inflation (% annual, CPI)	9.9	2.9	+
Adult literacy (%)	32.0	41.3	+
Composition of employment: agriculture	57.1	63.2	+
Composition of employment: industry	12.5	9.5	+
Composition of employment: service	26.5	27.3	+
Access to safe water (% of population)	80	97	+
Persons per hospital bed	3635	3307	+
Persons per physician	6886	4915	+
Daly per capita calorie intake (k.cal)	2191	2244	+
Income inequality ratio (ratio of top 10% to bottom 10%, income or consumption)	7.00	8.80	-
Gini index	25.9	31.6	
Poverty (<1US$/day or 2)		29.1	
Population below poverty line, national (%)	47.8	35.6	+
Human development index	0.32	0.48	+

Source: Author's compilation based on Muqtada (2003).

Rights at Work

Bangladesh has ratified seven of the eight conventions related to promotion, the safeguarding of freedom of associations and the progressive elimination of child labour, forced labour, and discrimination at work. However it has not yet ratified the convention No. 138 (minimum age convention), related to child labour. As pointed out earlier, the incidence of child labour in Bangladesh is high. Although the government has taken some measures to combat child labour, it would require some time before the incidence of child labour is brought down to an acceptable level. There are also other areas of concern. For example, although the freedom of association is safeguarded (except for EPZs and only in a limited form in the garment industry), there are problems in the development of labour institutions and movements. Importantly, the labour market regulatory framework applies to less than 3 percent of the workforce. This shows that the overwhelming majority of the labour force remains outside the purview of protective legislation. On the matter of discrimination in the workplace, there has been a perceptible improvement in female workers' access to jobs and educational attainment at all levels. The overall Gender Development Index (1995-2000) that assesses the relative position of the women in society when compared with men has significantly improved. In fact, over the past two decades Bangladeshi women have played an important role in the success of micro-credits, ready-made garment exports, reducing population growth, increasing child nutrition, and in the spread of primary education. The country has achieved gender parity in primary education and practically removed the gender gap that was apparent in secondary education. Recent evidence suggests that the country is close to achieving parity in life expectancy. While significant gender gaps still persist, the role of women in all walks of life has become increasingly visible and will be instrumental in bringing about wider social and economic changes in the future.

Work and Employment

Bangladesh's formal unemployment rate is less than 5 percent. However the underemployment rate is as high as 35 percent, which is approximately the same as the incidence of poverty in the country. The major area of concern is the slow growth of employment in the formal sector. The idea is that the enlargement of formal sector employment promotes formal employment relationships and allows the implementation of labour market regulations. With privatisation and foreign competition, formal sector employment has fallen in recent years. In the rural areas, the labour markets have remained loose and therefore real wages have not increased that much. Most farm and non-farm activities remain seasonal and casual in nature and work sharing is apparent in agriculture and non-farm activities. There has been an increase in the use of subcontract, temporary and casual work. Moreover the number of hours worked has showed a deterioration in recent years. About three-quarters of the employed workforce work for more than the standard number of hours per week. Given that the incidence of poverty remains high, this implies that work is not adequately remunerated and that there is a high incidence of working poor.

Social Protection

Social protection is miniscule in Bangladesh. It is only the protected workers in civil service, public enterprises, autonomous agencies and large private firms who enjoy varying schemes of pensions, provident fund, health and group/life insurances. The Labour Act of 1965 provides some unemployment benefits to workers of establishment that come within the purview of the labour code. Formal social protection is however not available to the majority of the workforce in the informal sectors. The income security of informal sector workers is weak and even modest shocks, such as natural disasters or political disturbances, reduce their consumptions below the 'threshold needed to retain productivity (World Bank, 2004).

Thus, without having formal mechanisms of social protection, the entire Bangladeshi workforce remains vulnerable. It is only through some government and non-government work and employment programmes during economic shocks and crises that the incomes and employment of the poor are somewhat protected. Therefore it is desirable that well-designed and well-coordinated safety net programmes ensure wider coverage and systematic protection of the poor. As a move in this direction, in recent years, social sector allocation in the Annual Development Programme has significantly increased (Muqtada, 2003; World Bank, 2004).

Social Dialogue

The last dimension of 'decent work' concerns social dialogue, which fosters democratic principles and cooperation among the business groups, workers groups and the government. This is present only in a limited form, as public and private sector employees constitute less than 5 percent of the workforce. In addition, only 3 percent of them have union membership. As the majority of the work force are not formally organised, they do not have the ability to negotiate formally. Within the unionised workforce, the density rate has declined over the past two decades. The number of strikes and lockouts and workdays lost as a result of such strikes has also declined. While these features bode well, most general and industrial strikes are triggered more on political considerations rather than to realise demands for the common workers. The multiple national federations of trade unions have close affiliation with the major political parties. Another important feature of the weak industrial relations system concerns the representation and voice of female workers, who are entering into wage work in fairly large numbers. The garment industry has remained practically exempt from introducing trade union rights and there is pervasive fear among female workers to organise. Thus female workers remain vulnerable in this industry.

SUMMARY AND CONCLUDING REMARKS

Until the 1960s agriculture directly employed about 80 percent of the labour force in Bangladesh. By the early-1990s this share gradually declined to about 60 percent. Although this structural change in employment was significant in an historical sense, one area of concern is that the share of employment in agriculture did not fall the way it was expected throughout the 1990s given that the share of agriculture in output fell sharply to about 18 percent. Therefore the agricultural productivity and the agricultural real wage rate did not rise the way it was expected. The second area of concern is that the shift of labour from agriculture to non-agricultural activities occurred primarily in the services sector, such as construction, retail trade, transport, hotels and restaurants, and community and personal services. The level of employment in large-scale manufacturing remained relatively low and appears to be shrinking primarily because of the closure of many state-owned, loss-making enterprises that have been adversely affected by competition from imports since opening up the economy in the mid-1980s. One positive development in the economy is that the employment opportunities in the private sector are rising. This has been due to the increasing importance that the government has accorded to the private sector. This is reflected in the steady deregulation, privatisation and opening up of the economy over the past two decades. Rising wage rates in the private sector reflect productivity gains but less job creation because employers appear to be less interested in hiring than using less labour more productively through the substitution of capital and an improvement of labour management. This has apparently created an elite group of skilled labourers who command high wages and other privileges in the middle of a large pool of unskilled, low-paid workers. Within manufacturing, incremental employment remains concentrated heavily in the textiles and garment industries, which account for about 70 percent of the manufacturing labour force. These workers are apparently poorly paid given the large army of 'surplus (women) workers' in the countryside who are willing to join the urban labour force if opportunities arise. Further, the increasing wage gaps between the private and public sectors are reflected in the rising income inequalities. The rising wage gaps in turn reflect the structural differences in the urban labour markets and the rigidities that prevent the homogenisation of work practices, skill requirements and developments.

As pointed out earlier, since the mid-1980s the Bangladesh economy has been deregulated and opened up for foreign trade and investment. Foreign capital flows in the form of overseas workers' remittances, foreign aid and loans and foreign investment have given an impetus to economic growth of about 5 percent per annum since the late 1980s and caused structural transformation of the economy in favour of non-farm and services sectors. Consequently, the labour markets have undergone structural change in terms of employment and work patterns. However this did not lead to the expected rush of workers to the urban areas. The significant improvement in the agricultural terms of trade since the beginning of economic deregulation in the mid-1980s, inherent rigidities in urban (formal) labour markets and the increasing urban pollution and environmental problems appear to have slowed the shift of labour from agriculture to manufacturing and services in the urban areas. Nevertheless the structural changes in labour and work patterns with modern economic growth are visibly reflected in the associated labour mobility from the rural to the urban areas, between the farm and non-farm activities within the rural areas, between the formal and informal activities within the urban areas and from both the rural and urban areas to overseas destinations for employment and to settle.

Additional changes in the labour markets have included the rise in the participation rate of women and the productivity and wage differentials across sectors. With such developments, the economy has recently moved to a higher growth path and exhibited some dynamism. It will take some time before the arrival of the Lewisian turning point in the rural labour market (that is, when no surplus labour would exist in the rural sector and there would be a steady rise in the agricultural real wage rate in this otherwise 'labour surplus' country. However the 'new generation' workers have gained a foothold in the economic growth pie. This follows the international pattern whereby economies that grow rapidly, find that their workers do well compared with economies that remain stagnant. There are winners and losers in economies in transition. For a small country like Bangladesh, globalisation has been both a challenge and an opportunity. There is a belief that globalisation has caused structural problem with regard to employment as some state-owned enterprises have been closed and many workers have lost their jobs. At the same time many job opportunities have been crated in many new areas due to globalisation. With the opening up the economy, trade union activities, which are heavily politicised, have been reduced sharply, especially in the private sector. They are not allowed in the export processing zones and only partly in the booming garment industry. The diminished trade union activity apparently has been beneficial to the economy and the welfare of the people. However there is scope for healthy trade union activities for the protection of workers' interests. Militant trade unions until recently have artificially maintained high real wages in the public sector where jobs remain protected. It has now been acknowledged by all concerned that any artificial increases in real wages are not good and cannot be sustained for a long period. In addition to the provision of trade union activities, with the increasing importance of private-sector employment in the urban areas, some of the global labour, trade and environmental issues, such as child labour, gender discrimination, unemployment, sickness and disability pensions and benefits and wage disparities have gained prominence in policy debate at both national and international forums.

The challenge for Bangladesh is to sustain the market-oriented, outward-looking development strategy so that it can generate enough productive employment in the private sector to absorb the growing labour force. This would require higher levels of human and physical investment, an improved business climate and greater flexibility in labour markets (World Bank, 2004). For Bangladesh, rapid economic growth remains the fundamental source of sustainable poverty reduction. This process would be easier if economic growth becomes employment-oriented and benefits the poor (ADB, 2005). As experiences of East Asia show, employment-oriented economic growth raises incomes of the poor and this helps to create societal consensus for economic reforms and prepare the community to make sacrifices that are needed for economic adjustment due to internal and external shocks. Additional income support should come from public expenditures that would provide benefits to the poor and those who remain outside the formal labour markets. To pursue this objective, the labour-intensive rural infrastructure development programmes should continue. Public works programmes could be designed in such a way that they create community assets in response to demands by, and for the benefits of, local communities (Muqtada, 2003; World Bank, 2004).

With the growing importance of the informal sector in employment generation, there is special need for a transformation of the informal sector as a source of productive employment. This can be done through introducing modern technology, promoting entrepreneurial skills, improving production organisation and marketing, strengthening rural-urban and external linkages and marketing chains, ensuring necessary infrastructure including electricity, transport and communication facilities, providing credit facilities, providing business advisory and development services, and ensuring conducive investment and policy regimes (Muqtada, 2003; World Bank, 2004). An improvement in rural infrastructure is crucial because it provides benefit to both the farm and non-farm economy. As the experience of China with township and village enterprises shows, a dynamic rural non-farm economy can contribute significantly to rapid economic growth (ADB, 2005). However, any major changes in informal labour markets cannot be brought about over a short period of time and unless there is sustained economic growth that generates societal demand for economic, social and political development.

REFERENCES

Abdullah, A.A. and Q. Shahabuddin (1997) 'Critical Issues in Agriculture: Policy Response and Unfinished Agenda', in Quibria, M.G. (ed.), *The Bangladesh Economy in Transition*, University Press Limited, Dhaka.

Ahmed, S. and Z. Sattar (2004) 'Trade Liberalization, Growth and Poverty Reduction: The Case of Bangladesh'. Processed. South Asia Region of the World Bank, Washington, D.C.

Alam, G.M.M,. Rahman, M.S. and Mandal, M.A.S. (2004) 'Backward and Forward Linkages of Power Tiller Technology: Some Empirical Insights from an Area of Bangladesh', *Bangladesh Journal of Political Economy*, Vol.20(1), pp.139-152.

Amin, A.T.M.N (1981) 'Marginalisation vs. Dynamism: A Study of the Informal Sector in Dacca City', Bangladesh Development Studies, Vol.9(4), pp.77-112.

Asian Development Bank (ADB) (2005) *Labor Markets in Asia: Promoting Full, Productive, and Decent Employment* (Special chapter of Key Indicators of Developing Asian and Pacific Countries), Asian Development Bank, Manila.

Bangladesh Bureau of Statistics (BBS) (various issues), *Statistical Yearbook of Bangladesh*, Dhaka.

Government of Bangladesh (GOB) (various years), *Bangladesh Economic Review*, Ministry of Finance, Government of Bangladesh, Dhaka

Hossain, Akhtar (1995) *Inflation, Economic Growth and the Balance of Payments in Bangladesh*, Oxford University Press, Delhi.

Hossain, Akhtar (1996) *Macroeconomic Issues and Policies: The Case of Bangladesh*, Sage Publications, New Delhi/Thousand Oaks/London.

Hossain, Ismail (2002) 'Export Processing Zones in Bangladesh and Industrial Relations', in Muqtada, Muhammed, Andrea M. Singh and Mohammed A. Rashid (eds.), *Bangladesh: Economic and Social Challenges of Globalisation*, The University Press Limited, Dhaka.

Hossain, M. (1988) *Nature and Impact of the Green Revolution in Bangladesh*, Research Paper 67, International Food Policy Research Institute, Washington, DC.

Hossain, M., M.L. Bose, A. Chowdhury and R. Meimzen-Dick (2002) 'Changes in Agrarian Relations and Livelihoods in Rural Bangladesh: Insights from Repeat Village Studies', in Ramachandran, V.K. and M. Swaminathan (eds.), *Agrarian Studies: Essays on Agrarian Relations in Less Developed Countries*. Proceedings of the International Conference on Agrarian Relations and Rural Development in Less Developed Countries, New Delhi.

International Monetary Fund (IMF) (2003) *IMF Country Report No. 03/194*, Washington, D.C., http://www.imf.org.

Khan, A.S. (2005) 'Impact of Globalization on Labor Market and Workers, Challenges and Opportunities: Trade Union Action', *Bangladesh Institute of Labour Studies*, (Processed), Dhaka.

Lewis, A. (1954) 'Economic Development with Unlimited Supplies of Labour', *Manchester School*, Vol.22, pp.139-191.

Muqtada, M. (2003) 'Promotion of Employment and Decent Work in Bangladesh: Macroeconomic and Labour Policy Considerations', Employment Strategy Department, ILO, Geneva.

Paul-Majumder, Pratima (2002) 'Organising Women Garment Workers: A Means to Address the Challenges of Integration of the Bangladesh Garment Industry in the Global Market', in Muqtada, Muhammed, Andrea M. Singh and Mohammed A. Rashid (eds.), *Bangladesh: Economic and Social Challenges of Globalisation*, The University Press Limited, Dhaka.

Rashid, Mohammed A. (2002) 'Globalisation, Growth and Employment', in Muqtada, Muhammed, Andrea M. Singh and Mohammed A. Rashid (eds.), *Bangladesh: Economic and Social Challenges of Globalisation*, The University Press Limited, Dhaka.

The Daily Star, http://www.thedailystar.net [accessed: August 17, 2005].

Todaro, M.P. and S.C. Smith (2003) *Economic Development*, Addison-Wesley, New York.

World Bank (2003), *Bangladesh: Development Policy Review*, Report No.26154-BD, Poverty Reduction and Economic Management Sector Unit, South Asia Region, World Bank.

World Bank (2004) *Labor Markets in South Asia: Issues and Challenges*, Unpublished Report.

END NOTES

1. To avoid ambiguity in the absence of consensus on various terminologies used to define employment and economic activity in poor countries, this paper uses the convention of including in the non-farm category those activities that are not directly related to the production, distribution and marketing of major agricultural products. Therefore, in addition to rural off-farm activities, non-farm activity includes the urban informal sector activity such as street selling and petty retailing, repair and other personal services, crafts and other manufacturing, construction work and non-mechanised form of transport, such as rickshaws. In the rural areas, non-farm (off-farm) activities include construction work, wood and bamboo crafts, fishing, rural transport, small-scale manufacturing, petty trading and personal services (Amin, 1981; Hossain, 1996).

2. According to the Lewis model, the real wage rate in the labour surplus rural sector remains constant and well below (say, about 30 percent) the industrial sector real wage rate. The industrial sector can therefore increase employment by drawing workers from the rural sector without raising the rural wage rate. It is only when the surplus labour in the rural sector is eliminated through industrialisation that there would be a rise in real wages in the rural sector. The main criticism of this approach to development is that if the size of surplus labour in the rural sector remains large and the industrial sector does not growth rapidly and raise the demand for labour, given the capital-intensive nature of its production, the rural wage rate may not rise

much unless there is an increase in agricultural productivity that would determine the supply price of labour for the rest of the economy (ADB, 2005; Todaro and Smith, 2003).

3. For a discussion of these indicators, see Lee and Wood in this volume.

4. This section is adapted from ADB (2005), Muqtada (2003) and World Bank (2004).

Chapter 6

THE CHANGING NATURE OF WORK IN ASIA:
THE PHILIPPINES[1]

Benedicto Ernesto R. Bitonio Jr.[2]

This chapter identifies some of the major developments affecting the labor market and the world of work in the Philippines over the last two decades. It takes a macro perspective of these developments and identifies the major issues that are seen to confront work and employment relations now and in the coming years.

THE MEANING AND NATURE OF WORK

The Meaning of Work

In its broad sense, work or employment is understood in the context of the normative notions of labor. In The Philippine Constitution, labor is a primary social economic force. The explicit policy of the State is to protect labor as the human component of the production process and as a partner with capital in a social and economic relationship (see ART. II, Section 18). The State is to regulate the relations between workers and employers, recognizing the right of labor to its just share in the fruits of production and the right of enterprises to reasonable returns on investments, and to expansion and growth. It also provides the norm that work or employment must be productive and gainful, and working conditions must be humane (ART XIII, Section

---

[1] Unless otherwise indicated, the statistics used in this paper are drawn from the Yearbook of Labor Statistics (2004) published by the Bureau of Labor and Employment Statistics (BLES) of the Philippine Department of Labor and Employment (DOLE) and BLES LABSTAT Updates, various issues.
[2] The author, a lawyer, was assistant secretary for policy and programs and undersecretary for workers' welfare and protection at the DOLE. He is now chairman of the National Labor Relations Commission, the country's labor tribunal. Until his appointment to his current post, he was for several years a professorial lecturer at the University of the Philippines School of Labor and Industrial Relations. This chapter is purely the author's own assessment of trends and is not an expression of any official position of the government on the issues covered.

3). Since 2001, the Philippines has adopted the advocacy of the International Labor Organization (ILO) for "decent work," defined as work that takes place under conditions of freedom, equity, security and dignity, in which rights are protected and adequate remuneration and social coverage is provided. All these attempt to capture the universal nature and meaning of work as a means of producing that which is of value, as a source of income and livelihood for oneself and one's family, and ultimately as a foundation of human dignity. Policy and academic discourse usually revolve on this broad formulation of labor and work.

Formal and Informal Sector Dichotomy

There is a dichotomy between formal and informal work or employment. The formal sector consists mostly of wage and salary workers which, in 2004, represented 16.4 million or 52.1% of all employed. As a rule, formal employment is covered by traditional instruments of labor protection as found in the Labor Code and other social legislations, such as labor standards, minimum wages, hours of work, occupational safety and health rules, security of tenure, collective bargaining and social security regulations. Accordingly, it is associated with better quality of work and more stable income. Since the financing of the costs of welfare such as social security and employee's compensation benefits are internalized into the wage system through mandatory contributions, wage and salary employment also implies a greater level of social protection for workers.

Informal employment is mostly found among own-account workers and unpaid family workers. It is also perceived to be most prevalent in agriculture. Informal workers are generally not covered by protective statutes. Policy and legal reforms in the 1990s, however, allow social security coverage to these workers through voluntary membership.[1]

A growing concern among workers, unions and policy makers is the trend that even in wage and salary employment, work is becoming increasingly informalized. Some employment situations, although formal in nature, constrain the application of protective statutes. Such is the case with non-regular or temporary work among wage and salary workers whose incidence has almost trebled in the last 15 years, as shown in a survey conducted by the Bureau of Labor and Employment Statistics (BLES) of the Department of Labor and Employment (the BLES Integrated Survey, or BITS).

Knowledge Work and Globalization

When it comes to understanding the extent of knowledge work in the economy, it is important to recognize three basic premises. First, there are jobs in the economy, particularly in the information, communication and technology (ICT) sector, which have high skill, technology and knowledge content that qualify them as knowledge work. There is also pool of Filipino workers who have the education and skills for these jobs. Though these jobs are increasing, their proportion to total employment remains small. Second, the Philippines is not a knowledge or technology leader. The knowledge and technology content of jobs is imported through foreign direct investments. Third, a major reason why investors come to the Philippines is to buy into the skills available in the local labor force. The presence of an educated and highly skilled labor force is still one of the country's main comparative advantages. Therefore, it can be said that the Philippines has some of the elements that characterize a knowledge economy, but on the whole it is still in the process of getting to that stage.

MACROECONOMIC INDICATORS AND DEMOGRAPHICS

Population and Labor Force Participation Rate (LFPR)

The population has been growing rapidly over the last 25 years. From 48 million in 1980, it reached 76.5 million in 2000, or an average annual increase of over 2.3%. Official statistics project the population to reach 85.2 million by 2005 and 93.9 million by 2010. Of the projected population in 2005, over 50 million will be from 15 to 65 years of age.

The LFPR in 1980 was at 59.6% as 17.2 million of the household population of 28.9 million 15 years old and over joined the labor force. In 1988, the LFPR increased to 66.1%, with 23.4 out of 35.4 million 15 years old and over joining the labor force.

The growth in LFPR appears to have crested over the last 15 years, with annual LFPR ranging from 64.4% in 1990, 65.8% in 1995, an all-time high of 67.4% in 2002, and 64.8% in the third quarter of 2005.

The fast growth of the LFPR in the 1980s was due to a marked increase in the percentage of females joining the labor force, which rose from 45% in 1975 to 51% in 1988. Since then, the sex distribution of the LFPR has remained stable at about 82 to 83% for males and 51% for females. As of 2004, 22.2 out of 26.4 million males and 13.6 out of 26.6 million of females of working age were in the labor force.

The Employment Picture

Overall outlook

The annual average employment rate between the years 1980 to 2004 ranged from a high of 92.1% in 1980 to a low of 87.4% in 1985. In 2004, the labor force was 35.8 million (66.7% LFPR) while the employment rate was 88.2%. The employment rate of males and females is about equal. Of those employed, 19.6 million (88.5%) were male and 11.9 million (87.6%) were female.

About 19.3 million or 54% of all employed worked full-time (over 40 hours a week). Those employed can be classified into wage and salary workers, own-account workers, and unpaid family workers. In 2004, wage and salary employment reached a historical high of 16.4 million or 52.1% of all employed. The public sector accounts for a significant share among wage and salary workers. In 2004, average employment in government and government corporations was 2.4 million, almost 15% among wage and salary earners. The share of own account workers has remained fairly stable, while there was a decrease in unpaid family workers from 13.7% in 1997 to 11.2% in 2004. Among the Millenium Development Goals indicators for labor, female share in non-agricultural wage employment was at 41.3% in 2003 and 40.7% in 2004.

Employment by industry and occupational groups

By industry, employment is grouped into three: 1) agriculture, which includes hunting, fishery and forestry; 2) industry, which includes mining and quarrying, manufacturing, electricity, gas and water, and construction; and 3) services, which includes wholesale and retail trade, hotels and restaurants, transport, storage and communications, financial intermediation, real estate, renting and business activities, public administration and defense including compulsory social security, education, health and social work, other community, social and personal services, private households with employed persons, and extra-territorial organizations and bodies. Industry and services are sometimes lumped together as the non-agriculture sector.

Industry distribution of employment has been shifting over the last 10 to 15 years. Until the 1980s, agriculture had the largest share in employment. In the early 1990s, services overtook agriculture. By 2004, 15.3 million were employed in services, or 48% of employment. The major factors that may have contributed to the decline in agriculture are rural-to-urban migration, mechanization and modernization, and cyclical climatic patterns such as the El Nino phenomenon.

While the trend in agriculture is one of gradual and consistent decline, it remains a significant share of employment. It accounted for 11.38 million or 35.9% in 2004. The occupations subsumed under agriculture like animal husbandry, forestry, hunting and fishing, remained the biggest employer among all occupational groups, accounting for 39.1% of total employed in 1997 and 36.7% in 2001. Likewise, in times of economic slack tending to slow down growth, agriculture serves as the catch-basin for those falling out of employment in industry and services.

Industry share to employment, which was 15.8% in 2004, has remained flat over the last decade. Even so, structural reforms and competition in the global market have been changing the industry mix. For instance, in the 1990s, the cement and steel industries, which previously thrived because of protectionist policies, shut down after tariffs on imports were lowered. Many pharmaceutical and garments companies also relocated their manufacturing operations to other countries. Liberalization of telecommunications, on the other hand, spurred employment growth in this industry group.

Employment by age and education level

The employed labor force is predominantly young. In 2004, about 60% of those employed were between 15 to 44 years old and almost 50% were between 25 to 44 years old. The 25 to 44 age bracket is also book-ended by employment of the youth or those from 15 to 24, and by employment of older workers or those from 55 and over. In April 2005, approximately eight million youth were in the labor force. On the other hand, there were about 4.2 million (13-14.5%) older workers in 2004. For the period from 1998-2004, about three-fifths of those 55 years old and over were economically active, indicating a preference for them to remain in the labor force rather than to retire from work.

The employment of college-educated workers, including college graduates or higher, has been increasing (8.09 million or 25.6% in 2004). However, a larger proportion of those employed (71%) have only basic education. In recent years, the percentage share of employed workers with up to elementary schooling has been going down (39.9% in 1997 to 34.8% in 2004), while the percentage share of those with secondary education has been going up (33.7% to 37.3%).

THE DEMAND FOR LABOUR

The demand for jobs by specific industries and the kind of skills needed to fill this demand largely shape the distribution and quality of employment. The BITS provides an important source of analytical data with respect to demand for jobs. According to the BITS, 2.413 million workers are employed in non-agricultural establishments with twenty or more workers. The nature of their employment is instructive.

Where the jobs are being generated

The major contributor to employment in non-agriculture is manufacturing, which had a payroll of over 894 thousand or 37.1% of employed workers in the covered establishments as of June 2004. Production workers constitute the second biggest occupational grouping across industries. Wholesale and retail trade had over 367 thousand or 15.2%; real estate, renting and business activities had over 269 thousand or 11.2%;[13] private education services had over 192 thousand or 8%; and transport, storage and communication had over 189 thousand or 7.8%.

Generally, employment in the establishments covered by the BITS is paid employment (wage and salary employment) and consists mostly of rank and file workers. The mode of payment is mostly time-rated (monthly or daily, and in some cases hourly) but there are variations across sub-industries. The establishments covered also reported a significant incidence of non-regular or temporary employment. Across industries, an average of 24.5% of all employed were engaged in non-regular work.

Manufacturing is the engine of the country's exports. It accounted for 80% of the country's total exports of US 3.6 billion dollars in 2003. Electronic, electrical equipment and parts, and telecommunication manufactures account for the biggest share at 69% of total exports. Machinery and transport equipment account for 4%. Garments account for 6%.

The sub-sectors within manufacturing are not diversified. More than half (54.9%) of manufacturing employment was shared by only five sub-sectors, with apparel (garments) and food products comprising the biggest groups at 15.9% each. Manufacturing of radio, TV and communication equipment and apparatus ranked second at 13.5%, followed by chemicals and chemical products at 4.7% and office, accounting and computing machinery at 4.6%.

The majority (93.3%) of those employed in manufacturing are full-time. It also had the biggest proportion of daily paid workers at 60%. Moreover, it had the most number of output rate workers, perhaps suggesting a link between competitiveness and modes of compensation that can be further explored.

Skills and Knowledge Content of Jobs

Generally, the primary job generators in industry do not require a high level of knowledge or specialized skills. This is especially true with respect to wholesale and retail trade and real estate as well as renting and business activities, which have been the fastest-growing sub-industries over the last decade. The demand for jobs can be filled in by the abundant labor pool since the skills sets required from workers are general skills, such as the ability to read and implement instructions, basic language skills, and mechanical skills including those requiring manual dexterity.

With respect to the ICT sub-sector, there are favorable trends. The critical role of ICT in the country's development and modernization has been recognized since the Philippine Development Plan for 2001-2004, and reaffirmed in the 2004-2010 Medium Term Philippine Development Plan (MTPDP). A survey conducted in 2001 indicates that the number of ICT users across all industries has reached 88.1%, with usage in ICT industries accounting for 93.6% and non-ICT industries 83.1%. Also in 2001, ICT-related activities contributed 4.2% to the country's Gross Domestic Product, with total expenditures reaching US 3.13 billion dollars, compared to less than two billion in 1995 (Development Data Group, World Bank).

ICT manufacturing remains the top exporter. But investments and job generation in business process outsourcing and call center operations have grown by leaps and bounds in the last five years. The Philippines is now among the world's top three countries providing outsourcing services. The nature of jobs being generated in these areas makes full use of the English proficiency of Filipinos. Many of these jobs also demand complex cognitive, computational or highly specialized skills acquired through higher education or specialized training. As such, these jobs could help push the Philippines forward and deepen its interconnectedness with the global knowledge economy.

KEY LABOR MARKET ISSUES

Youth unemployment, underemployment and levels of education

A key issue for the present and the future is youth unemployment. The LFPR of those between 15 to 24 years old is high at 49.1% in 2005 and has remained relatively constant. Youth unemployment stood at 23.9% in 2004, twice the national average. Even with the high youth unemployment rate, there is no indication that young people are postponing decisions to join the labor market in favor of more education. It has been suggested that since young unskilled workers are in relative abundance, youth unemployment can be addressed if the economy grows at a relatively rapid pace that permits the demand for unskilled or semi-skilled workers to increase. Raising the demand for this type of workers is helped by policies that permit industries like construction and labor-intensive light manufacturing to grow rapidly (Canlas 2005).

Underemployment, which indicates the inability of the labor market to optimally use the potentials of those who are employed, is also high (17.6% in 2004 and 21% in 2005). Underemployment cuts across age groups. A special concern is the case of older workers. In 2004, more than two thirds (70.8%) in the 55-59 age bracket were heads of households, even as more than half (53.1%) were engaged in part-time jobs or had worked less than 40 hours a week.

Another issue concerns the educated unemployed. From 2001 to 2003, the unemployed were better educated than the employed. For example, the majority of the unemployed had at least high school education (42.6%) while those with college education accounted for 34.3%. The incidence of unemployment also tended to increase with the years of education. In 2002, only 6.7% of those with at least elementary education were unemployed followed by those without formal education (9.3%), with at least high school education (13.2%) and with college education (15.4%). Employed professionals, technicians and associate professionals, considered most valuable to a developing nation, constituted 4.5% and 2.7% respectively.[2]

Coping With Surplus Labor

Entrepreneurship or self-employment, including cooperativism, is currently actively being promoted by the government not only as a temporary or alternative form of employment or source of income, but also as a permanent option for more value creation. A host of government agencies incorporate promotion of and capability building for entrepreneurship into their annual programs.

Occasionally, the State through its national government agencies and local government units, undertakes pump-priming measures to create temporary employment. The usual modes are public work projects such as construction and cleaning up operations, reforestation, and summer jobs for students. Apart from such projects, other publicly-provided means of coping with surplus labor are training and retraining programs with the view of expanding the skills sets of surplus labor in order to enhance their employability or absorption into available job opportunities. There is, however, a dearth of information correlating the effects of these schemes on employment patterns and practices.

Overseas employment

The Philippines is one of the major sources of overseas labor, sending about one million workers of various skills and education levels to different job destinations annually. The demand for Filipino workers is helped by their language skills, positive reputation in terms of skills and work ethics, and the fact that the Philippines has one of the most developed overseas employment services in the world. Those who qualify for overseas employment are most likely to have been employed in the Philippines before deciding to try employment overseas, or are repeat contract migrants who are part of the phenomenon called circular migration. The main push factor for migration is higher pay.

Overseas migration helps the economy cope with labor surpluses in two ways. Since the migrant worker is very likely employed, his or her departure will create employment opportunities for others. On the other hand, in 2004 and 2005, overseas Filipino workers remitted US 8.55 and US 8.83 billion dollars. These remittances can create a multiplier effect on the domestic economy, increasing the economy's capacity for job generation. Early concerns about "brain drain" have been tempered by the infusion of foreign exchange, as well as by the reality that, in the global economy, a country's human resources are part of a pool of resources that can be shared internationally. More recently, however, there has been a growing debate about the loss of critical skills, or skills needed for the economy to modernize, such as health professionals, teachers and airline pilots, because of better-paying opportunities overseas.

Employment services

One school of thought suggests that unemployment, underemployment and labor mismatches do not necessarily mean lack of jobs. There are actually jobs around, but there is a lack of information as to where these jobs are. Accordingly, policy has been oriented towards making labor market information a truly public good and strengthening employment facilitation services. The Labor Code and a subsequent legislation called the Public Employment Service Act (1999) provide for the setting up of employment services to facilitate job searching and matching of skills. The publicly-provided facilities are the public employment service offices in the local government units. The Department of Labor and Employment provides technical supervision over these offices as part of its mandate to administer a national employment service network. The backbone and infrastructure of this network, in which there has been a fair amount of public investment, is the Phil-Jobnet, a computerized job search, matching and counseling facility. Access to these services is free.

The Role of the State: Employment Regulation and Labor Standards

Under the Constitution, the State shall promote full employment and equality of employment, ensure security of tenure and just and humane conditions of work, promote and protect the right to self-organization and collective bargaining, promote workers' participation in decision-making processes directly affecting them, and promote shared responsibility and gain-sharing between employers and workers (ART. XIII, Section 3). The Civil Code recognizes that labor contracts are not just ordinary contracts but are vested with public interest that must yield to the common good. Therefore, these may be regulated through special laws. The Labor Code, first codified in 1974, is the primary enabling law that implements Constitutional objectives. The Code incorporates a number of international standards found in ILO conventions, including the ILO's eight core conventions.

The Code covers a comprehensive range of rights from pre-employment to post-employment. The human resource development policy is a combination of State provision of vocational training, regulation and accreditation of training institutions, and standard setting and skill certification. The employment policy concerns State provision of job facilitation services for local and overseas employment and regulation of recruitment activities. The Code provides minimum standards relating, among other things, to employable age, work hours, wage fixing, leaves, occupational health and safety, workmen's compensation and social security. The Code also protects security of tenure, classifies employees, prescribes grounds for termination of employment as well as separation pay where termination is due to economic causes, and provides remedies in case of illegal termination. Throughout the 1990s, legislations were also introduced on emerging policy areas, such as increased penalties against wage violations and gender discrimination, and affirmative measures for the employment of workers with disabilities.

The present regime of labor regulation follows the rights-based approach to regulating employment relations. Statutory rights are formulated as minimum labor standards that cannot be contracted away by the parties. Theoretically, this protects workers from the dangers of market failure, and therefore, leads to more predictable and stable employment relations. Nevertheless, there are difficulties in enforcement. There are also perceptions that the statutory standards are too high and too rigid, and consequently limit the flexibility of firms to innovate and expand, especially in a market-driven and rapidly changing business environment. The general debate, heightened by the pressures of globalization, can therefore be framed as a "State or market" dilemma, or the compatibility of regulation with employment, productivity and income growth.

Minimum Wages

By law, the authority to fix minimum wages is exercised by the regional wage boards, under the supervision of the National Wage and Productivity Commission (NWPC), an agency attached to the Department of Labor and Employment. The boards are tripartite in composition. The regional and decentralized structure was conceived to allow differentiated responses to regional differences in terms of levels of development.[3]

The NWPC estimates that there are about 2.6 million workers who are minimum wage earners. These workers are the primary beneficiaries in every wage round. But the wage boards have flexibility to mandate that minimum wage increases be made applicable not only to those actually receiving the minimum wage but also to those receiving beyond the minimum up to a prescribed ceiling. Thus, about 1.5 million more who receive more than the minimum wage but who are within the ceiling also directly benefit from wage increases. Beyond these groups, a wage round may also have upward spillover effects in the wage scale arising from adjustments to correct wage distortions.

As it has evolved, minimum wage setting obviously seeks to satisfy multiple and broader policy objectives other than simply protecting the low-skilled or setting a floor wage. The complex implications of minimum wage setting leaves many unanswered questions, including 1) the effectiveness of minimum wage as an anti-poverty measure, 2) the employment and dis-employment effects, if any, 3) whether or not minimum wage protects the currently employed but who are on the lower end of the wage scale, or actually undermines their job security, and 4) whether or not it effectively blocks workers, especially the young or new entrants and the low-skilled, from entering the labor market altogether.

Security of Tenure and Rules of Employment Termination

The Constitution and the Labor Code guarantee security of tenure to all workers. Employment is classified in the Labor Code as regular, employment for a fixed period (also referred to as term or contractual employment), or casual. Notwithstanding any written agreement to the contrary, and regardless of the oral agreement of the parties, employment is deemed regular when the employee has been engaged to perform activities which are necessary or desirable in the business or trade of the employer, except when the employment has been fixed for a specific project or undertaking the completion or termination of which has been determined at the time of the engagement of the employee or when the work or services to be performed is seasonal in nature and the employment is for the duration of the season. Employment is deemed casual if it is not classified as either regular or for a fixed period. However, an employee who has rendered at least one year of service, whether such service is continuous or broken, shall be considered a regular employee with respect to the activity in which he is employed and his employment shall continue while such activity exists.

In the context of the Labor Code, employment is presumed regular. A regular employee may not be dismissed from employment except upon just or authorized cause. Just causes refer to causes attributable to the fault of the employee, while authorized causes refer to those brought about by economic exigencies affecting the employer. Every case of termination from employment may be contested, and the law places the burden of justifying that the termination is for just or authorized cause on the employer.[4]

Termination of employment without just or authorized cause makes the employer liable for back wages, reinstatement of the employee and, in appropriate cases, damages. Termination for just cause exempts the employer from any liability to the employee. Termination for an authorized cause entitles the employee to separation or severance pay, unless the termination is brought about by closure due to proven serious business losses in which case the employer is exempt from liability.

Except when the dismissal is for just cause, termination of employment has costs. With respect to termination for authorized causes, one view is that the legal regime is inflexible and rigid, makes business adjustments difficult and costly, stymies firm-level responses to market forces, encourages litigation, and generally results in a less competitive labor market. The view has also been expressed that these rules protect insiders (the currently employed) at the expense of the outsiders (those who could otherwise compete for available jobs (e.g., Sicat 2005). The net effect, it has been argued but not empirically proven, is to inhibit hiring, make existing firms choose more technology and less labor, and encourage potential investors to choose other destinations with more flexible industrial relations regimes, thereby depressing demand for jobs.

There is an increasing use, in spite of, or arguably because of, the provisions of the Labor Code, of non-regular or temporary work particularly such arrangements as fixed-term or contractual employment, casual employment and subcontracting through agencies. The BITS estimates that the incidence of non-regular or temporary work in establishments employing twenty or more workers is 25% of the total workforce. It is clear from the Labor Code that regular, fixed period or contractual and casual employment are mutually exclusive. However, it appears from the survey that there is no distinction between the work being performed by regular workers and non-regular workers. Firms are motivated to employ non-regular workers to cut costs and to have a buffer to market fluctuations, thus giving them numerical flexibility. At the same time, it enables them to take advantage of labor surpluses in lower-skill categories by allowing them to recycle entry level pay and avoid the carrying costs of employing regular workers, such as seniority pay. It also enables them to avoid paying separation pay which is obligatory in the case of regular employment (Bitonio 2004). So far, the statistics suggest neither a positive nor negative correlation between increasing an incidence of non-regular work and growth in employment levels.

Industrial Relations and Unionization

The union and collective bargaining system in the Philippines is divided into public and private sector unionism. Public sector unionism is just starting to develop. Public sector unions are faced with the general limitation that they cannot bargain for terms and conditions of employment that are fixed by law.

Critical issues confront private sector unionism. Though Article 243 of the Labor Code defines the scope of the right to self-organization broadly to include all workers, whether covered by a formal employee-employer relationship or self-employed, this right is effectively available only to wage and salary workers covered by a formal employee-employer relationship. Union organizing and collective bargaining are decentralized and enterprise-based. In 2004, there were over 15 thousand registered unions with about 1.3 million members. Not every union, however, is able to conclude a collective bargaining agreement (CBA). In 2004, there were only 2,798 registered CBAs covering 555 thousand workers, representing roughly 43% of total union membership and 3.3% of wage and salary earners. Union and collective bargaining goals remain focused on traditional issues like wages, additional benefits, work security and job security.

In the past decade, the number of unions, union members and workers covered by CBAs has been declining. Unions typically blame economic liberalization as well as an overly strict implementation of the laws on self-organization for the decline. In reality, government has adopted, through tripartite consultations, major policy and procedural reforms that accommodate atypical work as well as changes in work practices at the firm level, such as simplified requirements for union organizing, recognition of associations for mutual aid and protection, and industry or multi-employer bargaining. In response, many unions have been making adjustments in their organizing and bargaining strategies. Nevertheless, the decline in membership continues. A relatively recent development is the emergence of cooperatives as major players in the economy. The possibility that cooperatives may have a replacement or substitution effect on unions is an emerging issue.

The State advocates free unionism and collective bargaining - and corollarily minimum government intervention in regulating employment relations – on the economic logic that decentralized negotiations will allow workers and employers to agree on the most efficient terms of employment. This logic favors the market mechanism more than the State in adjusting labor-management problems. While this logic remains sound and should be pursued, the statistics clearly indicate that it has not brought about desired outcomes. With profit margins of firms being competed away, unions have a weakened capacity to satisfy members' expectations in the traditional areas of bargaining like wages, additional benefits, work security and job security. As a result, the union strategy is to simultaneously pursue their interests in two fronts, one at the plant level and the other through advocacy for State intervention by way of policy and legislative reforms.

CONCLUSION: IMPLICATIONS OF THE CHANGING NATURE OF WORK AND FUTURE CHALLENGES

Policy Challenges

Given the characteristics of the Philippine labor market and the economy in the last two decades, employment generation, maximizing the potential of the current labor force, and improving the quality of employment are the main challenges for the Philippines. From a macro level, the basic problem is that the labor force is growing faster than the economy can generate jobs. There is an obvious need to address the rapid population growth. The natural consequences have been chronic labor surpluses and limited access to quality education, training and other social services. Limited access weakens the country's transformative and absorptive capacity and slows down its push toward the modern economy. Improving labor productivity and total factor productivity are essential. In this regard, underutilization of the workforce, as indicated by the country's underemployment rates, should also be effectively addressed.

While dealing with both the larger and more specific labor market issues, policy cannot ignore some basic realities brought about by the changing nature of work.

Some of these realities challenge the basic foundations of formal employment. First, with global competition, firms must benchmark their performance, productivity and practices not with local firms but with the most competitive firms at the regional or international level. Second, the life cycles of jobs, even those with relatively lower knowledge and technology content, are also becoming shorter. Coupled with the increasing incidence of non-regular work, this suggests a more rapid labor turnover. It also raises fears concerning job, income and employment security, and overall social anxiety. Third, the country's advantage in attracting investments is the availability of educated and trained human resources. But in a global playing field, Filipino workers must brace themselves for stiffer competition. And fourth, the rights-based system, founded on international labor standards and explicit statutory protection, has always been considered to have the virtuous effect of positively motivating workers to perform better and to produce more, thereby increasing the capacity of firms to make profits. Nevertheless, there is a great deal of debate about its compatibility with new work arrangements and productivity. The debate should lead to a practical consensus.

Conversely, policy must be mindful not to create a divide between an old economy built on lower-skilled work and informal arrangements, and a new economy built on knowledge work. For workers whose skills equip them to participate in the knowledge economy, the jobs being created in the global economy provides them an opportunity to enhance their incomes, as well as improve their living standards and quality of working life. But at the same time, there is the threat of insecurity and exclusion for those who are not so well situated or equipped with regard to their skill base. A situation where a minority of the labor force is able to benefit from knowledge work, while a majority must make do with less skilled, less remunerative and less secure work can create social tensions.

Steps Forward

Proper responses to labor market issues will be critical for the Phillipines. The MTPDP is a useful instrument in enabling the various institutions and actors to have a coherent and coordinated development plan that will benefit as many workers as possible while promoting business competitiveness. In the field of labor and employment, this plan can be enhanced through social dialogue. Some specific measures, with the view of infusing dynamism in the labor market are considered next.

First, it is important to have sound institutions to promote labor market efficiency and work-to-work transitions, including labor market information and facilitation networks, access to further skills acquisition and enhancement, measures to smooth out consumption in case of income discontinuity, portability of social security benefits, and simpler and faster dispute settlement procedures.

Second, public and private sector investments in human resource development, education, training and technology should continue. There is much room for knowledge work to expand its share of total employment. Efforts in this direction should be supported through proper incentives. On the other hand, upgrading the skills of those with low levels of education and training should be part of the overall goal of human capital formation. Creative ways to finance access to education and training opportunities should also be developed.

Third, with reference to knowledge work, there is indeed fast employment growth in specific areas that can qualify as knowledge work. But care must be taken to understand both the sustainability and limits of this growth. State policy should avoid picking winners and losers. The MTPDP has taken the prudent path of encouraging growth sectors while giving as much attention as possible to traditional employment generators. It is recommended that this path be maintained.

Fourth, further empirical research on critical issues should be pursued in order to inform policy debates and responses. Among these issues are minimum wages, the role of unions and other non-state actors in promoting employment, youth employment, underemployment, the phenomenon of the educated unemployed, and the rising incidence of non-regular work.

Fifth, the framework of State regulation needs to be reviewed. The Labor Code has proven to be an extremely useful instrument for workers' protection, equality and social justice. However, the need to bring it up to speed with changing work environments is both legitimate and urgent. While the scope of labor regulation has broadened, the real policy question is whether the assumptions of the regulatory framework are still valid given the changing nature of work. This issue is framed, on one hand, by the legitimate interests of workers for labor protection and, on the other hand, by market forces that may tend to erode the effectiveness of the very instruments that provide protection. There is much room for research and policy debate toward a better understanding of the content, design and relevance of regulation within the rights-based system and the need of the economy to improve its competitiveness.

Change and the Political Process

The Philippines has a liberal and pluralist political system. Employers, workers and their organizations are only three of many represented in a system that provides channels of participation for all groups. Participation operates through an overlay of institutions. In Congress, there is an avenue to embed workers' interests through labor representation in the party-list system. Outside Congress, there is also an avenue to embed both workers' and employers' interests through mandatory representation in tripartite policy-making and consultative agencies. The accountable use of democratic mechanisms, including people's participation, tripartism and social dialogue, can bring about social and political consensus.

The State speaks through the political process. It is ultimately through this process that responses to critical macroeconomic and labor market issues and the allocation of scarce resources to address these issues will be determined. It is therefore important to pay attention to the way the political process intermediates workers' and employers' interests amid a changing world. The kind of policy decisions taken, in combination with market forces, will have a profound effect on the behavior and interactions of the traditional industrial relations players, individual workers and firms, and other non-State actors. These factors will also shape the pace, depth and extensiveness of change in the country's workplaces, as well as the opportunities that such change will create for the Phillipine economy.

REFERENCES

Bureau of Labor and Employment Statistics (BLES), (2004) Department of Labor and Employment, Philippine Yearbook of Labor Statistics.

BLES. LABSTAT Updates, (2005) No. 5, Employment Patterns in the Wholesale and Retail Trade Industry.

BLES. LABSTAT Updates, (2005) No. 7, Employment Patterns in the Transport, Storage and Communication Industry.

BLES. LABSTAT Updates, (2004) No. 7.

BLES. LABSTAT Updates, (2005) No. 8, Employment Patterns in Real Estate, Renting and Business Activities.

BLES, LABSTAT Updates, (2005) No. 9.

BLES.LABSTAT Updates, (2005) No.10, Employment Patterns in the Private Education Services Industry.

BLES. LABSTAT Updates, (2005) No. 13, Employment Patterns in the Manufacturing Industry.

Bitonio, Benedicto Ernesto Jr. R. (2004) "Labor Flexibility and Workers Representation in the Philippines" An initial version of this article was presented at the 5th Asian regional Congress of the International Industrial Relations Association, Seoul, Korea, in June 2004.

Canlas, Dante B. (2005) "Labor Market Regulation: Does it Promote or Hinder Full Employment and Workers Welfare?" Paper presented at the National Tripartite Policy Conference on Wages and Productivity, Manila.

Constitution of the Philippines.

The New Civil Code of the Philippines.

Labor Code of the Philippines, as amended.

National Economic and Development Authority (NEDA), (2004) Medium Term Philippine Development Plan (MTPDP) 2004-2010.

Sicat, Gerardo P. (2005) "What it will take to reform RP's labor market." Paper presented at the National Tripartite Policy Conference on Wages and Productivity, Manila.

END NOTES

---

[1] Made possible through Republic Act No. 8282 (Social Security Law of 1997) and Republic Act No. 7875 (National Health Insurance Act of 1985).

[2] NEDA. MTPDP 2004-2010, p. 111.

[3] See Republic Act No. 6727 [1989], otherwise known as the Wage Rationalization Act.

[4] See ARTS. 277 (b), 280, 283, and 284, Labor Code of the Philippines.

Chapter 7

GLOBALISATION OF THE MALAYSIAN ECONOMY AND THE WTO: PROBLEMS AND PROSPECTS FOR THE MALAYSIAN INDUSTRY AND THE WORKFORCE

Amir Mahmood and Ming Yu Cheng

INTRODUCTION

Over the past two decades, there has been a noticeable transformation of the Malaysian economy. Rapid and sustained economic growth has been accompanied by: falling poverty, falling unemployment, improved human development and low inflation. Specifically, an integration of the Malaysian economy with the rest of the world through inward Foreign Direct Investment (FDI) and trade has played a key role in transforming Malaysia from a resource-based economy to one that participates in high-skilled and technology-intensive sectors in the global markets.

Largely, this shift can be attributed to an adherence to trade liberalisation and foreign investment policies that have helped the country to reap the benefits of globalization with regard to production and competition in global markets (Athukorala, 2001). Up until now unilateral trade and investment liberalisation policies have helped Malaysia to strategically steer the manufacturing and services sectors towards enhanced competitiveness. Recently however, the surge in Free Trade Agreements, regional economic integration, China's accession to the World Trade Organisation (WTO), competitive trade and investment policies by regional competitors and the Doha Round of multilateral trade negotiations have all posed new challenges for Malaysia.

While the above developments offer opportunities to the export sector through expanded market access, they also force domestic import-competing industries, which thus far have received protection, to become competitive. For Malaysia, both scenarios have far reaching implications in a number of areas. Specifically, these include: structure of production, value chains, industrial reorientation, resource allocation, Malaysia's position in regional production chains, employment, and the workforce. The focus of this study is to evaluate the impact of the increasing globalization of the Malaysian economy on industrial reorientation and the resulting labour market outcomes.

The study is organised into 4 sections. Following the introduction, section 2 entitled, 'A Contemporary Overview of the Malaysian Economy' highlights the Malaysian growth experience and analyses the associated structural changes in the economy. This section analyses the role of the manufacturing sector as the engine of Malaysian economic growth, employment, value added, and exports. Two key globalisation drivers; trade and foreign direct investment have greatly influenced the performance of the Malaysian economy and its structural transformation. Consequently, this section traces the trade and FDI trends, at both aggregated as well as disaggregated levels, while analysing the above nexus.

Section 3 evaluates the Malaysian trade policy instruments, intended objectives, and their ramifications for Malaysian industry and the workforce under different scenarios. This section provides a critical analysis of labour market outcomes and workforce issues that are directly, as well as indirectly, attributed to globalization in general and trade and investment liberalisation in particular. Finally, section 4 provides conclusions and policy implications drawn from the study.

AN OVERVIEW OF THE MALAYSIAN ECONOMY

During the past few decades, the Malaysian economy has shown resilience by withstanding negative economic shocks and sustaining high rates of economic growth. This rapid economic growth has been accompanied by a marked structural transformation of the Malaysian economy. Among other factors, the macro policy initiatives undertaken by the Malaysian government, including a unique policy response to the Asian Financial crisis, played a key role in helping Malaysia to sustain a healthy growth path. These polices include: import substitution policies in the

1960's; initiatives towards export promotion and industrialisation during the 1970s; deregulation, privatisation, and the promotion of heavy industries during the mid-1980s; foreign direct investment-driven growth policies and the promotion of greater intra-industry and inter-industry trade in the early 1990's; initiatives towards technology-led growth in the late 1990s, and a post-Asian Financial Crisis policy response that helped the country to recover within a short period of time (Tham, 2000; Hajinoor and Saleh, 2000; Okposin, Hamid & Boon, 1999; Okposin and Cheng, 2000). This rapid economic growth in Malaysia has been accompanied by low inflation, falling unemployment, falling poverty, reductions in income inequality, and rising per capita income. Specifically, Malaysian per capita income, GDP per capita (PPP, current international US$) rose from US$ 2185 in 1980 to US$ 9, 760 in 2004 (World Bank, 2005).

Since the 1980's, the country has sustained average economic growth of over 6 % per annum. While in the 1980's the economy grew at an average rate of 5.2% per annum, the pre-Asian Financial Crisis era (1990-97) saw the GDP growth hovering at over 8%. The short-term growth implications of the Asian Financial Crisis for the Malaysian economy were damaging, with GDP growth declining by 7.4% in 1998 (Asian Development Bank, 2005). The post-crisis (1999-04) turnaround, in which the economy grew at an annual rate of 5.3 % (see Table 1), demonstrates the interplay of the post-crisis policy response of the Malaysian government and the capacity of the agriculture, manufacturing and services sectors to overcome an exogenous shock in a relatively short period.

The impact of the Asian Financial Crisis was not, however, uniform across sectors. The manufacturing sector witnessed a decline of 13.4 per cent in 1998, followed by industry decline of 10.6 per cent, which includes manufacturing mining, construction, water, and gas, services (-5%) and agriculture (-2.8%) (World Bank, 2005). The turnaround of the Malaysian economy from this very difficult situation was quite remarkable. As Table 1 shows, all sectors have contributed to mitigate the negative impact of the financial crisis during the post-crisis period.

Table 1. Growth of Output by Sector, Malaysia 1980/90 to 1999/2004

(% Growth)

Gross domestic Product			Agriculture			Industry[1]			Manufacturing[2]			Services		
1980-90	1990-96	1999-04	1980-90	1990-96	1999-04	1980-90	1990-96	1999-04	1980-90	1990-96	1999-04	1980-90	1990-96	1999-04
5.2	8.7	5.3	3.8	1.9	2.9	7.2	11.2	6.4	8.9	13.2	7.8	4.2	8.5	4.8

Source: World Bank,1999a, World Bank 2005

Notes: [1]Industry Value added ISIC divisions 10-45 and includes manufacturing (ISIC divisions 15-37). It comprises value added in mining, manufacturing, construction, electricity, water, and gas. Value added is the net output of a sector after adding up all outputs and subtracting intermediate inputs (World Bank, 2005)

[2]Manufacturing value added refers to industries belonging to ISIC divisions 15-37 (World Bank, 2005)

During 1980-2004, the share of the agricultural sector to GDP declined from 23 per cent in 1980 to 10 per cent in 2004. The industry contribution to GDP grew from 41 per cent in 1980 to 48 per cent in 2004. The manufacturing sector, which is also a part of the industry sector, increased its share from 22 percent in 1980 to 30 per cent in 2004. The structural change in the Malaysian economy also witnessed an expanding role of the services sector, with its share in GDP growing from 36 per cent in 1980 to 42 per cent in 2004 (Table 2). Among other factors, these changes were an outcome of deliberate government policies to guide the economy away from the agricultural sector towards the manufacturing and services sectors. During this period, government policies emphasising export-led growth, trade and foreign direct investment played a pivotal role in the expansion of the manufacturing sector.

Table 2. Structural Change in the Malaysian Economy

(% of GDP)	1980	1990	2000	2004
Agriculture	23	15	8	10
Industry	41	42	50	48
Manufacturing	22	24	32	30
Services	36	43	40	42

Source: World Bank, 2005

The Malaysian manufacturing sector can be segregated into "Export-Oriented Industries" (EOI) and "Domestic-Oriented Industries" (DOI). In 2004, the share of EOI and DOI in total manufacturing production was 53 and 47 per cent, respectively (Ministry of Finance, 2005). The EOI include electronics and electrical, rubber and wood based products, and textiles and clothing. Whereas, the major players in the DOI include: plastic and chemical products, food and beverages, construction-related products, and transport and equipment. One of the distinguishing features between the EOI and DOI is the discriminatory protection treatment afforded to the DOI. While EOI operates under liberal trade arrangements, DOI usually enjoy considerable effective rates of protection, where although imports of raw materials are encouraged free of duty, protection increases as a product moves up in the value chain. It is the DOI sector, such as the Malaysian automobile industry, which now faces major challenges due to further trade and investment liberalisation. Conversely, declining market access barriers in the global markets have put further competitive pressure on the EOI. For instance, a slowdown in the global economy is bound to reduce the demand for semiconductors, an industry that constitutes 35 per cent of the total manufacturing production (Ministry of Finance, 2005). Despite the growing openness of the economy, industry protection remains to some extent. For example, heavy industries, such as the automobile industry, and infant industries such as biotechnology still require protection.

GLOBALISATION OF THE MALAYSIAN ECONOMY

Globalization and economic integration in various forms, such as free trade agreements and WTO-induced multilateral trade liberalisation, have played important roles in transforming the Malaysian economy from being agricultural-based in the 1960s and 1970s to the current services-and knowledge-based economy. In the early stages of economic development, foreign direct investment in Malaysia was concentrated mainly in the import-substitution industries. In the 1970s and 1980s, foreign investors were encouraged to relocate their production-bases to Malaysia in order to take advantage of low-cost production. These foreign direct investments focused basically on producing standard technology products and re-exporting these products to other developing markets (Sieh and Yew, 1997). Thus, the presence of these foreign firms has induced significant trading activity and generated substantial employment and output in the manufacturing sector. Latterly, the open economy policy has not only made it possible for Malaysian firms to venture into new markets and expand trade into global markets, but it has also allowed for the creation of new industries, such as the call centre industry and a range of high-tech industries.

That said, greater openness is not without its costs. As a small and open economy where trade is occupying more than 200 percent of its annual GDP, Malaysia is subject to global volatility and the transmission of external shocks. During the 1997 Asian Financial Crisis, Malaysia experienced its greatest shock since independence because of its extensive linkages with the global economy. Many firms, especially small and medium sized businesses went bankrupt, while others were forced to go through a series of business restructuring. As a result, it is a challenge for Malaysian firms, especially small and medium enterprises, to sustain their competitiveness while enjoying the benefits of globalisation.

The structural transformation of the Malaysian economy can be attributed to an increasing globalisation of the Malaysian economy, which is underpinned by a host of drivers such as, trade & investment liberalisation, the openness of financial markets, advances in information and telecommunication technologies and the privatisation and deregulation of state owned enterprises (Shakur, 2006). However, it is the phenomenal growth in world trade, investment flows, and advancement in technology that has hastened the process of economic globalisation (OECD, 2005). One of the simplistic measures of a country's globalisation is the country's trade (export plus imports) as a percentage of GDP. In the context of Southeast Asian economics, with the exception of Singapore, the pace of globalisation of the Malaysian economy has been more rapid than in any other country in the region (World Bank, 2005). As Figure 1 indicates, with a relatively modest increase until mid-1980, trade as a percentage of GDP in Malaysia grew at a much faster rate in subsequent periods. In 2004, Malaysian trade as a percentage of GDP stood at 221 per cent, significantly higher than for other countries at this level of development.

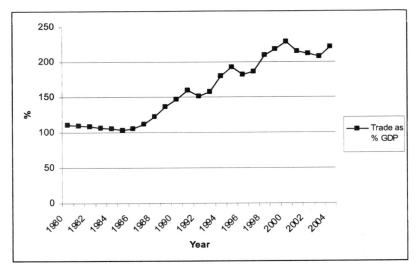

Source: World Bank, 2005

Figure 1. Globalisation of the Malaysian Economy (Trade as % GDP)

Trade, is not however, the only indicator of the increasing globalisation of the Malaysian economy. Foreign direct investment into domestic as well as export oriented industries has proved to be the catalyst in linking Malaysia with the regional and global production networks. The role of inward FDI in Malaysian economic growth, through its contribution to fixed capital formation, domestic value added, employment, exports, industrialisation and technology transfer cannot be underestimated. During 1985-1995, the annual average inflow of inward FDI stood at US$2.9 billion, contributing 14 per cent to gross capital formation in the country. By 2004, FDI inflows were in the range of US$4.6 billion, representing 19 per cent of the gross capital formation (UNCTAD, 2005). That is a significant recovery from its 2003 level of US$2.5 billion, which amounted to 11 per cent of the gross capital formation (Figure 2). The significance of FDI inflow for gross capital formation, and thus employment generation, cannot be underestimated as gross capital formation has followed the FDI trends (World Bank, 2005).

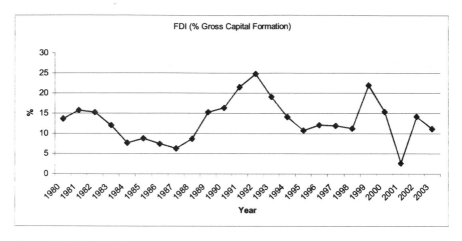

Source: World Bank, 2005

Figure 2. Inflow of FDI (as % of Gross Capital Formation)

The interplay of market-friendly trade and investment policies and a stable macroeconomic environment led to an export and FDI-led economic transformation of the Malaysian economy. In particular, the stance of the Malaysian government towards unilateral trade liberalization, regional economic grouping, and bilateral free trade arrangements, provided the necessary stimulant for a rapid globalization of the Malaysian economy. Besides, successive rounds of trade negotiations under GATT, and on-going trade WTO-led trade and investment liberalisation have provided further opportunities and challenges for the Malaysian economy.

TRADE LIBERALISATION, WTO, & THE MALAYSIAN WORKFORCE

Malaysia joined the WTO in 1994. At the Fourth Ministerial Conference of the WTO in Doha, the Member countries agreed to reduce, or as appropriate, eliminate tariffs, including the reduction or elimination of tariff peaks, high tariffs, and tariff escalation, as well as non-tariff barriers, in particular on products of export interest to developing countries.

While a successful conclusion of the Doha Round will lead to further globalization of markets and production, and thus more market opportunities for the Malaysian export sector, this opening up of possibilities will also have a dampening impact on relatively protected industries. Adverse labour market outcomes in industries such as fabricated metal products and machinery; basic metals; non-metallic mineral products; chemicals; paper, printing and publishing; food and beverages, wood and furniture, textiles and leather, transport equipment; plastic and rubber, can be significant. While Malaysia exhibited a relatively low average applied MFN (Most Favoured Nation) rate of 8.1 per cent in 2005, the incidence of tariff peaks[1] and tariff escalation was prevalent in the above industries. For instance, while the average applied tariff rate is below 10 per cent, the rate exceeds 20 per cent on 16.9 per cent of tariff lines, with some of the product lines in the protected sectors possessing a tariff rate of over 100 per cent (WTO, 2005). Apart from these tariff peaks, a reduction of which will have significant labour market sectoral repercussions, a dismantling of tariff escalation will further reinforce adverse employment outcomes for the affected sectors. In common with many developed, as well as developing countries, Malaysia's tariff structure exhibits a noticeable element of "tariff escalation", whereby raw materials are allowed to be imported largely duty-free or at a lower rate. Then again, processed intermediates have higher tariffs, and final goods have even higher import duties. In other words, the effective tariff protection granted to finished products is higher than for nominal tariffs. For instance, the applied MFN tariff average on manufacturing raw material is 3.7 per cent; 9.0 per cent on semi-processed output; and 10.4 per cent on fully processed outputs. The net impact of such a policy is that the tariff protection increases with the stage of processing, making the final stage of manufacturing more vulnerable to a decline in the incidence of tariff escalation. In Malaysia, the incidence of tariff escalation is prevalent in industries such as textiles & clothing, rubber products, paper and paper products, and basic metals. For instance, the applied average tariff on raw materials for textiles and rubber products is negligible but the fully processed domestic output in this sector attracts protection of around 15 per cent.

The Malaysian textiles and clothing sector is already under pressure due to trade liberalisation, as a direct outcome of the complete removal of quota restrictions under the WTO Agreement on Textile and Clothing (ATC)[2]. Malaysian firms are coming under increasing pressure from other low-wage countries in South and Southeast Asia. China is posing the primary competitive threat[3]. Moreover, the integration of the textile and clothing sector into the world trading system is affecting the pattern of regional production, and thus employment, in Asian economies, with Malaysia being no exception. For instance, in 2004, the textile and apparel production declined by 9.9 per cent and in 2005, this sector witnessed a further drop of 4.3 per cent (Ministry of Finance, 2005).

GLOBALISATION, LABOUR MARKET OUTCOMES, AND THE MALAYSIAN WORKFORCE

The unemployment rate in Malaysia is one of the lowest in the region. It was below three per cent in the few years before 1997 and slightly increased to an average of 3.5 per cent following the financial crisis of 1997. In addition, the effects of the inflow of foreign direct investment and trading activity on employment are not only limited to static employment relocation, it also allows for dynamic interaction with domestic capabilities that enhance the skills, technology and knowledge level of local workers. Thus, it is not only the quantity of employment that has increased; globalisation has also improved the skills and labour quality of the workforce in Malaysia.

Following expanding economic activity and improved labour productivity, the average real wages in Malaysia have generally been on the rise for the past two decades. Table 3 shows the average real wage index (1996=100) and the official unemployment rate from 1988 to 2005. With the exception of a few years following the financial crisis in 1997, the real wage index has been on an increasing trend throughout the period studied. Improved labour productivity has provided workers with greater negotiation power in securing better rewards for their contribution. However, not all workers are equally endowed with such power as globalisation does not favour unskilled workers who compete in the free market. According to Lustig's study (1998), free trade has led to a rise in the wages of skilled workers, while simultaneously depressing the wage rate for unskilled workforce. Free trade, therefore, not only lowers the wages of unskilled workers, it may also drive them out of the job market in sectors that compete with cheap imports, especially in the manufacturing and service sectors. As a remedial measure, the Malaysian government has set up the Human Resources Development Fund (HRDF) to encourage firms to provide continuous on-the-job training that is designed to improve the capability of unskilled workers in upgrading their skills.

Table 3. Average Real Wage Index and Unemployment Rate in Malaysia (1988-2005)

Year	Average real wage index (1996=100)	Recorded unemployment (%)
1988	74.042	7.2
1989	74.511	6.3
1990	75.333	5.1
1991	80.867	4.3
1992	85.416	3.7
1993	87.055	3
1994	92.666	2.9
1995	95.461	2.8
1996	100	2.5
1997	104.535	2.5
1998	99.588	3.225
1999	98.957	3.425
2000	99.394	3.1
2001	99.955	3.675
2002	100.159	3.475
2003	101.112	3.6
2004	103.6	3.55
2005	105.6	3.6

Source: Economists Intelligence Unit, Country Data (1995)

In the 1970s and 1980s, when trade activity was focusing on the export of low-cost and low-value products, and when foreign investors were attracted by the low wages offered by the Malaysian workforce, Malaysian workers were obliged to perform low skilled jobs as operators or assemblers in factories set up by foreign investors. Today, things have changed as globalisation and rapid technological innovation have resulted in the need for different types of workers in Malaysia. Structural change in the economy, as a response to the intensification of competition and capital-intensive investment, has resulted in increased demand for skilled workers. In addition, more job creation has been observed in sectors that require substantial technical knowledge and skills. This shift in the industrial structure has greatly increased demand for skilled labour. However, there are problems in meeting the demand for skilled labour. While workers are updating their skill level to meet demand, there remain acute skills shortages and mismatches that have been considered as one of the major weaknesses undermining Malaysia's ability to compete in the global market (see World Bank Investment Climate Survey Report, 2005).

Structural changes in the Malaysian economy, underpinned by forces of globalisation, have had a profound impact on the dynamics of the labour market. This has resulted in the share of agriculture in total employment falling from 37.2 per cent in 1980 to 13.7 per cent in 2004. This decline in employment in the agricultural sector was offset by the emergence of "industry sector" employment, which includes the manufacturing and services sub-sectors. For instance, the employment share of the "industry sector" grew from 24.1 per cent in 1980 to 36 per cent in 2004. For the services sector, these figures were 38.7 percent and 50.3 per cent respectively (Table 4). The main reason for this surge in manufacturing sector employment has been the rapid growth of the export and domestic market - oriented industries.

Table 4. Employment Share (% Share of Total Employment)

Employment Share	1980	1990	2000	2004[a]
Agriculture	37.2	26	18.4	13.7
Industry	24.1	27.5	32.2	36
Services	38.7	46.5	49.5	50.3

Source: World Bank, 2005; [a] Ministry of Finance, 2005 (calculated from Table 2.22)

Globalisation brings three key impacts to the labour market, namely: employment, wages and labour use. The expansion of the economy as a result of trade and foreign direct investment has, without doubt, increased demand for domestic workers, thus creating enormous employment opportunities. Though the influx of foreign investment and trade oriented production has caused some workers to lose their jobs, due to changing demands in the labour market, the overall effect on the Malaysian labour market has been positive.

Table 5 provides insight into the structural changes in FDI inflows and the resulting employment outcomes. While the absolute levels of FDI inflows for every industry sectors witnessed an increase, their relative share to the total inflow exhibited varying trends. For example, the share of the transport equipment industry declined from 19.4 per cent of the total FDI inflow in 1985 to only 1.94 per cent in 2004. Conversely, the share of the electrical and electronics industry increased from 11.5 per cent in 1995 to 51.93 per cent in 2004. The decline in the relative share of the transport equipment industry related FDI can be attributed to the changing investment climate in this sector. This is due to trade liberalisation within the ASEAN region and the inherent comparative disadvantages faced by the Malaysian transport equipment sector. Then again, a significant rise in the relative share of electrical and electronics- related FDI highlights the attractiveness of the investment climate, labour market conditions, and the rising global demand for electronics products. In 2004, this industry also contributed 28 per cent of the FDI-induced employment for the year. The contribution of employment by FDI in the "miscellaneous" sector shows a gradual diversification of FDI inflows into non-traditional segments in manufacturing.

Another aspect of the FDI inflows is a move away from the low skilled and resource intensive sectors towards skilled labour, knowledge, and capital intensive segments of the economy. This is evident from the declining relative contribution to FDI by industries such as textiles and textile products, paper products, rubber and rubber products (Table 5). The on-going trends of inward FDI, which are shaped by the internal, as well as external environment, clearly signal declining FDI-induced direct and indirect unemployment in protected, resource-intensive, and low skilled labour-intensive segments of the market. As the Malaysian economy becomes more integrated within and outside of ASEAN, the related structural unemployment problems may, however, become more prevalent.

Table 5. Foreign Direct Investment in Approved Projects by Industry and Employment Generation - 1985-2005

Industry	% Share in Total FDI (RM)			Employment Outcomes (000)		
	1985	2004	Change[4]	1985	2004	Change[5]
Food manufacturing	6.1[1]	2.93	-3.17	2.0[2]	2.93	+1.5
Textiles & textile products	3.3	2.80	-.05	6.3	5.9	-0.4
Paper, printing & publishing	10.6	10.36	-0.24	1.1	3.1	+2.0
Chemicals & Chemical products	3.1	4.23	+1.13	0.9	3.1	+2.2
Petroleum & gas	0.1	6.18	+6.08	0.0	0.4	+0.4
Rubber & rubber products	3.1	0.84	-2.26	1.3	3.3	+2.0
Non-metallic Mineral products	11.6	2.90	-8.7	2.9	3.2	+0.3
Basic metal products	15.4	2.01	-13.39	1.5	2.6	+1.1
Fabricated metal products	4.6	5.60	+1	1.2	8.6	7.4
Electrical & Electronic products	11.5	51.93	+ 40.43	7.60	24.5	+ 16.9
Transport equipment	19.4	1.94	-17.46	3.3	6.7	3.4
Miscellaneous[3]	11.2	8.28	-2.92	6.8	23.7	16.9
Total	100	100	-	34.3	88.6	8.7

Source: Ministry of Finance (2005)
Notes: [1] % share of total FDI in RM millions; [2] Figures in parentheses refer to employment outcomes in thousands; [3] This includes beverages, and tobacco, wood and wood products, furniture and fixtures, plastic products, scientific and measuring equipment, leather and leather products, machinery manufacturing ; [4,5] Calculated by the authors; [6] Based on overall FDI inflows (RM Millions) figures

It is evident that although the structure of Malaysian manufacturing has diversified, the electronics and electrical sector is the key driver of employment in manufacturing. For instance, in 2004, the electronic and electrical sectors accounted for 36.6 per cent of total employment in the manufacturing sector (MIDA, 2005). While this sector has widened the employment opportunities available in Malaysia, the export-FDI oriented nature of this sector has made the labour market outcomes vulnerable to external demand shocks. Moreover, increased global competition, due to reductions in market access barriers, the emergence of new competitors with lower labour costs, and a rapid diffusion of technology adds further pressure on the competitiveness of the Malaysian electrical and electronics sector and its capacity to absorb more labour.

Given the dominance of the electronics and electrical sector, and its impact upon economic growth, exports, and employment, it is imperative for this sector to sustain and enhance its competitiveness. While globalisation has helped this sector to expand rapidly due to falling trade and investment barriers, a relative similarity of export patterns in selected ASEAN and other low cost emerging Asian economies poses new challenges. Further, the sustainability of this sector depends to a large extent upon external demand for electronics and electrical products, making this sector vulnerable to negative demand shocks. Also, in order to maintain competitiveness in the sector, it is vital to increase innovation, creativity and skills amongst employees and workers. While this demands a more targeted focus on skill enhancement, it might also demand changes in traditional manager/employee relationships, and human resources policies both at the government and firm levels. (Todd, Lansbury & Davis, 2004) To a large extent, it is the interplay of the above factors that will determine whether this sector will continue to dominate economic growth, export and labour market outcomes.

An interesting feature of the labour market outcomes has been the urbanisation of the labour force due to rural-urban migration. Urbanisation has increased from 34% in 1980 to 63% in 2005 (Athukarola 2001; Government of Malaysia 2005). However, the rate of urbanisation has been successfully matched by a rate of expansion in urban activities, avoiding the increase in urban unemployment and poverty that has occurred in many other rapidly industrialised countries.

Globalisation, higher education levels, and the improved health of women have also changed the gender composition of the Malaysian labour force. In 2005 women accounted for 48% of the working population aged between 15 and 64 years, while female labour force participation in 2005 amounted to 45.7%, up 1% from 44.7% in 2000. As can be seen in Table 6 women are mostly employed in manufacturing, wholesale and retail trade and agriculture (Economic Planning Unit, 2006).

Table 6. Gender Distribution of Malaysian Labour Force (%)

Sector	Male (2000)	Female (2000)	Male (2005)	Female (2005)
Agriculture, Forestry, Livestock and Fishing	17.3	11.9	15.2	9.0
Quarrying and Mining	0.6	0.2	0.6	0.1
Manufacturing	24.5	33.5	27.0	31.7
Construction	11.8	1.5	10.2	1.4
Electricity, Gas and Water	1.1	0.2	1.3	0.3
Transport, storage Communication	6.7	1.8	7.8	2.4
Wholesale and Retail Trade, Hotels and Restaurants	16.0	19.0	17.0	18.7
Finance, Insurance, Real Estate and Business Services	5.0	6.1	6.1	7.8
Other Sectors	17.0	25.8	14.9	28.6
Total	100	100	100	100

Source: Economic Planning Unit, 2006

Successive Malaysian governments have made concerted efforts to lift the female labour force participation rate by reducing gender disparities in education and providing vocational training opportunities for women. Apart from these initiatives, the Malaysian government has initiated a series of targeted training opportunities in entrepreneurship, business skills and ICT aimed at increasing female participation in entrepreneurial activities. The Malaysian government and NGOs have been active in implementing programs, such as micro-credit schemes, to reduce the incidence of poverty among women-headed households. These efforts reduced the incidence of poverty among women-headed households from 12.5% in 2002 to 11.5% in 2004 (Economic Planning Unit, 2006).

As a result of women's improved education levels, their participation in higher level positions has also increased. Table 7 shows the considerable increase in the number of women employed in higher-level positions in retail trade and services sector, while women in low-paid jobs have declined considerably.

Table 7. Employment by Gender and Occupation (%)

Occupation	Male 2000	Female 2000	Male 2005	Female 2005
Senior Officials and Managers	8.0	4.8	9.4	5.4
Professionals	5.1	7.2	5.5	7.5
Technicians and Associate Professionals	10.9	14.1	12.6	14.0
Clerical Workers	5.2	18.3	4.6	17.2
Service and Sales Workers	12.9	13.3	12.3	17.7
Skilled Agricultural and Fishery Workers	17.5	10.0	14.7	9.9
Craft and Related Trade Workers	11.5	4.4	15.2	5.0
Plant and Machine Operators and Assemblers	16.2	15.8	15.9	11.5
Elementary Operations	12.7	12.1	9.8	11.8
Total	100	100	100	100

Economic Planning Unit, 2006

While the Malaysian unemployment rate has been steady at 3.5 per cent during the first half of this decade, the industrial re-orientation of the Malaysian economy, underpinned by increasing globalisation and the emergence of low-wage competitors, has also led to some adverse outcomes for workers, irrespective of their gender. This includes retrenchments, pay cuts, layoffs, increased graduate unemployment, and the importing of low-skilled foreign workers to ease shortages in plantation, manufacturing, domestic help and construction (Bank Negara Malaysia, 2006).

In recent years (2002-05), most retrenchments have taken place in those areas that are vulnerable to external factors, that is, the manufacturing and the services sector. In terms of their professional orientation, over 50 per cent of retrenched workers have been production related workers, followed by professional and technical workers. Among the main reasons cited for retrenchments were: high production costs, reductions in demand for products, the sale of companies, company reorganisation and automation, relocation to foreign countries, relocation locally and closure of companies (Bank Negara Malaysia, 2006). A closer examination of the above factors indicates that it is the interplay of competitive and cost pressures that underpins the key reasons for retrenchment. It is important to note that, with the emergence of regional production networks, increased foreign access to Malaysian markets and the globalisation of production are key contributing factors behind these retrenchments.

While retrenchments are an extreme response to cost and competitive pressures, the emergence of a flexible labour market is a feature of the changing nature of the Malaysian workplace. Globalisation-led competitive pressure requires continuous innovation and lower costs. While innovation involves further investment, research and development and is risky, drops in unit labour costs necessitate increases in productivity levels that are higher than corresponding wage increases. Conversely, high-skilled innovative labour, demands higher salaries, which often conflicts with cost-controls (Todd et al 2004). Kanapathy (2001) reported that skill shortages are affecting around 50% of 300 multinational companies surveyed in Malaysia, with more than 60% reported in the manufacturing sector, and the lowest reporting fewer than 40% in the banking sector. The main areas of skill improvement required to address these skill shortages were reported to be; management, interpersonal and communication skills, planning, new technology and job-related IT-skills. In manufacturing there was also detected a need for improving basic numeracy (30%) and literacy (28%) skills. It was also found that local graduates lacked proficiency in English, which hampered technology transfer to local firms.

Increasing the skills and knowledge base of its population remains one of the main foci of the Ninth Malaysia Plan (2006 to 2010) which proposes to take the leap towards a fully-fledged knowledge economy. To counter the skills shortage, the Malaysian government has introduced several measures to promote skills and competence development. For example, they have reformed the education system which now teaches mathematics and science in the English language (ADB 2006). It has also created incentives for training and skills enhancement through the Human Resource Development Fund (HRDF). According to figures from 1998, more than 80% of firms in the manufacturing sector and around 30 % of firms in the services sector benefited from these government-supported training courses. The government training reportedly had a success rate of 50-60% (Kanapathy 2001). Further, it is stated that Malaysia is behind other APEC countries in firm-based training.

To move towards a flexible labour market, the Malaysian government has been promoting a Productivity-Linked Wage System (PLWS). The Malaysian wage system relies predominantly on a pre-determined annual increment that is negotiated every three years by a company's labour union on behalf of its employees. The PLWS links the wage increment to productivity, ensuring that wage increments do not exceed productivity growth. In practice, the PLWS consists of fixed and variable components. The fixed part, which is a basic wage, ensures income and consumption stability. The variable portion depends upon a worker's productivity, performance of the economy, and the company profitability. On the positive side, PLWS rewards productivity in terms of higher wages, it can motivate workers, add to cost advantage and provide a flexible wage structure to adjust with the changing external environment. There is clear evidence that an increasing number of Malaysian firms embrace PLWS. For instance, from a sample of 322 collective agreements in 2004, 62 per cent were based upon PLWS. In the agricultural sector, a total of eight collective agreements were based on PLWS. In the services sector, 77 per cent had PLWS components, while this figure was 53 per cent for the manufacturing sector (Ministry of Finance, 2006). The system, however, is not without its limitations. For workers, a PLWS based wage system adds uncertainty to job security and instability to income and consumption.

Industrial relations in Malaysia has been under tight government control since independence in order to maintain economic stability and attract foreign investment (Kuruvilla and Erickson, 2002; Todd et al 2004). Unionism has, therefore, been restricted and remains at 12% of the workforce (Todd et al 2004), and in some sectors (such as electronics) unions are virtually non-existent (Kuruvilla and Erickson, 2002). While minimum wages are set by the authorities, these apply only to certain sectors. (ILO, 2006a). Although, tripartite arrangements for collective agreements have been introduced but they remain slow to gain acceptability. (Kuruvilla and Erickson, 2002; Todd et al, 2004).

The changing working environment with higher skills and salaries might also have led to the reduction of person days lost due to strikes and lockouts in recent years. In the difficult years after the financial crisis the numbers of person days lost due to strikes and lockouts peaked in 1999 reaching 10,555 in 12 different conflicts, mainly in the agricultural and manufacturing sectors. In 2002 only 1638 days were lost in only 4 conflicts (ILO, 2006b).

Increasing globalisation has also put the focus on workers' benefits, such as pensions, unemployment, and social security benefits, highlighting the need to provide social safety nets to workers. The key role of the workers' benefit scheme is to smooth lifetime consumption, alleviate poverty, and provide insurance against inflation and longevity (Asher and Nandy, 2006). In the Malaysian context, while no welfare or unemployment benefits programs exist, the government has programs in place, such as the Employees Provident Fund (EPU), a compulsory savings scheme and the provision of social security benefits. These are the two main schemes that protect Malaysian workers against any loss of income due to sickness, injury, old age or death. The EPU is a compulsory saving scheme, in which both employees and employers contribute, 11 and 12 per cent of the monthly wage to the employee's account. The main objective of this scheme is to provide retirement benefits to employees. It also caters for supplementary benefits for employees whereby they can utilize part of their savings for certain purposes before reaching retirement age, such as, house ownership (Lawyerment, 2006).

The social security scheme provides coverage to eligible employees through the Invalidity Pension Scheme (coverage to employees against disability and death unrelated to employment) and the Employment Injury Insurance Scheme (this covers eligible employees against occupational accidents and illnesses, including those arising during commutes to and from work). These schemes are designed for workers earning wages that do not exceed RM 2,000 (US$526) per month. Once covered, workers remain covered irrespective of their wages. Under the Employment Injury Insurance Scheme, employers contribute 1.25 per cent of the employee's wages, whereas there is no contribution required from employees. However, in the case of the invalidity Pension Scheme, both employees and employers contribute 1 per cent of an employee's wages (MSC, 2006).

Competitive pressure, inflow of FDI, and low level of unemployment have led to acute shortages in some segments of the labour market, necessitating the importation of foreign labour. As a result, Malaysian authorities allowed an inflow of foreign workers so as to alleviate labour market shortages and to discourage foreign firms from relocating their production elsewhere (Athukorula 2001). Migrant workers are mainly from Indonesia, Bangladesh (where there was a ban in 1998), the Philippines, Thailand, Pakistan, Nepal and Vietnam, with Indonesians constituting the largest group (more than 80%) (Iredale and Piper, 2003).

In 2004, the government reported that of a total workforce of 11.29 million, there were 1.7 million foreign workers with work permits (Economic Planning Unit, 2006). Foreign workers account for 17 per cent of the total employed labour force. A vast majority of these workers are employed by the manufacturing (32 per cent), plantation (24 per cent), and construction (18 per cent) sectors. Apart from filling the labour shortages in some segments of the labour market, the inflow of temporary migrants in Malaysia also points to reluctance on the part of the local workers to accept jobs under the prevailing wage conditions. In this case, foreign workers provide a cheap and readily available substitute to a relatively expensive and demanding local work force. This enables low-wage industries to prosper, but provides little incentive for companies to move towards high wage, high productivity strategics (Rasiah, 1995, in Todd et al 2004).

Another significant trend is the rapid feminisation of Asian migrants, who in worker supplying countries such as Indonesia, Philippines and Sri Lanka now comprise a majority of migrants. Women migrants are employed in low-paid, poorly protected sectors such as domestics or entertainers/sex work. Similarly to the increase in migration, there has been an upsurge in organised employment recruitment agencies possessing varied ethical standards. According to Malaysian officials, there are currently 240,000 women migrant domestic workers, of which 90% are from Indonesia. The increase in domestic workers was, in part, a response to Malaysian women moving into more secure and higher paying factory jobs (Human Rights Watch 2004).

Another unintended outcome of globalisation has been an increase in irregular (illegal) migration. According to Women's Aid Organisation (WAO) (2003), there are an estimated one million unauthorised foreign workers in Malaysia. However, due to the sensitivity of this information, several authors have pointed to the lack of transparency in the figures (Wickramasekara 2002). This high level of unauthorised workers is being addressed by the authorities in the form of amnesties. However, workers and their children caught without permits during non-amnesty periods risk detention and corporal punishment such as whipping (Human Rights Watch 2004; Iredale and Piper, 2003). Malaysia's stop-go policies regarding migrant labour are a result of the changing economic and social circumstances and the government's response to changing labour and skills shortages.

CONCLUSIONS AND POLICY IMPLICATIONS

Globalisation increases linkages among nations. During the past two decades, these linkages have benefited small developing and agricultural-based nations, such as Malaysia, to jump-start its industrialisation process. As a country that depended heavily on commodities exports, Malaysia has diversified and transformed to become a country that exports manufacturing and electronics as well as electrical products. Through active international trade and financial flows in the past two decades, new technology, knowledge as well as financial capital were transferred directly and indirectly to Malaysia, which enabled the nation to build up its competitiveness in the process of industrialising the economy.

During the past few decades, Malaysia has witnessed significant economic growth and a structural transformation of its economy. These outcomes are associated with increasing globalisation of the Malaysian economy, with trade and FDI acting as the key drivers of globalisation and structural change. The unilateral, regional, and multilateral trade and investment liberalisation policies of the past three decades have provided a favourable environment for an unprecedented inflow of FDI and an impressive trade performance. The emergence of WTO, as a regulator as well as a facilitator of international trade, and on-going negotiations under the Doha Round to liberalise market access will further accelerate the pace of globalisation. These latest developments provide challenges as well as opportunities for the Malaysian agriculture, manufacturing, and services sectors. A successful conclusion of the Doha Round of negotiations will exert considerable competitive pressure on the relatively protected and domestically oriented Malaysian industries.

In recent Malaysian economic history, the manufacturing sector has played a lead role in terms of its contribution to economic growth, value added, employment and exports. Given its dominance on the Malaysian economic scene, the performance of the manufacturing sector, in terms of production and exports, is a key determining factor for the overall economic performance of the country. Being a small open economy, the buoyancy of the manufacturing sector, in turn, depends upon the external markets and economic environment, adding vulnerability to the Malaysian economy. Given the dominance of the electrical and electronic sector in manufacturing output, exports, and employment, these vulnerabilities cannot be underestimated.

Further trade liberalisation, the removal of tariff peaks, and tariff escalation will lead to competitive pressure on a number of relatively protected Malaysian industries such as fabricated metal products and machinery, basic metal and non-metallic mineral products, chemical, paper, printing and publishing, food and beverages, wood and furniture, textiles and leather, transport equipment; plastic and rubber products. Malaysia is already coming under increasing competitive pressure from the low-wage economies of the region. While export-oriented industries will gain from enhanced market access, employment losses in the above list of industries are imminent. An added dimension to these employment vulnerabilities is the changing nature of FDI. While the initial wave of FDI occurred in labour intensive, employment-creating, industries, the latest inflow of FDI has been in capital and knowledge-intensive segments of the economy.

The globalisation-led structural change of the Malaysian economy has a profound impact on its labour market outcomes. While the unemployment rate remained low, positive wage outcomes have been skewed towards the highly-skilled work force, underpinning the further marginalisation of the unskilled work force. This dichotomy in wage structure is a direct outcome of the ongoing industrial reorientation of the Malaysian economy in which Malaysia is losing its comparative advantage in the production of low skill-intensive products to low-wage economies in the region.

The industrial reorientation and globalisation-induced competitive pressures have led to retrenchments of workers, pay cuts, layoffs, increased graduate unemployment, flexibility in the labour market, productivity-linked wage outcomes, non-contractual bounces, and the importing of foreign workers to ease shortages in plantation, manufacturing, domestic help, and construction. Increased trade and investment liberalisation, which is internal as well as external to ASEAN, has led to a spread of value chains and the emergence of regional production networks, reducing the bargaining power of workers to negotiate better outcomes. While the introduction of the Productivity-Linked Wage System (PLWS), rewards productivity and efficiency, it also adds uncertainty, insecurity, and instability in wage outcomes. In order to avoid the demands of the local work force and to add flexibility to the employment outcome, Malaysian firms have been resorting to foreign work forces, which are willing to work under given or lesser conditions.

While in the industrialised countries, the social safety networks have helped to moderate the adverse labour outcomes of globalisation-led industrial reorientation, the same is not the case in many developing countries. Malaysia is no exception. The present social security and worker benefits schemes in Malaysia are limited in terms of their coverage, scope, and impact. Most importantly, these schemes were not designed to mitigate the impact of the changing industrial reorientation of the economy due to emergence of regional production networks, import of cheap foreign work force, and a changing comparative advantage of the Malaysian industry. To achieve its vision to become a developed country by the year 2020, it is imperative for Malaysia to provide an institutional environment that generates optimum labour market outcomes.

REFERENCES

Asher, M. and Nandy, A. (2006) *Social Security Policy in an Era of Globalization and Competition: Challenges for Southeast Asia*, National University of Singapore, www.spp.nus.edu.sg/docs/wp/wp06-06.pdf.

Asian Development Bank (ADB), (2005*). Key Indicators of Developing Asian and Pacific Countries,* Accessed on January 1 from http://www.adb.org/Documents/Books/Key_Indicators/2005/pdf/MAL.pdf Viewed 1/1/06

Asian Development Bank (ADB) (2006) "Malaysia". *In Asian Development Outlook 2006.* Accessed on 1st June 2006 from http://www.adb.org/Documents/Books/ADO/2006/documents/mal.pdf

Authukorala, P. (2001) Employment Intensive Development: the Malaysian Experience, Research School of Pacific and Asian Studies, Australian National University, Canberra. Accessed on April 4 from http://rspas.anu.edu.au/economics/staff/athu/Athukorala%20Malaysia%20paper%202001.pdf

Bank Negara Malaysia, (2006). *Annual Report 2005*, Kulala Lumpur

Chitose, Y. (2003) *Effects of Government Policy on internal migration in Peninsular Malaysia: A comparison between Malays and Non-Malays.* International Migration Review. Vol. 37. No.3, Winter, 2003. New York.

Economic Planning Unit (2006) *Ninth Malaysian Plan*, Putrajaya: Prime Minister's Department

Hajinoor, S. M., and Saleh, Z. M (2000) "Malaysian Industrialization and External Trade Capability and Timing of Structural Changes", a paper presented at the National Seminar on Strengthening the Macroeconomic Fundamentals of the Malaysian Economy, Kuala Lumpur, 5-6 June.

Human Rights Watch (2004) *Labour Migration in Asia..* Accessed on June 20, 2006 from http://hrw.org/reports/2004/indonesia0704/4.htm

International Labour Organisation (ILO) (2006a) International Labour Relations Records. Malaysia. Minimum Wages Databases. Accessed on 1st June 2006 from http://laborsta.ilo.org/

International Labour Organisation (ILO) (2006b) International Labour Relations Records. Malaysia. Strikes and Lockouts. Accessed on 1st June 2006 from http://laborsta.ilo.org/

Iredale, R. and Piper, N. (2003) Identification of the obstacles to signing and ratification of the UN convention on the protection of the rights of migrant workers. The Asia – Pacific Perspective. International Migration and Multicultural Policies Section UNESCO. October 2003.

Kanapathy, V. (2001) "Skills shortages, Training Needs and HRD Strategies of MNCs in Malaysia". *In Skills shortages, Training Needs and Human Resource Development Strategies of Multinational Companies in APEC Member Economies. Human Resource Working Group.* Asia Pacific Economic Cooperation(APEC), and Centre for Asia Pacific Social Transformation

Studies(CAPSTRANS), University of Newcastle & University of Wollongong, November

Kuruvilla, S. and Erickson, C.L. (2002) "Change and Transformation in Asian Industrial Relations". *Industrial Relations*, Vol. 41, No.2. April Oxford UK.

Lawyerment (2006) Employee Provident Fund. Accessed on May 24 from http://www.lawyerment.com.my/library/doc/empl/epf/

Lustig, N. (1998) From Structuralizm To Neostructuralizm: The Search For A Heterodox Paradigm. In *The Latin American Development Debate*, ed. Patricio Miller Boulder: Westview.

Malaysian Industrial Development Corporation, MIDA, (2005) The Electrical and Electronics Industry. Accessed on January 20, 2006 from http://www.mida.gov.my/beta/view.php?cat=5&scat=9&pg=102

Ministry of Finance. (2005) *Economic Report 1999/2000* Economic and International Division, Kuala Lumpur, Malaysia

Ministry of Finance, (2006) *Economic Report 2005*, Kuala Lumpur, Malaysia.

MSC, (2006) Human Resources, Accessed on May 10, 2006 from http://www.msc.com.my/xtras/business/human_resource.asp

Okposin, Samuel Bassey., and Cheng, Ming Yu (2000) *Economic Crises in Malaysia: Causes, Implications & Policy Prescriptions*, Subang Jaya: Pelanduk Publications.

Okposin, Samuel Bassey., Hamid, Abdul, and Boon, Ong Hway (1999) *The Changing Phases of Malaysian Economy*, Subang Jaya: Pelanduk Publications.

OECD, (2005) *OECD Handbook on Globalisation Indicators*, Paris. Accessed on February 27, 2006 from http://www.realinstitutoelcano.org/materiales/docs/ OCDE_handbook.pdf

The Economist, *Economists Intelligence Unit,* Bureau van Dijk Electronic Publishing

Rasiah, R. (1995) "Labor and industrialization in Malaysia" Journal of Contemporary Asia, 25 (1), pp.73-92

Shakur, Mohammed. (2006) "The Globalization of the Malaysian Economy" Available on-line, Accessed on February 16, 2006 http://www.freewebs.com/ suaraanum/0310b02.htm

Sieh, L. M. and Yew, Siew Yong (1997) "Malaysia: Electronic, Autos, and the Trade-Investment Nexus" in *Multinationals and East Asian Integration*, ed. Dobson, W. and Chia, S. Y. IDRC/ISEAS.

Tham, Siew Yean, (2000) "Trade and Investment Policies in Malaysia: Countering the Challenges of Globalization", a paper presented at the National Seminar on Strengthening the Macroeconomic Fundamentals of the Malaysian Economy, Kuala Lumpur, 5-6 June.

Todd, P., Lansbury, R. and Davis, E. (2004) Industrial relations in Malaysia: Some Proposals for Reform. *International Industrial Relations Association 5th Asian Conference*. Accessed on 1st June 2006 from http://www.kli.re.kr/iira2004/pro/papers/PatriciaTodd/pdf

United Nations Conference on Trade and Development (UNCTAD) (2005) *World Investment Report 200.* Accessed on March 17, 2006 from www.unctad.org/fdistatistics

Wickramasekara, P. (2002) *Asian Labour Migration: Issues and Challenges in an Era of Globalization.* International Migration Papers no. 57. International Migration Programme. International Labour Office, Geneva.

Women's Aid Organisation (2003) Protection of foreign domestic workers in Malaysia: Law and Policies, Implications and Intervention. Paper presented at the Programme Consultation Meeting on the Protection of Domestic Workers Against the Threat of Forced Labour and Trafficking, Hong Kong SAR, February 16-19.

World Bank (1999a) *World Development Report*, New York: Oxford University Press.

World Bank (1999b) *World Development Indicators*, CD-ROM, Washington, DC.

World Bank (2005) "Malaysia: Firm Competitiveness, Investment Climate, and Growth" Report No. 26841-MA

World Bank (2005) World Bank Development Indicators (2005). Washington DC. Available at Accessed on March 28 from http://www.worldbank.org/data

World Trade Organisation (WTO) (2005) *Trade Policy Review Malaysia*. Accessed on February 17, 2006 from www.wto.org

---

[1] Tariff peaks are defined as tariffs of 15 percent or higher, or about three times the average tariff level in industrial countries.

[2] According to ATC, the MFA was to be phased out gradually and integrated into world trading system in four stages by 2005.

[3] From, China's garments exports are no longer have any quota restriction in EU and after 2009 its exports to the US will also be free from quota restriction leading to an increased market share (Asian Development Bank, 2000)..

Chapter 8

THE IMPACT OF THE GLOBAL ECONOMY ON THE LABOUR MARKET IN THAILAND

Sujinda Chemsripong

The objective of this chapter is to focus on aspects of change in the labour market which are linked to economic globalization in Thailand. In particular, this chapter will:

a) outline the implications of globalization with regard to the transformation of the labour market;

b) examine the impact of recent internal and external crises in Thailand on the labour market and

c) review policy implications for the labour market under globalization.

THAILAND OVER THE PAST THREE DECADES

The past three decades have been witness to major changes in the Asian labour markets. These changes have been associated with the globalization process and the integration of national economies into the international economy (Gita Sen, 1999). Thailand, possesses distinctive characteristics in the labour market and, since the 1980s, it has opened itself up to the global economy. Currently, a high percentage of its income comes from exporting – around 66 per cent of GDP compared to 24 per cent twenty years earlier. During the period 1987-90 Thailand experienced a growth rate of 11.2 per cent and has steadily maintained this pattern for the past two decades, although rapid changes in economic and social structure have had a significant impact on the labour market (Acosta, 1998).

As international trade developed, the manufacturing sector expanded, and as a result, large numbers of process and casual workers have been needed. These factors have assisted in shifting the excess supply of labourers from the agriculture sector to urban centres (Jackson, 1997). This is ironic, since following the financial crisis in 1997, labourers who had been laid off from the manufacturing sector were forced to return to the farming sector (Acharya, 2000).

In contrast, a shortage of labour supply in some agricultural sectors and in unskilled fields encouraged workers to emigrate from neighbouring countries such as Burma, Cambodia and Laos to Thailand. The emigration pressures in the country of origin, economically and politically, plus the demand for labour in Thailand, provided intensive preconditions for attracting migrant labour to Thailand (Angsuthanasombat, Nakhorn & Wanabriboon 2001). This labour supply has been especially important in the informal sectors that are associated with personal service work and labouring.

CHANGES IN DEMOGRAPHY

Changes in the composition of demographic forces not only affect labour supply but also participation rates. Due to the intense efforts of the Thai government to place stringent controls on birth rates, the growth of the labour force has drastically declined. The National Economic and Social Development Board statistics (2004) indicate that there is a tendency for a domestic labour shortage to occur in line with birth reduction rates. As the population of Thailand increased from only 55.8 million people in 1990 to 62.2 and 64.7 in 2000 and 2005, respectively, it is evident that the birth control policy driven by the government has had an impact on birth rates.

Table 1 shows that, for the next decade, the population will stabilise with a forecast population of 70.9 million people in 2018. Moreover, it demonstrates the changing demography of the population, with the share of young people falling and the share of older people forecast to increase. That said, this is a phenomena that is present among nearly all Western economies.

Table 1. Population Structure, 2000-2018

Population Structure	2000	2004	2005	2009	2010	2018
Population (million)	62.2	64.1	64.7	66.5	67.0	70.9
Children (%)	24.7	23.3	23.0	21.6	21.3	19.5
Work force (%)	65.9	66.6	66.7	67.1	67.0	65.0
Dependency ratio (%)	51.7	50.1	49.9	48.0	48.1	53.8
Under 14 years (%)	37.4	34.9	34.4	32.2	31.7	30.0
Over 60 years (%)	14.3	15.2	15.5	16.9	17.4	23.8

Source: National Statistics Office (NSO) Population Forecasting of Thailand, 2000-2025 (2004)

LABOUR FORCE IN THAILAND

Table 2 demonstrates a slight increase in the labour force and a slight decline in the participation rate, reflecting the changing demographic composition of the population, especially with regard to its ageing profile. This is also reflected in the growing dependency rate (the share of the population who are not employed).

Table 2. The Labour Force, 1996-2004 (%)

Labour Force Status	1996	1997	1998	1999	2000	2001	2002	2003	2004
Total	100	100	100	100	100	100	100	100	100
Labour Force	53.7	53.8	53.0	53.0	53.2	53.9	54.0	54.3	54.9
Not in labour force	46.3	46.2	47.0	47.0	46.8	46.1	46.0	45.7	45.1
LF Participation rate	74.0	73.5	72.2	71.6	71.5	72.1	71.8	71.9	72.4
Employed rate	95.4	96.8	92.7	93.7	94.2	94.8	96.4	97.2	97.2
Unemployed rate	1.7	1.5	4.4	4.2	3.6	3.2	2.2	2.2	2.1

Note:
1. during 1996 – 2000, survey 4 rounds per year: in February, May, August and November and average a year between round 1 and 3,
2. since 2001 survey each month in whole year and average between February and August

Source: NSO, Report of the Labour Force Survey, (2004).

Over the period 1996 to 2004 employment and unemployment rates were stable, except for the financial crisis in 1997. Statistics from the NSO (2004) indicate that Thailand's unemployment rate increased from 1.5 percent to 4.4 per cent in 1998 but decreased to 2.1 per cent in 2004.

CHANGES IN LABOUR DEMAND: PRODUCTION AND EMPLOYMENT STRUCTURE IN THAILAND

Agriculture contributed to approximately 40 per cent of GDP and over 80 per cent of the population was engaged in agricultural activities during the 1960s and 1970s. Rice was the major crop and primary products for export included rubber, maize, kenaf and tin (Krongkaew, 1995).

An import substitution policy was launched as part of the first and second economic plan in order to promote foreign direct investment, especially with regard to manufacturing in Thailand. This resulted in an internal migration of labour from the agricultural sector to the industrial sector (Chalamwong, 1998).

The decline in the economic importance of agriculture and the rapid growth of the industrial sector were signs of the success of the export promotion strategy that was implemented in conjunction with the fifth plan (1982-86) and continued with the sixth plan (1987-91) (Chemsripong, 2005). Many policies, such as tax holidays and import tax exemptions for investors for a period of five years, were implemented to encourage foreign investment into the manufacturing and services sector. Industries such as chemical, electrical, food, textile, hotels and shipping expanded over this period (Suphachalasai, 1995).

Through this strategy, Thailand's manufactured products became competitive in both the foreign and domestic markets. Changes in the industry distribution of production can be explained through two factors: inward factors, such as the economic development policy and outward factors such as globalization.

Thailand has implemented a trade liberalization policy (referred to as outward factors) to extend Thailand's export markets and external investment. The main factor that attracted foreign investors to Thailand was the cheap labour supply which can be used to reduce production costs for relocating industries, especially in the value-added manufacturing areas such as in fertilizer, steel, auto parts, cement and the textile industries (Chalamwong, 2004).

The value of manufactured exports has risen dramatically since 1985. Exports of technology-based products such as food, electronic, petrochemical and the steel industry increased significantly from 22 % of total exports in 1992 to 37 % in 1998 (WTO, 1995). During the same period resources-based products declined from 11.3 to 9.2 % of total exports and labour-based products fell from 21.6 to 11.7 % of total exports (Poapongsakorn, and Tangkitvanich: 2000). As a result of this expansion, the number of skilled workers employed has increased.

EMPLOYMENT BY SECTORAL DISTRIBUTION OF THE WORK FORCE

Table 3 shows production trends for the period 1999-2004. It demonstrates the growing share of services that occurred at the expense of both the agriculture and manufacturing sectors.

As a result of changes in the composition of production (Table 3) there are accompanying changes in the sectoral distribution of employment. The share of the agricultural workforce is declining while that of manufacturing and services is increasing. Table 4 demonstrated that, by sector, the major changes in the period 1996-2004 were in plant and machine operators, unskilled occupations, trade workers, service workers, clerks, technicians and senior officials.

Table 3. Gross Domestic Product (GDP) as the market price classify by sector 1999-2004 (% GDP)

Gross Domestic product (GDP)	1999	2000	2001	2002	2003	2004
Agricultural	10.0	10.3	10.4	9.4	10.0	9.8
Agriculture, hunting & forestry	8.3	8.6	8.7	7.4	8.2	8.2
Fishing	1.6	1.6	1.6	1.9	1.7	1.6
Non-Agricultural	89.9	89.7	89.5	90.5	89.9	90.1
Mining & quarrying	2.1	2.1	2.1	2.4	2.6	2.6
Manufacturing	36.0	36.4	36.1	33.6	34.7	35.1
Electricity, gas & water supply	3.0	3.2	3.3	3.2	3.2	3.1
Construction	2.9	2.5	2.4	3.0	2.9	3.1
Wholesale & retail trade, etc	15.9	15.7	15.2	15.9	15.4	14.7
Hotel & restaurants	3.7	3.7	3.8	5.6	5.0	5.1
Transport, storage& Communication	9.4	9.6	10.0	8.2	7.8	7.7
Financial intermediation	3.1	2.7	2.7	3.1	3.4	3.6
Real estate, renting & business	4.0	4.0	3.9	3.1	3.0	2.9
Public administration & defence, etc	3.2	3.1	3.2	4.4	4.4	4.4
Education	2.8	2.7	2.7	3.8	3.7	3.7
Health & social work	1.3	1.3	1.4	1.9	1.8	1.8
Other community, social & personal service activity	1.8	1.9	1.9	1.5	1.6	1.7
Unknown	0.1	0.1	0.1	0.1	0.1	0.1
Total	100	100	100	100	100	100

Source: National Economic and Social Development Board, Office of the Prime Minister, 2004.

EMPLOYMENT BY GENDER

Over time, official labour force participation rates for women are significantly lower than those for men, even though the share of women in the adult labour force grew from around one-third in 1970 to over two-fifths in 1997 and by more than a half in 2004. This increase in the female labour force is a result of changes in the age structure of the population and the relative increase in women's labour force participation rates.

Table 4. Employment by Industry: 1996-2004 (per cent)

Industry	1996	1998	2000	2002	2004
Agricultural	45.2	45.4	44.2	42.3	38.5
Agriculture, hunting& forestry	43.5	44.1	42.9	40.8	37.3
Fishing	1.7	1.3	1.3	1.5	1.2
Non-agricultural	54.8	54.6	55.8	57.7	61.5
Mining and quarrying	0.2	0.2	0.2	0.1	0.1
Manufacturing	14.0	13.9	14.7	15.4	16.5
Electricity, gas & Water supply	0.4	0.5	0.4	0.3	0.3
Construction	8.5	5.4	4.9	5.5	6.0
Wholesale& retail trade, Repair etc.	13.2	13.6	13.9	14.9	15.8
Hotel and restaurants	4.2	5.1	5.7	6.1	6.5
Transport, storage& communication	3.2	3.3	3.1	3.1	3.3
Financial intermediation	0.8	1.0	0.8	0.8	0.9
Real estate, renting and Business	1.2	1.4	1.6	1.5	1.9
Public administration & defence, etc	3.1	3.5	3.6	3.0	2.8
Education	2.7	3.1	3.0	2.9	2.9
Health & social work	0.9	1.2	1.4	1.4	1.6
Other community, social & personal service activity	1.6	1.7	1.7	1.8	2.1
Private households	0.7	0.7	0.7	0.7	0.7
Extra-territorial organizations	- -	- -	- -	- -	- -
Unknown	0.1	- -	- -	0.0	0.1

Source: NSO Report of the Labour Force Survey (2004).

Table 5 indicates specific cross-sectional data in 2004 whereby nearly 38 per cent of male workers and 32 per cent of female workers held two or more jobs. Sectors that are dominated by men are construction, transport, storage and communication, public administration, defence and social security. Females dominate employment in the hotels, education, private household, health and community services sectors.

Table 5. Employment by Industry and gender in 2004 (In percent)

Industry	Total	Female	Male
Total	100	100	100
Agricultural	41	38	43
Agriculture, hunting & forestry	39	37	41
Fishing	1	1	2
Non-Agricultural	59	61	56
Mining and quarrying	0	0	0
Manufacturing	15	18	13
Electricity, gas & water supply	0	0	0
Construction	5	1	8
Wholesale & retail trade, repair etc	15	16	14
Hotel and restaurants	6	9	4
Transport, storage & communication	3	1	4
Financial intermediation	1	1	1
Real estate, renting & business act.	1	1	2
Public administration & defence, etc.	2	2	3
Education	3	3	2
Health and social work	1	2	1
Other community, social & personal service activity	2	2	1
Private households with employed persons.	0.8	1	0
Extra-territorial organizations& bodies	- -	- -	- -
Unknown	0	0	- -

Source: NSO, Report of the Labour Force Survey (2004).

EMPLOYMENT BY STATUS, FIRM SIZE AND EDUCATIONAL ATTAINMENT

Table 6 indicates that the private sector employed nearly 40 per cent of workers and that this share increased between1996-2004. Own account workers and unpaid family workers, which accounted for more than 50 per cent of the workforce in 1996, have declined dramatically since 2000. Conversely, there has been an increase in the share of employees (both in the private and public sectors) and a decline in the share of non employees - principally own account workers and family workers. The distribution of businesses by size across sectors and their employment share was nearly 85 per cent of the whole establishment in 2002 represented by small (100-299 people) and medium (300-499 people) enterprises.

Table 6. Percentage distribution of employed people by employment status, 1996-2004 (%)

Employment status	1996	1997	1998	1999	2000	2001	2002	2003	2004
Total	100	100	100	100	100	100	100	100	100
Employer	2.6	2.4	2.5	3.0	3.2	3.1	3.3	3.3	3.1
Government employee	7.5	7.7	9.0	8.6	8.4	8.8	8.1	7.8	8.4
Private employee	35.0	34.4	32.3	31.6	33.1	34.4	34.1	35.6	38.4
Own account worker	31.3	30.4	32.4	32.5	31.8	31.5	31.7	31.4	30.5
Unpaid family worker	23.6	25.0	23.8	24.2	23.2	22.2	22.7	21.7	19.4
Group worker	-	-	-	-	-	0.1	0.1	0.1	0.2

Source: NSO, Report of the Labour Force Survey (2004).

According to the United Nation Demographic Population (1992), Thailand has a literacy rate of 93 per cent across the population. The National Economic and Social Development Board also indicated high education rates among Thais (Pongsapich, 1994). However, the success of improving human capital has also been associated with a shortage of unskilled labour. As a result, Thailand has imported labour as a way of meeting demand for unskilled labour (Siampukdee, 2005).

THE CROSS BORDER MIGRATION OF LABOUR

Through globalisation, trade liberalization in goods and services has had an impact on the labour market; resulting in both an over supply and a shortage of labour. That is a labour mismatch has arisen as the labour market has lagged behind the changes that have occurred in product market conditions. Labour shortages, occurring as a result of the changed production structure, have emerged in a number of occupations including engineering, accounting, technical and related workers, administrative, executive and management. These problems were exacerbated by the emigration of many Thais who had possessed these skills since the 1980s.

Over one million Thai workers have left to work abroad since 1980 and have accordingly earned foreign currency to help with the country's current account deficit. The two main factors which contribute to emigration rates are a combination of persistent income inequality (referred to as push factors) and the high income differential gained from working overseas (referred to as pull factors). On an annual basis, the number of Thai workers going overseas decreased slightly from 202,296 in 1995 to 185,436 in 1996. The share of overseas workers in the major geographical destination, East Asia, declined while other major destinations such as ASEAN, the Middle East and Western countries increased slightly.

There is also a shortage of unskilled and semi-skilled labour, especially in agriculture. A study conducted by the Asian Research Centre of Migration of Chulalongkorn University (2000) revealed that industries where labour was in short supply in 2000 were agriculture, fisheries, livestock, rice mills, construction, mining, cargo shipping, warehouse and grain storage. Moreover, the numbers of unfilled vacancies are growing each year (Pitayanon, 2001). To meet this shortage, foreign workers are being sourced from 3 countries - Burma, Laos and Cambodia.

Two main reasons causing the induction of labour from Thailand's neighbouring countries to Thailand are: better wages (more than 10 times compared with Burma and 5 times compared with Laos and Cambodia). Burma is the main source of official and illegal labour in Thailand. Figures from the labour ministry show that labour from Burma increased from 38 thousand people in 1987 to 500 thousand in 1995 and to 733,000 in 1996 (Nontitat, 1995 cited in Chalamwong & Cewillar, 1996). The demand for immigrant labour increased in the labour intensive agriculture sectors, such as rubber, sugar, and fisheries and in the product handling sectors in areas such as cargo shipping, warehouse, and grain storage. The figures from the NSO show that the number of migrant temporary applications in 1997-2003 approved increases from 15,728 cases in 1997 to 20,737 in 2003 (Soraj, 1995).

Government policy has been to arrange for the registration of immigrant labour. The long term government solution was to organize immigrant labour and set a suitable policy for them in order to protect the influx of legal and illegal labour in the long run (Cabinet resolution on 25/06/1996). On the basis of Thai labour emigration to other countries, it is recommended that the government develop emigrant employment up to the standard of international alien labour (Chalamwong & Amornthum, 2002).

The impact of trade liberalization in goods and services has increased labour mobility within SE Asia, especially in the ten sectors affected by the General Agreement on Trade in Service (GATS) in telecommunications, construction, engineering, wholesale and retail trades, education, environmental, money and banking, tourism, entertainment and transport. As a result, the labour market has become more competitive and open through GATS, with more cross border labour flow occurring. The government has, in the past, attempted to control the number of migrant workers entering Thailand, but with limited success.

POLICIES ON SKILL DEVELOPMENT

To solve the unemployment problem associated with the economic crisis, the government had to improve the position for those laid off by developing their work skills. Training Promotion for unemployment created new employment opportunities. In this regard, informal workers and immigration workers play an important role in globalisation.

To help solve the labour shortages the government has attempted to address the problem of most people in rural areas not being able to continue their studies at the secondary education level. Specifically, the government encouraged educational institutes to offer studies in the science and technology fields. This was intended to assist in meeting future labour demands by distributing scholarship or funding grants for labour shortage areas to the level of undergraduate education, masters and PhD degrees.

CONCLUSIONS

By studying the Thai labour market and the process of globalization over the past three decades, it is apparent that there are some typical features that need to be understood. These features include:

1. The population comprising children of less than 15 years of age has been declining, while the number of adults aged 40 years and over has been increasing. Together with the increase of the population which is not a part of the labour force, such as house workers and school children, the labour force in Thailand has decreased. This ageing phenomena is a factor that has affected many countries.

2. Production structures have been changing from agricultural to non- agricultural, especially in the manufacturing and services sectors. Demand for labour to work in assembly line production manufacture is increasing. Women workers, who are characteristically more adept in handling intricate operations than men, have generally been employed in these production areas.

3. In some sectors, such as construction, housekeeping, and for those in casual work – occupations and contracts which may constitute dirty, dangerous, and hard work, have attracted migrants out of their home countries to Thailand.

4. A large percentage of employment by occupation in the Thai labour market has remained agricultural, including fishery, elementary occupations and retail trade.

5. Employment status by gender has revealed that women workers participate more in non-agricultural sectors, in particular the manufacturing sector, retail and wholesale trade, hotel and restaurants, education, and in service activity. In contrast, men's employment participation is mostly based in agriculture, construction, and defence.

6. Change of production in the future may be geared towards service sectors, mostly in communication, computers, transportation, trade and education. Because of that, the labour market also needs to upgrade with the availability of skilled labour, particularly in science, engineering, and computing, more than ever before. The

government should pay full attention to this issue, as, in the near future when the change of production completes its phase, it might be too late for those who influence the Thai labour market to act.

In the past decade, many policies have been launched to solve the shortage problems of the Thai labour market that are associated with the challenges of globalization. However, for the future the policies have to address the importing of labour from abroad. To deal with the influx of labour or illegal labour in the long run, the Thai government need to limit the registration of immigrant labour or set higher qualification standards for those who want to apply for work permits.

With regard to the export of Thai labour to other countries, the Thai government should develop that labour by educating and training up to international labour standards. It is advocated that the Thai government set up training centres classified by the types of jobs required including the offer of a training certificate on completion.

To prevent the unemployment problems associated with globalisation, the Thai government has to arrange job creation for the unemployed in order to create new employment opportunities. The government should provide training by supporting some budgets to training centres either in universities or institutes. These strategies can assist in creating new entrepreneurs who can run their own business and create more informal workers in the Thai economy.

To fill the gaps occurring due to the skilled-labour shortage, the government has supported increased funding s for secondary education s - but this is not enough. It is recommended that the Thai government further support and provide more financing loans for secondary and higher education. Also, the Thai government needs to encourage educational institutes to generate more graduates in the science and technology fields, so as to meet the demand of labour in the future by distributing scholarships or funding grants for labour shortages to the level of under graduate and graduate education.

Labour mobility will continue to be high within the country in response to job opportunities and to the development of new sectors associated with the ongoing expansion of export sector activity in the economy. There remain challenges linked to skill shortages, insufficient investment in training and improved labour standards in the export sector.

Thailand has to adjust to internal pressures associated with population ageing and a shifting demographic profile. Changes in the composition of labour demand, especially related to the ongoing process of opening up the economy to international trade, require both skilled and mobile labour. With respect to labour migration Thailand is situated close to neighbouring countries that offer pools of cheap and unskilled labour for the agriculture and manufacturing sectors. However, skilled Thai workers in turn can access jobs elsewhere where wage rates are much higher than in Thailand. There will remain a tension between allowing the inflow of cheap unskilled labour while at the same time skilled labour is migrating elsewhere.

Overall, the experience in Thailand over the past three decades highlights the opportunities and challenges associated with the process of globalisation. Job generation and material development has advanced, yet there remains problems with developing skills within the country, the workforce remains gendered and the benefits of growth are very unevenly distributed across the population.

REFERENCES

Books and articles (In Thai)

Chalamwong, Yongyuth. and Cewillar Ramond. (1996) "Rapid Growth of Thai Economy: A Rethinking of the impact on Thai Labour market" *Thai Economy, National Research Institute*, pp. 263-298.

National Statistics Office (NSO), (2004) "Survey of labour force survey" *National Statistics Office*, Technology information and communication department.

National Economic and Social Development Board (NESDB) (2004) "Report of Social" in *NESDB Social Outlook* 1 issue 2 June 2004.

In English

Acharya, Sarthi. (2000) *"Labour Markets in Transitional Economies in Southeast Asia and Thailand: A study in Four Countries"* (online at www.idrc.ca/uploads/users/102865652201)

Acosta, Lilibeth, (1998) *The impact of ASEAN Free Trade Area (AFTA) on Selected Agricultural Products in ASEAN Countries.* Peter   Long Frankfurt.

Angsuthanasombat, Kannikar., Nakhorn, Bharat Na and Wanabriboon, Phan. (2001) *"The Situation and case study of informal labour in Bangkok: The aftermath of the economic crisis"* (on line at http://www.caw.jinbo.net/pdf/thailand.pdf)

Chalamwong, Yongyuth. (1998) "Economic Crisis, International Migration and the labour Market in Thailand". *TDRI Quarterly Review*, 13(1):12-21

Chalamwong, Yongyuth. (2004) Country Report: Thailand. " Thaksinomics, labour Market and International Migration in Thailand" *Thailand Development Research Institute Foundation (TDRI)* (on line at http://www.jil.go.jp/foreign/event_r/event/documents/2004)

Chalamwong,Yongyuth. S. Amornthum. (2002) "Thailand: Improving Migration policy Management with Special Focus on Irregular Labour Migration: Analysis of Thai Labour Market" submitted to International Organization for Migration (IOM)/ *International Labour Organization* (ILO), TDRI March 2002 (online at http://www2.hawaii.edu/amornthu/paper/IOM.pdf)

Chemsripong, S. (2005) "The political economy of the manufacturing industry" in *Thailand in EconomicDevelopment Issue and policies*. Narayana Serial publications New Delhi (ed), pp.191-227.

Gita Sen (1999) "Partnership on globalization liberalization and sustainable human development" in Occasional paper *Gendered labour Markets and globalisation in Asia*, UNCTAD/UNDP

Institute of Asian studies, Chulalongkorn University (2000) "Report on Shortage of Unskilled Labour in Thailand in year 2000" submitted to *Department of Employment, Ministry of Labour and Social Welfare*, July 2000, Bangkok.

Jackson, Kenneth. (1997) "Free Trade, Fair Trade: Trade Liberalisation, Environmental and Labour standards", Department of Economics *University of Auckland New Zealand* UNEAC Asia Paper No.4.

Krongkaew, M. (ed) (1995) *"Thailand's Industrialization and Its Consequences"*. New York: St. Martin's Press.

Nontitat,Wut (1995) "Cheap and Vulnerable" *Bangkok Post*, 17 December 1995.

Poapongsakorn, Nipon. and Tangkitvanich, Somkiat. (2000) "*Industrial Restructuring in Thailand: A critical assessment*" (on line at www.tcf.or.jp/data/ 2000127_28_Nipon_poapongsakorn_Somkiat_Tang_kitvanich.pdf.)

Pongsapich, Amara (1994) "International Migrant workers in Asia: the case of Thailand"-proceeding of the international conference on Trans-national migration in the Asia- Pacific region: problems and Prospects. No.1-2, December 1994. *Chulalongkorn University-Bangkok Thailand.*

Pitayanon, Sumalee. (2001) "Migration of labour into Thailand", Chulalongkorn *Journal of Economics*, 13 (2): 1-42

Soraj Pavit (1995) "Employers Want Clear Policy to End Staffing Uncertainties" Bangkok Post, 17 December 1995.

Suphachalasai, Suphat. (1995) "Export led Industrialization," in Medhi Kronkaew, Medhi (ed) (1995), *Thailand's Industrialization and its Consequences.* New York: St. Martin Press.

Siampukdee, Usamard (2005) "Sustainable Development of people Crossing Border: State's Policy towards Burmease Migration workers in Thailand". Chiang Mai University Department of Political Science (online at http://sylff2005.ui.edu/ downloads/full).

World trade organization (WTO) (1995) "Thailand's economic success set to continue as exports keep growing" (online at http://www.wto.org/english/tratop_e/)

APPENDIX

Table A1. Number of population classify by sex and age 1990-2020

Age	1990		2000		2006		2010		2020	
(year)	M	F	M	F	M	F	M	F	M	F
Total	55839		62405		65470		67230		70503	
	27941	27898	31105	31301	32557	32913	33422	33807	35018	35486
0-4	2788	2709	2628	2557	2523	2474	2448	2376	2277	2207
5-9	2906	2809	2703	2640	2566	2517	2519	2452	2345	2278
10-14	2978	2872	2751	2681	2676	2616	2591	2529	2421	2356
15-19	2936	2828	2881	2795	2722	2661	2682	2627	2501	2442
20-24	2793	2696	2941	2849	2835	2761	2722	2665	2566	2516
25-29	2567	2512	2875	2778	2907	2817	2838	2761	2644	2603
30-34	2311	2277	2680	2623	2852	2744	2877	2782	2668	2623
35-39	1948	1972	2425	2446	2647	2592	2779	2676	2763	2700
40-44	1507	1541	2193	2218	2378	2428	2535	2516	2783	2702
45-49	1260	1320	1846	1910	2155	2217	2258	2349	2662	2583
50-54	1138	1198	1406	1474	1837	1927	2029	2119	2390	2410
55-59	944	996	1139	1236	1387	1486	1670	1795	2072	2217
60-64	682	723	974	1083	1044	1175	1213	1342	1777	1944
65-69	486	531	742	848	846	990	908	1064	1357	1564
70-74	326	391	469	553	616	746	683	841	873	1063
Over 75	371	524	452	612	566	762	673	915	919	1279

Source: National Economic and Social Development board, Office of the Prime Minister, 2000.

Chapter 9

AN INVESTIGATION INTO THE TRANSFER OF HRM POLICIES AND PRACTICES OF US AND JAPANESE COMPANIES BASED IN VIETNAM

Anne N. Vo

This chapter aims to examine the interaction between 'country-of-origin' and 'country-of-operation' effects in determining human resource management (HRM) policies and practices in multinationals (MNCs) in the context of globalisation. As national institutional patterns can penetrate a firm's internal operations, this study investigates the transmission and adaptation of the home country's HRM policies and practices within the MNC subsidiaries in the developing host country. Based on an investigation of the reward systems and performance management practices of a sample of US and Japanese companies based in Vietnam, this chapter argues that while 'low power' environments pose little in the way of formal constraint mechanisms they can facilitate the penetration of novel HRM practices. Findings also suggested a complex and challenging situation exists for MNC operations, requiring a very high level of adaptation and flexibility on the part of the host country firm.

INTRODUCTION

Recent trends concerning regional integration, the removal of trade barriers, deregulation, the opening of previously closed national markets to international competition, the rise of Asian countries and the integration of Central and Eastern Europe and China into the world economy have inevitably provoked speculation in relation to a globalised world. This has led to a renewal of the debate on the identity of firms and the convergence/divergence of their behaviour patterns. Despite the strength of the globalisation phenomenon which supports the theory of a 'borderless world', stateless firms (Ohmae, 1990) and the homogeneity of firms' structure and behaviour (Bartlett and Ghoshal, 1989), many authors argue that the nation state continues to be a key element in the understanding of MNCs' management practices across borders (Porter, 1990; Whitley, 1992; Lane, 1995).

Globalisation is not a homogeneous process. Instead, it increases inequality across countries, especially between developed and developing countries (Guillén, 2001). It emphasises the dependency of peripheral developing countries on investment from centre economies. In this context, the features of capitalist development are not simply expressed in a uniform fashion across borders. They are, in many respects, refracted in a distinctive fashion within specific national states. For example, even though developing economies have become increasingly internationalised and integrated into the global system, their firms are, like those in East Asia, in a weaker position in the 'global commodity chains' (Gereffi, 1996). Japanese transplants in Malaysia for instance produce mature goods which compete in world markets mainly on price, engage in relatively low value activities, particularly mass assembly, undertake limited product design work, and engage only in highly limited ways in process innovation (Wilkinson, Gamble, Humphrey, Morris & Anthony, 2001). The globalisation processes of uneven development, interdependence between equals and those who are less equal alongside interactions of conflicting and common interests, within which national state institutions are embedded, do not simply sustain a single and homogenous pattern of firm behaviours.

The relationship between national features and firm distinctiveness has been highlighted by the institutionalist school of thought. Institutionalists argue that firm activities bear the imprint of specific national institutional arrangements (Orrù, Biggart & Hamilton, 1997; Hollingsworth and Boyer, 1997; Lane, 1995; Whitley, 1999), as they 'gravitate towards the mode of coordination for which there is institutional support' (Hall and Soskice, 2001: 9). Firms are also likely to reflect their national origins with regard to behaviour in their foreign operations (Ferner, 2000). This is because to varying degrees, the particular features of the home country become an ingrained part of an MNC corporate identity influencing their international orientation as the general approach. Furthermore, in some cases, the particular configuration of the home system can give MNCs an advantage when competing outside their home countries (Taylor, Beechler and Napier 1996).

Many authors have attempted to answer the research question: how far do national states influence the international transfer of MNCs' management practices? The literature on MNCs and the transfer of HRM practices across countries suffers from a lack of research on the application of these issues in developing countries. One key question is centred on the formation and implementation of HRM systems in subsidiaries within weak host countries. This chapter addresses the transfer of HRM practices in relation to how institutional differences (distance) operates to mediate the transfer of such practices. It aims to investigate the transmission and adaptation of the home country's HRM policies and practices at MNC's subsidiaries in a low power host country.

In exploring the question of the effect of nationality on multinationals' behaviour, the literature reviews an analysis of the transfer of HRM policies and practices between different national business systems. The empirical study is based on eight main case studies of US and Japanese MNCs operating in Vietnam in automotive and fast moving consumer goods (FMCG) industries. The chapter discusses two different yet related HR issues – the reward system and performance management practices of the sample firms. It argues that developing and transitional economies, such as Vietnam, may facilitate the penetration of novel forms of economic organisation. Then again, they suggest a complex situation for MNC operations and require from them a very high level of flexibility, and in some cases compromise, when forming and implementing transferred managerial practices.

THE TRANSFER OF HRM POLICIES AND PRACTICES BETWEEN DIFFERENT NATIONAL BUSINESS SYSTEMS

Comparative institutionalism theory has been widely used to study the diffusion of organisational practices across countries. Operating in more than one country, MNCs confront a multitude of different and possibly conflicting institutional pressures (Ferner and Quintanilla, 1998; Westney, 1993). Since it is vital for MNCs to establish and maintain organisational legality in all their host environments, they need to conform to the legal environment, particularly on labour issues as well as be responsive to the cultural environment. Furthermore, as argued by Birkinshaw and Hood (1998), subsidiaries possess their own capabilities and resources such as consumption market, resources, and efficiency, which are desirable to the parent company. MNCs therefore are under pressure to adopt local practices in the host countries (Kostova and Zaheer, 1999; Ghoshal and Barlett, 1988; Taylor et al., 1996). At the same time, an important source of competitive advantage for the MNC is the utilisation of organisational capabilities worldwide (Ghoshal and Barlett, 1988; Nohria and Ghoshal, 1997). Hereby lies the central question in the literature on MNCs: the extent to which their various foreign subsidiaries act and behave as local firms (local adaptation) versus the extent to which their practices resemble those of the parent firm (global integration). This is the core research question addressed in this chapter.

There is some evidence that the home country exerts a distinctive influence on the way labour is managed in MNCs. Ferner (1997, 2000) argues that the parent company is embedded in an institutional environment located in the home country. To varying degrees, the particular features of the home country becomes an ingrained part of each MNC's corporate identity and shapes its international orientation as the general philosophy or approach taken by the parent company in the design of the HRM systems used in its overseas subsidiaries. Thus, ''ethnocentricity' and 'polycentrism' have been seen as traits characteristic of multinationals of different national origins: thus Japanese and American companies tend to be more ethnocentric than their European counterparts, other things such as sector of operation being equal' (Ferner, 1994: 88; see also Barlett and Ghoshal, 1989; Johansson and Yip, 1994; Kopp, 1994; Dicken, 1998; Berggren, 1999).

Taylor et al. (1996) assert that business system differences, including cultural distance and institutional distance, are the most important constraints on the 'context generalisability' of HRM practices. Kostova and Zaheer (1999) argue that each subsidiary of the MNC is faced with the task of establishing and maintaining both external legitimacy in its host environment and internal legitimacy within the MNC. As suggested by institutional theorists, organisations may achieve legitimacy by becoming 'isomorphic' with the institutional environment (DiMaggio and Powell, 1991). However, they do not necessarily adapt to the local environments, but, rather, manage their legitimacy through negotiation processes with their multiple environments (Kostova and Zaheer, 1999, Doz and Prahalad, 1984). Adaptation and hybridisation result from these processes. Hybridisation' refers to the mixing of two or more different practices. For example, if a Vietnamese subsidiary (a joint venture between a Japanese partner and a Vietnamese partner) has a salary policy which is based on that of the Japanese parent company (the nenko system) while their benefit policy is the same as that of the Vietnamese parent company their reward system would be considered a 'hybridisation'.

Almost all empirical studies that look at the cross-border transfer of HRM come to the conclusion that a certain amount of change is always necessary to successfully implement a HRM system that has been developed in the home business system. Ferner and his colleagues for instance have observed that in recent years, elements of Anglo-American business practices are being incorporated into the German business system. The authors term this process 'Anglo-Saxonisation', but argue that it occurs 'in the German manner' (Ferner and Quintanilla, 1998; Ferner and Varul, 2000).

The transfer of HRM/IR policies and practices between two economies needs to be seen as part of the global economy. Smith and Meiksins (1995) argue that 'countries can be slotted into [global] commodity chains relative to societal endowments, and have their comparative superiority and inferiority reinforced'. The 'dominance' (Elger and Smith, 1994) or inferiority of a business system strongly determines what and how the HRM system is transferred from one business system to another. From the home country perspective, Elger and Smith (1994) argue that the dominance, largely in economic terms, of a home system itself is one mechanism of diffusion. Dominant states are more able to exert or invite dissemination and adoption of their version of capitalism in other national systems. 'Firms from strongly integrated and successful economies may carry over national character to subsidiaries when locating abroad, and transfer home country practices rather than adopt the practices encountered in the host country' (Smith and Meiksins, 1995: 262). For example, the post-war era witnessed American economic and political dominance of the international political economy. This period saw a dissemination of American managerial and production techniques in the world; while the1980s witnessed the transitory dominance of Japanese companies and the 'Japanisation' of production and management systems in the US and other parts of the world.

From the host country perspective, the superiority/ inferiority of the host system determines its relative openness or receptiveness to dominant 'best practice' (Whitley, 1992). In a permissive/open host country environment which poses fewer constraints on firms, the introduction of country of origin practices is easier (Whitley, 1992). In contrast, MNCs may be prevented from transferring country-of-origin practices into a constraining/closed host country environment which is highly regulated and distinctive (Whitley, 1992). Moreover, the subsidiaries can utilise their resources (expertise about local environment and market, specialist knowledge, culture and so on) to block diffusion (Edwards, Ferner and Sisso, 1993).

The literature on MNCs and the transfer of HRM practices has concentrated overwhelmingly on the Triad of the European Union, America and Japan and the interactions amongst firms which are of those nationalities and located within these locations (Barlett and Ghoshal, 1989; Guest and Hoque, 1996; Tempel, 2001; Evans, Lank & Farquhar, 1989; Quintanilla, Ferner & Varul, 2001; Edwards, Chris and Coller,1999; Schmitt and Sadowski, 2003 to name but a few). This reflects the heavy concentration of FDI amongst the Triad (Hirst and Thompson, 1999). Meanwhile, little is known about the same phenomenon in developing economies, which are located in weak and disadvantageous positions in the global commodity chains. There are a series of related analytical questions to be answered in this niche: What are the possible constraints and opportunities placed by a low power host country on the operation of MNCs coming from dominant economies? Are MNCs from dominant countries less likely to adopt local practices in weaker host countries and more likely to transfer their own practices? Or are many aspects of their progressive systems lost when firms work in permissive environments? What mechanisms do MNCs develop to cope and adapt to constraints and take advantage of opportunities? These are the research questions that this chapter attempts to answer.

RESEARCH METHODOLOGY

To highlight the power disparity between home and host systems, MNCs originating in America and Japan and operating in Vietnam were chosen as the object of research. In terms of HRM, American and Japanese MNCs are in dominant positions in the world economy. They also have very distinctive ways of managing their labour forces, rooted in differences in their institutional systems. For example, Whitley (1999) argued that America represents what he describes as an arm's length type of business environment whilst Japan symbolises a collaborative one. Each of these environments generates a characteristic type of firm, isolated hicrarchy and cooperative hierarchy respectively (Whitley, 1999). Of 61 countries and territories investing in Vietnam, Japan and the US have been key investors. Regarding implemented capital, Japanese is the biggest investor in Vietnam. Meanwhile, even though the US ranks 11th in implemented capital, its presence in Vietnam has significant political and economic meaning. Some substantial investment projects are subsidiaries of U.S. companies funneled through third countries or offshore tax havens. As such, they are not credited to the U.S., thereby underestimating the 'real' value of overall U.S. investment in Vietnam.

The specific reason for choosing Vietnam as a host country example is that Vietnam is an emerging, developing and transitional economy, which offers a context for research as a low power host country. Vietnam has poor infrastructure, including physical structures and legal structure, a high degree of environmental volatility for the operations of both international and local firms, and is craving foreign capital to foster industrialisation. In 1986, the Vietnamese government introduced a comprehensive reform program, known as Doi Moi (reform), to liberalise and deregulate the economy from a hard-line socialist economic system to a more market oriented one. Although the results of the economic reforms were very encouraging, the fact remains that Vietnam is a very poor country. In 1998, 37 percent of the Vietnamese population was living below the poverty line (World Bank, 2002). In 2003, Vietnamese GNI per capita was USD 430. This is already a real achievement for the country, considering that in 1992, it had a per capita income of about USD 220. Meanwhile, FDI constitutes an essential part of the industrialisation and development of the Vietnamese economy. It is the biggest source of capital inflow to the economy, except for long-term borrowings (World Bank, 2003). Vietnam is seeking different paths to transform its political, economic and social systems, and is willing to engage with and learn from other economies in this process. As a result Vietnam is in a less favourable power position to influence the operation of foreign companies.

The aims of this research were pursued through a case study research strategy. As such qualitative methods provided a sophisticated instrument to capture the often subtle, complex, and changing ways in which companies operate allowing for investigations into the behaviour of different actors (headquarters, subsidiary, government, union, etc.) under intertwined forces of influence at different levels (global, national, sectoral and work place level). Most importantly, it enabled investigation into how policies actually operate in practice once they are transferred to the Vietnamese subsidiary. Although a quantitative method is very useful for achieving a broad overview of patterns, it is unable neither to successfully capture the complexity of the phenomenon nor to explain the differences in behaviour patterns of companies of different nationalities.

Interviews were conducted at nineteen economic organisations. Of those, eight foreign invested companies constituted the main research cases; three state-owned enterprises (SOEs) are directly linked with them, as they are the Vietnamese partners of some joint ventures; the rest are considered pilot case studies (see table 1). In order to capture the various industrial effects, if any, half of the main cases were selected from the automotive sector and the other half from the fast moving consumer goods (FMCG) industry. Organisational factors such as firm function, age, size and ownership type which impact on HRM practices and their potential transfer were also recorded. In total, 184 interviews were carried out, of which 121 interviews were with the main case organisations. The interviews in Vietnam were complemented by other interviews and questionnaires sent to the headquarters of the same companies.

Table 1. Main case studies

	Company	Branch of activity	License granted	Opening day	Capital (million USD)	Capital shares	Mode of entry	No. of employees
1	US Auto	Car assembling	1995	1997	102.70	US 75%, VN 25%.	Greenfield	331
2	JP Auto1	Car assembling	1995	1996	89.61	Japan 70%, Singapore 10%, VN 20%.	Greenfield	444
3	JP Auto2	Motorcycle assembling and limited producing	1996	1997	104.00	Japan 42%, Thailand 28%, VN 30%.	Greenfield	937
4	JP Auto3	Motorcycle assembling and limited producing	1998	1999	80.27	Japan 46%, Malaysia 24%, VN 30%.	Greenfield	342
5	US FMCG1	Shampoo, conditioner, bar soap, household products	1994	1995	83.00	In 1995: US 70%, VN 30%. Since 1998, US 93%, VN 7%	Greenfield	184
6	US FMCG2	Toothpaste, toothbrushes, bar soap, shower cream, softeners	1995	Jun-1996	40.00	In 1995, US 70%, VN 30%. Since 1999, US 100%	Brownfield	310
7	US FMCG3	Sanitary napkins, tampons, tissues, diapers (import – packaging only)	1995	1995	13.20	Originally Thailand 70%, VN 30%. In 1997, US 51%, Thailand 19%, VN 30%. In 1999, US 70%, VN 30%. Since 2000, US 100%	Brownfield	600
8	JP FMCG	Shampoo, conditioner, hair styling, skin care, and household products, sanitary napkin	1995	Jan-97	39.50	100% Japan	Greenfield	310

THE TRANSFER OF REWARD AND PERFORMANCE MANAGEMENT SYSTEMS OF US AND JAPANESE MNCs TO THEIR VIETNAMESE SUBSIDIARIES

Home and Host Country Effects

US and Japanese MNCs are renowned for their distinctive styles in setting reward systems and appraisal practices. On one hand, US firms have wide experience with various forms of gain-sharing, profit-sharing and group and individual incentives in the effort to link compensation and performance (Strauss, 1990). They emphasise openness and employee participation in the performance management (PM) process. The individual 'ought to' have an active role in the setting of goals and needs to have the right to challenge a supervisor who makes unreliable decisions about pay issues (Lawler, 1990: 232). On the other hand, the Japanese wage system is characterised by a seniority based wage structure (nenko) which regulates pay rises according to age and length of service in the organisation (Littler, 1982). Individual performance appraisal is conducted by the immediate supervisor. This is often done according to a subjective assessment of personality and behaviour (Abo, 1994; Kumazawa and Yamada, 1989). This study of US and Japanese MNCs' reward systems and PM practices offers a chance to compare different international approaches.

The Vietnamese business environment poses little formal constraint to the design and implementation of MNCs' remuneration and PM systems. Foreign invested companies are free to apply either their own reward system or the Vietnamese one (Circular number 11/LDTBXH-TT, Article 2a). However, employers are required to make some contribution to two publicly managed funds: social insurance and medical insurance. Employers are to contribute 15 percent of gross salary for social security (employees contribute 5 percent), and 2 percent for health insurance (employees contribute 1 percent).

However, companies have been faced with bifurcated labour market conditions. At the skilled end of the labour market, companies encounter the problem of insufficient labour with required qualifications and experience in some fields such as computing, marketing, human resource management and similar. In this context, job-hopping in a bid for a higher salary has become popular. The labour market thus places pressure upon companies in designing their remuneration and PM practices to keep their employees, or at least the valuable ones. On the other hand, one of the biggest attractions of investing in Vietnam is the abundant and cheap low skilled labour force. Since 1990, the Vietnamese government has reduced the minimum salary level in foreign invested companies three times, from 50 USD to 30 USD per month in a bid to attract more foreign investmenti.

The Transfer of Reward Systems

Salary

Companies identify their strategies and positions in the industry salary market following HQs' general policy and/or direction. For example, US Auto's global compensation & benefit (C&B) philosophy was 'to provide a total compensation package that was fully competitive with other leading companies in each country in which the company operates' (Global C&B guidance). These include automotive companies and companies from a variety of industries in which US Auto competes for people. This global view was reflected in the C&B package that US Auto Vietnam offers - that is fully competitive with the largest and best managed companies in a variety of industries, and particularly those in the car industry.

Compared to the US firms, the strength of the Japanese MNCs did not lie in the attractiveness of their wages and benefits packages. The amounts paid by the Japanese-owned companies are often lower than wages paid by American firms in the same industry. The US firms occupy all market leader positions, whilst Japanese firms are usually market followers. US Auto's C&B package was higher than that of JP Auto1, JP Auto2 and JP Auto3, while US FMCG1, US FMCG2, and US FMCG3 were ahead of JP FMCG. Especially, for the higher paid categories of employees (top management and management) salaries paid by Japanese subsidiaries were significantly below that of the US firms. This may reflect the attitude of the Japanese subsidiaries in that they do not attempt to recruit the most highly qualified host country managerial and professional employees because they tend not to assign vital posts and responsibilities to them.

Allowances and benefits

While salary practices were centrally designed, various types of allowances and benefits were left open to the subsidiaries to decide on what was 'suitable to the Vietnamese situation', as stated by US Auto's C&B Specialist. Even though the value of these may vary significantly, companies appeared to offer very similar types of allowances and benefits, which also resembled those offered by their Vietnamese SOE partners to their employees. Benefits offered were in the form of uniforms, subsidised lunches, accident insurance, company's good purchase program, commuting for staff, cars for top executives, gifts on personal days, mobile phones, end-of-year celebrations, Company Family Day, sporting activities, annual health checks and similar.

Bonuses

As far as bonus practice is concerned, the Labour Code indicates that the employer is responsible for paying a fixed bonus to those employees who have worked for more than one year when the company reaches 'break even' point. The payment should be no lower than one month's salary and is paid to all permanent employees.

Seven out of eight companies studied provided a fixed bonus in compliance with the Labour Code to all of their permanent / regular employees. Some of them provided much more than the law requires by providing an extra one month salary (14th month salary) as a fixed bonus. Two of the companies, US Auto and US FMCG3 had not met the break even points, thus they were not tied to this regulation yet. However, US Auto still guarantees a 13th month salary fixed bonus, while US FMCG3 did not deliver any fixed bonus but claimed that their employees' average income surpassed the required 13th month payment. A fixed bonus was paid either at the year-end or before the Lunar New Year holiday (Tet holiday).

There is also evidence that some companies which were not part of this research project did not provide any form of bonus, simply paying12 months of fixed salary after reaching their break-even points. This obviously violates the Labour Law, but its enforcement is questionable.

In many cases, allowances/ benefits and bonuses were used to adjust individual packages and most importantly, to minimise social, medical insurance costs and to avoid the high personal income tax. Taking advantage of the ambiguous regulations regarding C&B polices in foreign invested companies, many firms (including JP Auto3 and US Auto) developed a so-called '70/30 style' of C&B package, in which companies and individuals came to a verbal agreement that a company pays 70 percent of the agreed salary as 'fixed salary', the remaining 30 percent are paid in the form of non-salary payment (benefits, bonus). Applying this structure, companies only contribute to the social insurance and health insurance funds on the basis of 70 percent of what they actually pay to their employees and accordingly avoid or reduce the high personal income tax. The '70/30 style' C&B package gets the support of the higher income groups, namely professionals, managers and top managers, who aim at short-term benefits in terms of reduced income tax. This is because employees have to contribute 6 percent of their salary (of which 5 percent is for social security and 1 percent for health insurance) to state-controlled funds, but receive the same amount of money and the same kind of health services, regardless of their higher contribution. Therefore, social insurance and health insurance are seen as more for the benefit of the lower income group while the high-income group only reluctantly contributes to these government-controlled funds.

Nonetheless, a majority of big companies, especially the leading ones, did not utilise this payment structure. The C&B specialists interviewed explained that this practice is based on the assumption that the related authority (company trade union, local trade union, local Ministry of Labour, Invalid and Social Affairs) will turn a blind eye to this practice as long as the company does not violate the minimum payment level. However, in the event of being audited, the company must be able to verify their proportion of allowances/ benefits and bonuses. Moreover, a cut of social security payment leads to a smaller pension paid to employees in the future. Thus, the strategy is not for employees' long-term benefit, and can possibly cause labour relations problems for the company. In fact, the main reason for applying the 70/30 arrangement is to reduce income tax for higher paid managers.

In July 2002, the government adjusted the income tax system, which reduced the tax rate levied on the high-income group, and stated that, in future, the 70/30 regulations would not be accepted. This situation forced companies to abandon the 70/30 arrangement to avoid legal problems.

Pay for performance

Performance related pay (PRP) which rewards individual performance was evident in all the studied firms. The relationship between individual PRP and performance related pay is explained in Table 2.

Table 2. The relationship between performance rating and performance related pay*

	Performance grade	Performance related pay
US Auto	A, B+, B, C	Each performance grade allocated a PRP index. An 'A' rate will get a higher index than a 'C' rate. For example, considering variable pay of a Production Technician: • Approximate monthly earning: 1,500,000 VND • If he is rated A: 1.50 x 1,500,000 = 2,250,000 VND (per annum) This means an additional 187,500 VND in their monthly pay
JP Auto1	S (special), A, B, C	• If rated S: extra 2 month salary • If rated B+, B-: extra 1.5 month salary • If rated C: no extra pay
JP Auto2	S (special), A, B+, B-, C	• If rated S: extra 2 month salary • If rated B+, B-: extra 1.5 month salary • If rated C: no extra pay
JP Auto4	A, B, C	Depending on the rating employees will receive PRP from 15% - 6% of their basic salary.
US FMCG1	1 (performing above expectations), 2 (performing according to expectations), 3 (performing below expectations)	• Employees rated 1 are in the highest salary band/curve (higher frequency of salary rises and large amounts) • Employees rated 2 are in the middle salary band/curve • Employees rated 3 are at the lowest salary curve and basically flat lining or going backwards if including inflation.
US FMCG2	Exceptional, meet expectation, below expectation	• Depending on their performance, employees will be sorted in 3 distribution curves, exactly as US FMCG1. • Applied for staff and upper level only
US FMCG3	Exceed expectation, meet expectation, does not meet expectation, not rated (for temporary workers)	• If rated 'exceed expectation': extra 2 month salary • If rated 'meet expectation': extra 1.5 month salary • If rated 'does not meet expectation': no extra pay
JP FMCG	No formal system exists	

* This applied to all permanent employees, if not otherwise mentioned

The main difference between firms originating from the US and those from Japan, in relation to remuneration practices, lies in how they define the basic salary. The Japanese firms have the distinctive 'age-linked salary'. JP Auto1, and JP Auto2 claimed the use of the so-called 'life module' in defining the level of salary they pay to their employees[ii]. JP FMCG used the same principle but abandoned it a few years later. The Vietnamese life module was the result of research conducted in Vietnam by C&B specialists from the Japanese headquarters with the support of the Vietnamese staff at the subsidiaries. According to the life module, the salary of the employee is supposed to increase in pace with his/her promotion in firms (from team member to team leader to supervisor and so on) and his/her personal needs (from being single to being married, having children or buying a house).

Thus, in the form of age-linked payment, the seniority wage (*nenko*) system manifested itself in the remuneration system of big Japanese firms in Vietnam. However, the companies did not attempt to implement a fully-fledged Japanese style seniority based wage system. First of all, the HRM Manager of JP Auto1 and JP Auto2 claimed that greater weight was given to individual merit in determining wages and promotions, due to the much greater influence of the external labour market compared with Japan. Secondly, due to the limited number of qualified professionals in the Vietnamese labour market, in order to attract candidates for their vacancies, the starting salary paid by these Japanese subsidiaries was relatively higher than what would be expected by firms adhering strictly to the *nenko* principal (compared to their headquarters).

The life module salary is in line with the stable long-term employment philosophy of JP Auto1 and JP Auto2. However, it is interesting to look at the value of the *nenko* system from the perspective of the Vietnamese employees. Interviewed employees, especially the white-collar ones, did not find the implied promise of steadily rising wage rates throughout a long-term career with the same company sufficiently credible and /or desirable. Most of them considered it merely a technique used to calculate salary level. What they really looked at was the final salary paid to them at the present time rather than any long-term future benefits. One interviewed manager said:

'My parents had been working all their lives in this one big SOE. They believed that they would be looked after when they retired. They indeed were, until the day that the [centrally planned] system collapsed. After the currency reform and some inflation storms what they receive today is not enough to live on for half a month...This generation suffers from this 'unsecured' feeling, not knowing what might happen tomorrow...Promises and long-term plans are nice but we care more for the present.'

On the other hand, the *nenko* system loses its attractiveness, because its salary increase rates and promotions come relatively slowly. Vietnamese employees, especially ones with high skills or in managerial categories, consider that job hopping will, in all likelihood; provide them with a much higher salary and better benefits than staying with one organization would.

While highly centralised and complex remuneration systems were evident in most of the case studies, JP FMCG opted for localised policies regarding reward systems. Before 1999, JP FMCG employees enjoyed 'seniority benefit'. However, it was dropped when Japanese managers considered it 'unnecessary' in the Vietnamese context. The company's remuneration was then extremely simplified. JP FMCG's salary system was divided into two categories: white-collar employees and blue-collar employees. The wage of blue-collar employees was calculated based on their working days per month (35,000 VND/day). Conversely, the salaries of professionals and the upper levels of JP FMCG were negotiated on an individual basis with Japanese managers, most often with the Japanese General Director. He also personally decided on salary increases without any systematic salary structure being in place. However, the extremely simplified salary structure appeared to function fairly well in the context of a small subsidiary organisation.

The effect of both the global and local host environments on the design of the reward systems were evident. Compensation practices were highly centralised in terms of defined positions in the salary market, the permitted salary range and the compensation structure, which put a great deal of emphasis on individual performance. However, there were instances of centralised policies being translated into practices and procedures in a manner which was suitable to the local situations and preferences, such as allowances and benefits, fixed bonus practices and the *nenko* system. The Vietnamese legislation regarding salary in foreign invested firms does however leave certain gaps that MNCs can take advantage of to minimise labour costs and reduce income tax –evident in the '70/30' reward style.

The Transfer of Performance Management Practices

PM practices in the US firms

PM systems in the US firms studied were marked by a high level of employee participation and by the openness of the process. Firstly, employees were required to engage in defining their performance targets. The companies shared their business objectives and targets with employees, and actively encouraged them to suggest strategies by which these targets could be achieved. Secondly, the evaluation of individual performance was open for discussion and if employees disagreed with the performance evaluation rated by their supervisors or colleagues, they could voice their concerns and ask for a re-evaluation. Immediate supervisors and HR Managers were responsible for organising interviews to 'check and balance', so as to minimise unfairness or bias. The final ratings were decided by both parties.

Advanced PM tools and techniques were widely applied in the US firms, illustrated by the use of the 360-degree feedback and forced distributions in all the case studies. The 360-degree feedback was applied solely for top management, which means that less than ten employees in each company were subject to this type of performance review. Forced distributions of performance were seen as a sharp tool in the US firms to not only evaluate individual performance but also to create competition to push up performance amongst employees. It is noted that, while the distribution of performance was a popular practise in the Japanese firms and Vietnamese SOEs studied, the 'forced' element was what made the US firms different and more aggressive in their attempts to link performance and the pay system.

Table 3. Forced distribution system applications in the sample companies

Company	Forced distributions and the direct influences on employees	
	White-collar employees	Blue-collar employees
US Companies		
US Auto	A (5-10%), B+, B, C. 'Looser' forced distributions are applied for blue-collar workers.	
US FMCG1	1 (15 - 20%), 2 (65-70%), 3 (15%).	
US FMCG2	Exceptional (15%), meet expectation, below expectation (5%)	Ratings are the same as white-collar group. However, forced distribution is not applied.
US FMCG3	Exceed expectation (4-5%), Meet expectation, Does not meet expectation (1-2%), Not rated (for temporary workers).	Ratings are the same as white-collar group. However, forced distribution is not applied.
Japanese companies		
JP Auto1	S (special), A, B, C. No forced distribution is imposed. However normally S and A occupy 5%-10%. A global forced distribution system is being considered.	
JP Auto2	S, A, B+, B-, C. No forced distribution is imposed by headquarters. However company distributes rankings as follows: normally S is accounted for about 3%, A 10% and B+ 20%.	
JP Auto3	A, B, C. No forced distribution is imposed, however, the number of A is normally around 5-10%.	
JP FMCG	Ratings are conducted but no forced distribution. There are four ratings: outstanding (91-100 marks/100), very good (81-90 marks), satisfaction (71-80 marks), need improvement (61-70 mark) and under satisfaction (under 61 marks).	

Mendonca and Kanungo (1990) believe that performance appraisal practices that involve with a confrontational mode of feedback during the appraisal discussion may not be effective in developing countries where 'face saving' is important. Nevertheless, it is argued that the problem of direct criticism is more a potential than real difficulty, and that cultural values are not overwhelming constraints to the implementation of PM, as long as expatriates and local managers are sensitive with the issue. Interviewed managers reported that they had good and thorough discussions with their Vietnamese employees, which also covered negative issues.

The 360-degree feedback included upward ratings which would be unfamiliar to the Vietnamese and might be considered incompatible in a hierarchical society. Meanwhile, the forced distribution system promoted competition amongst colleagues, and thus may damage their harmonious relations. Presumably, the transfer of these technologies into the Vietnamese subsidiaries could be faced with strong reactions and even refusal to participate from local employees. However, in practice, no particular constraint on the implementation of the 360-degree feedback and forced distributions was recorded. The smooth transfer of this HRM practice might have been the result of a newly liberated business system, at the macro-level and a cultivated 'American culture', at the micro-level. The break down of the centrally planned economy leading to the collapse of the communist model of an egalitarian ideal of income distribution makes the 'capitalist country's way of distributing principles, which are strongly based on individual performance more acceptable to Vietnamese employees, who have come to consider performance related payment as an important dimension of modern PM practices. At the company level, employees have a positive perception of American standards of 'fairness' and 'straightforwardness', which reflect a common perception concerning the way Americans conduct business in particular and of Westerners in general. This is generally seen as a refreshing and welcome working environment.

PM practices in the Japanese firms

The studied Japanese firms reported a system of top-down alignment. This means that white-collar employees were expected to take on additional duties, as occasionally demanded. In some companies, target setting was a one-way process, with little engagement of the subordinates (JP Auto3, JP FMCG)iii. Individual objectives were set, but not written down, which appeared to significantly damage the reviewing process. Performance appraisal was conducted on a strictly top-down basis and supervisors' decisions were considered final. PM processes in the studied Japanese companies involved neither upward evaluation nor face-to-face discussion.

Although top down appraisal practices, which heavily depend on Japanese managers' personal evaluation, were in line with some aspects of Vietnamese culture, such as respect for authority and hierarchical order, the Vietnamese employees in this study were dissatisfied with the Japanese firms' PM practices. This may be explained by the fact that this practice was opposed to the Vietnamese customary practice – which has been predominant in SOEs for decades – of the 'democratic' sounding of opinions in performance appraisal, which means that opinions from a wide range of employees were gathered at 'Appraisal Committees' in order to achieve a 'democratic' evaluation of employees performances. Although these Appraisal Committees operated in a hierarchical order, the evaluation of individual performance was conducted openly in the presence of employees and their colleagues. This is to say that national cultural traits and their influences on firms' behaviours were indeterminate and complex. In this case, respect for authority and hierarchy were traditionally implemented in a fashion that stressed openness and 'democratic' participation in decision-making.

In brief, distinctive patterns of national PM were evident in this study. The US firms emphasised financial measurements, supported by non-financial ones, in performance appraisal. In addition, the PM process was facilitated by the use of advanced management tools and techniques. In contrast, PM in the Japanese firms was characterised by a more informal structure of regular performance review, which was conducted in a strictly top-down manner, suffering from bias and a lack of openness. Cultural influence was acknowledged in this research, such as difficulties involved in providing and receiving direct criticism although it is argued that this should not be seen as an overpowering obstacle as it can be overridden by a strong company culture.

CONCLUSION

The aim of this research study was to examine the transmission and adaptation of the host country's HRM policies and practices within MNC's subsidiaries in a developing host country, in this case Vietnam. Overall some important conclusions were reached.

Primarily this research confirms that the globalisation process does not simply sustain a single and homogenous pattern of firm behaviour and that greater economic efficiency in work systems within a country does not automatically lead to the dispersal of these practices to other countries. Even if it can be demonstrated that a particular set of HRM practices contributes significantly to superior performance in home country operations, a MNC has to determine whether it wishes to transfer these practices. This research argues that MNCs may consider that the transfer of HRM policies and practices is not necessary for successful operation within a Vietnamese context. In the case of JP FMCG, they basically decided to stop the transfer of their home practices to the Vietnamese subsidiaries. Instead, there was a high degree of localisation of managerial practices (even though the same conclusion cannot be drawn for transferring production technology). The first few attempts to copy home practices (the nenko system) quickly disappeared in the Vietnamese environment. The argument is strengthened when some attempts to compare their practices with regard to other subsidiaries are made. Elsewhere, JP FMCG is described as a 'classic global company' where international operations are largely formulated and controlled by headquarters. Their global strategy seeks to build competitive advantage by treating the world as a single, largely undifferentiated marketiv. Instead of home-grown methods, the company seeks to use fairly universalistic forms of 'common sense' management, experimenting, learning and copying pieces from other firms in a haphazard and eclectic manner. Thus, the low degree of transfer might be attributed to the perceived lack of necessity and assumptions concerning the importance of particular management practices.

It is argued that a developing country poses a minimal *formal mechanism of constraint* to the design and implementation of MNCs' remuneration and PM practices. The Vietnamese government has been conscious of the necessity to keep the base level of salary in foreign invested companies at a minimum level and to reduce personal income tax rates. In this context MNCs are allowed to design and/or implement suitable rewards and performance management systems. That said, companies are faced with an *informal mechanism of constraint* in the form of a default labour market and job-hopping practices. This encourages the implementation of attractive and effective reward systems. The combination of these factors might explain the transfer of well-developed and standardised reward and PM systems in the sample firms.

The home country effects were also evident in this study. For example, MNCs kept tight control of the reward systems in the Vietnamese subsidiaries. A well-defined salary position, permitted salary ranges, and the practice of variable pay which strongly emphasises individual performance were exercised. There were also instances of adaptation to local situations as seen in fixed bonuses, allowances and benefits practices. These practices were very similar in the studied firms and resemble those found in Vietnamese SOEs. Gaps in legislation and weak law enforcement mechanisms have seen companies develop practical tactics to reduce labour costs, such as the '70/30' salary package.

The distinctiveness of the US and Japanese traditions of rewarding and appraising employees was also evident in their Vietnamese subsidiaries with some minor adaptations. In the US firms, the PM process was closely linked with financial measurements and individual performance. The companies also applied a wide range of advanced PM tools and techniques, including the use of 360-degree feedback and forced distributions of performance. Conversely, the Japanese *nenko* system was transferred to Vietnam in the form of an age-linked payment. Some adaptations of the *nenko* system were apparent, such as a greater weight being given to individual merit and a higher starting salary.

Finally, although it was not a focus of this research, this chapter acknowledges certain cultural influences with regard to the practices of PM. However, the successful implementation of the US 360-degree feedback and forced distribution system and the limitations of the Japanese top-down appraisal process illustrate the transience and indeterminacy of national cultural traits. In opposition to Hofstede (1980) and other culturalists who see some unchanging national differentiation with regard to culture, this chapter illustrates that cultural values can actually evolve in some situations. The transitional period in Vietnam, which witnessed the fall of the centrally planned system and its promises, is receptive to new and seemingly contrasting practices. It remains to be seen how these develop over time.

REFERENCES

Abo, T. (ed.) (1994) *Hybrid factory the Japanese production system in the United States*, New York Oxford: Oxford University Press.

Bartlett, C.A. and Ghoshal, S. (1989) *Managing across borders the transnational solution*, Great Britain: Mackays of Chatham PLC, Chatham, Kent.

Berggren, C. (1999) 'Introduction: between globalisation and multidomestic variation', in Belanger, J., Berggren, C., Bjorkman, T. and Kohler, C. (eds.) *Being local worldwide: ABB and the challenge of global management*, New York: Cornell University Press.

Birkinshaw, J. and Hood, N. (1998) 'Multinational subsidiary evolution: capability and charter change in foreign-owned subsidiary companies', *Academy of Management Review*, 1998, Vol.23, No.4, pp.773-795.

Dicken, P. (1998) *Global shift [transforming the world economy]*, 3rd edition, London: Paul Chapman Publishing Ltd.

DiMaggio, P.J. and Powell, W.W. (1991) 'The iron cage revisited: institutional isomorphism and collective rationality in organization fields', in Power, W.W and DiMaggio, P.J. (ed.) *The new instutionalism in organizational analysis*, Chicago and London: The University of Chicago Press, p.41-63.

Doz, Y.L. and Prahalad, C.K. (1984) 'Patterns of strategic control within multinational corporations', *Journal of International Business Studies*, Vol.15, No.2, pp.55-72.

Edwards, P., Ferner, a. and Sisson, K. (1993) *People and the process of management in the multinational company: A review and some illustrations*, Warwick Papers in Industrial Relations, Coventry: IRRU.

Edwards, T., Chris, R. and Coller, X. (1999) 'Structure, politics and the diffusion of employment practices in multinationals', *European Journal of Industrial Relations*, Vol.5, No.3, pp.286-306.

Elger, T. and Smith, C. (1994) 'Global Japanization? Convergence and competition in the organisation of the labour process', in Elger, T. and Smith, C. (ed.) *Global Japanization? The transformation of the labour process*, London: Routledge.

Evans, P., Lank, E. and Farquhar, A. (1989) 'Managing human resources in the international firm: Lessons from practice', in Evans, P, Doz, Y. and Laurent, A. (ed.) *Human resource management in international firms*, London: Macmillan

Ferner, A. (1994) 'Multinational companies and human resource management: An overview of research issues', *Human Resource Management Journal*, Vol.4, No.3, pp.79-102.

Ferner, A. (1997) 'Country of origin effects and HRM in multinational companies', *Human Resource Management Journal*, Vol.7, No.1, pp.19-37.

Ferner, A. (2000), *The embeddedness of US multinational companies in the US business system: implications for HR/IR*, Occasional Paper No. 61, Leicester: De Montfort University Business School.

Ferner, A. and Quintanilla, J. (1998) 'Multinationals, national identity, and the management of HRM: "Anglo-Saxonisation" and its limits', *International Journal of Human Resource Management*, Vol.9, No.4, pp.710-731.

Ferner, A. and Varul, M. Z. (2000) '"Vanguard" subsidiaries and the diffusion of new practices: A case study of German multinationals', *British Journal of Industrial Relations*, Vol.38, No.1, pp.115-140.

Gereffi, G. (1996) 'Commodity chains and regional divisions of labor in East Asia', *Journal of Asian Business*, Vol.12, pp.75-112.

Ghoshal, S. and Bartlett, C. (1988) 'Creation, adoption, and diffusion of innovations by subsidiaries of multinational corporations', *Journal of International Business Studies*, Fall, pp.365-388.

Guest, D. and Hoque, K. (1996) 'National ownership and HR practices in UK greenfield sites', *Human Resource Management Journal*, Vol.6, No.4, pp.50-74.

Guillén, M. (2001) 'Is globalization civilizing, destructive or feeble? A critique of five key debates in the social science literature', *Annual Review of Sociology*, Vol.27, pp.235-260.

Hall, P. and Soskice, D. (2001) *An introduction to varieties of capitalism*, in Hall, P. and Soskice, D. (ed.) *Varieties of capitalism: The institutional foundations of comparative advantage*, Oxford: Oxford University Press.

Hirst, P. and Thompson, G. (1999) *Globalization in question*, 2nd edition, Polity Press.

Hollingsworth, R.J. and Boyer, R. (1997) 'Coordination of economic actors and social systems of production', in Hollingsworth, R.J. and Boyer, R. (ed.) *Contemporary capitalism the embeddedness of institutions*, the USA: Cambridge University Press.

Johansson, J. and Yip, G. (1994) 'Exploiting globalisation potential: US and Japanese strategies', *Strategic Management Journal*, Vol.15, No.4, pp.579-601.

Kopp, R. (1994) 'International human resource policies and practices in Japanese, European, and United States multinationals', *Human Resource Management Journal*, vol.33, No.4, pp.581-599.

Kostova, T. and Zaheer, S. (1999) 'Organisational legitimacy under conditions of complexity: the case of the multinational enterprise', *Academy of Management Review*, Vol.24, No.1, pp.64-81.

Kumazawa, M. and Yamada, J. (1989) Jobs and skills under the lifelong nenko employment practice, in Wood, S. (ed.) *The transformation of work? Skill, flexibility and labour process*, London: Unwin Hyman.

Lane, C. (1995) *Industry and society in Europe. Stability and change in Britain, Germany and France*, Edward Elgar.

Lawler, E. (1990) *Strategic pay*, San Francisco: Jossey-Bass.

Littler, C. (1982) *The development of the labour process in capitalist societies*, London: Heinemann.

Mendonca, M. and Kanungo, R.N. (1990) 'Performance management in developing countries', in Jaeger, A.M. and Kanungo, R.N. (ed.) *Management in developing countries*, London: Routledge.

Nohria, N. and Ghoshal, S. (1997) *The differentiated network. Organizing multinational corporations for value creation*, San Francisco: Jossey-Bass Publishers.

Ohmae, K. (1990) *The borderless word*, London: HarperCollins.

Orrù, M., Biggart, N.W. and Hamilton, G.G. (1997) 'Organisational isomorphism in East Asian', in Powell, W.W. and DiMaggio, P.J. (ed) *The new institutionalism in organizational analysis*, Chicago: University of Chicago Press.

Porter, M. (1990) *The competitive advantage of nations*, London/Basingstoke: MacMillan.

Quintanilla, J., Ferner, A.. and Varul, M. (2001) 'Country-of-origin effects, host country effects and the management of HR in multinationals: German companies in Britain and Spain', *Journal of World Business*, Vol.36, No.1, pp.107-128.

Schmitt, M. and Sadowski, D. (2003) 'A rationalistic cost-minimization approach to the international transfer of HRM/IR practices: Anglo-Saxon multinationals in the Federal Republic of Germany', *International Journal of Human Resource Management,* Vol.14, No.3, pp.409-430.

Smith, C. and Meiksins, P. (1995) 'System, society and dominance effects in cross-national organisational analysis', *Work, Employment & Society*, Vol.9, No.2, pp.241-267.

Strauss, G. (1990) 'Toward the study of human resources policy', in Chelius, J., and Dworkin, J. (ed.) *Reflections on the transformation of industrial relations*, Metuchen, NJ: IMLR Press.

Taylor, S., Beechler, S. and Napier, N. (1996) 'Toward an integrative model of strategic international human resource management', *Academy of Management Review*, Vol.21, No.4, pp.959-985.

Tempel, A. (2001) *The interaction of country-of-origin and host country effects on human resource management practices in German and British multinational companies*, Paper for conference on multinational companies and human resource management: between globalisation and national business system Conference, De Montfort University, Leicester.

Westney, D.E. (1993) 'Institutionalization theory and the multinational corporation', in Ghoshal, S. and Westney, D.E. (ed.) *Organization theory and the multinational corporation*, Basinnstoke/ Hampshire: St. Martin Press.

Whitley, R. (1992) 'Societies, firms and markets: The social structuring of business systems', in Whitley, R. (ed.) *European business systems firms and markets in their national contexts*, SAGE publications.

Whitley, R. (1999) *How and why are international firms different? The consequences of cross-border managerial coordination for firm characteristics and behaviour*, Presented to Sub theme 3 "Business System In Their International Context" of the 15th EGOS Colloquium held at the University of Warwick, 4th – 6th July 1999.

Wilkinson, B., Gamble, J., Humphrey, J., Morris, J. and Anthony, D. (2001) 'The new international division of labour in Asian electronics: work organisation and human resources in Japan and Malaysia', *Journal of Management Studies*, Vol.38, No.5, July, pp.675-695.

World Bank Organisation (2002) *World Fact Book 2002*, [Online], Available: http://www.odci.gov/cia/publications/factbook/index.html [12th January 2003].

World Bank, Report No. 25050-VN, (2003) *Vietnam delivering on its promise development*, [Online], Available: http://www-wds.worldbank.org/servlet/ WDSContentServer/WDSP/IB/2002/12/14/000094946_02120304010865/Rend ered/INDEX/multi0page.txt, [12th January 2003].

---

[1]
- On 29th August 1990, the Ministry of Labour, Invalids and Social Affairs (MOLISA) issued Decision number 365/LDTBXH-QD regulating that the minimum salary of employees in foreign invested companies is 50 USD/month.
- On 5th May 1992, MOLISA issued Decision 242/LDTBXH-QD regulating two levels of minimum salary: 35 USD/month for Ha Noi and Ho Chi Minh City; and 30 USD/month for the rest of the Country.
- On 1st April 1996, MOLISA issued Decision number 385/LDTBXH-QD regulating three levels of minimum salary:
  - ➤ 45 USD/month for enterprises located in Ha Noi, and Ho Chi Minh City.
  - ➤ 40 USD/month for enterprises located in Hai Phong, Vinh, Hue, Da Nang, Bien Hoa, Can Tho, Ha Long, Nha Trang, Vung Tau.
  - ➤ 35 USD/month for enterprises located in other provinces and cities, or enterprises which use a large amount of manual workers in agriculture, forestry and fishery.
  - ➤ 30 USD/month for enterprises located in under-developing and lack of infrastructure areas, and those which use a large amount of manual workers and are faced with financial difficulties, with the approval of MOLISA.

[2] This conclusion excludes JP Auto3 that refused to offer explanations of their salary structure. However, they do acknowledge the existence of a seniority factor in their salary structure.

[3] Kaizen, improvement suggestions on the other hand is a bottom-up process.

[4] Reference is withheld to maintain anonymity for the company.

Chapter 10

MEDIA AND COMMUNICATIONS WORK IN INDONESIA: TRANSFORMATIONS AND CHALLENGES FOR WOMEN

Pam Nilan and Prahastiwi Utari

INTRODUCTION

This chapter addresses issues of globalisation and work in Asia by examining trends and challenges for female workers in the media and communications industries in Indonesia. Indonesia has been one of the last countries in the region to begin recovering from the 1997 Asian currency crisis and is currently in a period of slow growth. However, the ICT (Information and Communication Technology) sector is growing rapidly, and this has a direct effect on media and communications workplaces. At present women constitute only a small minority of professional workers in this occupational field, even though they graduate from communications degrees in Indonesia in much larger numbers than men. Due to gender-biased deficiencies in their professional ICT training, and the negative effects of traditional gender stereotyping in Indonesia, female media and communications workers are likely to find that the advanced ICT aspects of globalisation do not empower them as workers, but instead, contribute to their increasing marginalisation in the workplace.

BACKGROUND

The percentage of women in the formal sector of the Indonesian labour market increased from 35 per cent in 1980 to 41 per cent in 2003 (WorldBank, 2005), and presumably has increased further as the economy continues to strengthen. Real GDP growth in 2004 was 4.9 per cent (BPS, 2005), up from less than 1 per cent in 1997. The increase in females participating in the formal labour market to over 46 per cent of women is mainly due to the high unemployment rate for men (CIRCLE, 2002: 3), an outcome of both the 1997 economic crisis, the steady decline in agriculture, and urban drift. The urban population of Indonesia rose to 45.6 per cent in 2003 (BPS, 2005) indicating a change in labour market emphasis. Growth in areas such as manufacturing, food technology, and financial services has been matched by growth in the media and communications services and industries. Indeed, one might argue that given the influence of globalisation in the new era of technology in Indonesia, print and visual media journalism, advertising, public relations, music, video and film production now constitute some of the most attractive and well-paid forms of new work. However, according to our research, women do not always fare well in this occupational field.

We focus here on three closely-related aspects of globalisation and work in Asia. The first is the global spread of legislative protections for workers, the second is the effect of advanced information and communication technologies, and the third is the transnational icon of the young Asian career woman. In this chapter these three aspects are discussed in general terms, then we look at how these trends are realised in our Indonesian data on the experiences of female workers in the field of media and communications.

DATA AND METHODOLOGY

The research project referred to in this chapter involved a study of the educational and workplace experiences of female media students and workers in Indonesia. The project uses data that was collected in 2001 and 2002. Specifically, between June and September 2001 the following data was collected: a survey of 180 female communication studies undergraduates from first to final semester at a state university in Central Java; interviews with 40 of those female students; interviews with 40 sets of parents of those students; a focus group with ten sets of parents of female communications students; and interviews with 15 communications lecturers from the same university. Individual interviews and a focus group were also conducted with established female media workers in Solo. In addition, interviews were conducted with media industry bosses in Solo and Yogyakarta.

Between January and March 2002 further interviews and a focus group were conducted in Jakarta with female media workers, and interviews were conducted with media industry bosses in Jakarta. In total, 23 media employers or managers were interviewed for the whole project. Five were from newspapers, three from radio, five from television, four from advertising, three from public relations, and three from on-line media. In total, 46 female media workers were interviewed for the whole project. Thirteen worked for newspapers, nine for radio stations, seven for television stations, six for public relations firms, six for on-line media companies, and five for advertising agencies. In interpreting this data, the Indonesian author of this chapter drew upon her own extensive experience as a lecturer in communications, and also as a practicing female radio journalist and broadcaster. All tape recorded material was transcribed and translated from Indonesian to English by the two authors. Some of this data is utilized in order to explore the transformations and challenges for women training for, and working in, the media and communications field in Indonesia.

INDONESIAN LABOUR LAWS AND PROTECTIONS: FEMALE MEDIA AND COMMUNICATION WORKERS

Since the early 1980s, Indonesian workers have been protected by more internationally ratified labour laws and human rights agreements than ever before, including laws that prohibit discrimination on the basis of gender. Yet, female workers in communications and media industries continue to experience gender discrimination in initial employment, highly gender-stereotyped assignment of workplace duties, and sexual harassment at work. Employers and male colleagues in this study were found to show little, if any, awareness of legal constraints on their behaviour. Even the female workers themselves appeared relatively uninformed about their rights. The circulating *global* human rights discourse (consisting of various international conventions and protocols) has been signed to by many countries in Asia. However, in Indonesia the *local* 'letter of the law' in regard to these international agreements has yet to be taken seriously, and female workers are not getting the protections they need.

In 1984 Indonesia ratified the United Nations Convention on the Elimination of all forms of Discrimination Against Women (CEDAW). The United Nations Human Rights Convention. A number of other agreements relevant to protecting the rights of women have also been agreed. For example, in 1988 the Ministry of Manpower Circular No. 4 (04/MEN/88) on the Implementation of the Convention on the Elimination of Discrimination against Women Workers was sent to all Heads of Provincial Offices of Manpower throughout Indonesia. It required company regulations and collective agreements to include equal pension age limits and equal medical benefit costs for male and female workers, and requested them to ensure that employment arrangements did not include any forms of discrimination against women workers, in accordance with *UURI 7 – 1984*, the 1984 law which outlaws discrimination against women.

Yet, discrimination on the basis of gender, remains a significant problem in Indonesia according to the ILO (2002: 9; see also Mariani, Armando, Hasyim, Heri, Mutmainnah & Ilvas, 2000: 75). Discrimination begins during recruitment when male workers are preferred over women, then moves on to lower pay, less involvement in decision making, and different ages for retirement. Women are paid, on average, only about 68 per cent of men's wages (Gardner, 2003: 7). The curious nature of the Indonesian Marriage Law *(UURI 1 – 1974)* means that female *workers* are defined as single, even if they are married – 'the underlying assumption being that married women do not work and that the husband is the primary income earner' (Gardner, 2003: 7). This means that the tax rates of female workers are higher, and women are not paid family allowances where employers offer them. Indonesia does have some specific laws to protect the interests of women in the workplace, for example *UURI 7 – 1984, UURI 39 – 1999* and *UURI 13 - 2003,* but these laws do not appear to be widely acknowledged, respected or implemented by employers and regulatory bodies.

Quite a few of the bosses interviewed in this study openly expressed the view that most media jobs were unsuitable for women,

> *I would suggest that it is better for a woman not to choose a job as a media*
> *worker. It is a hard and risky job. It needs more mental and physical*

preparation than the regular jobs that women choose (Mr. BS, newspaper editor-in-chief).

His argument was similar to many other media and communications employers. They were convinced that only men were suited to most kinds of media work, for example,

> *It is a job that demands we are outside the home with unlimited working hours and high-risk practices. It is difficult for women to do this given their limitations* (Mr AM, radio coordinator).

> *If the deadline is near, our volume of work increases up to one hundred and eighty per cent. It means we have to stay up and work all night until it's finished. This work is a daily reality for certain media workers. Physically, it is difficult for this to be done by women* (Mr MH, newspaper editor).

Both these comments refer to the gendered moral discourse that respectable Indonesian women (especially married women) do not work beyond daytime hours, particularly not all night in teams consisting of mostly men. This discourse takes its credibility in part from the Ordinance on Measures Limiting Child Labour and Nightwork for Women created in 1925, which prohibited women from performing nightwork between 22.00 p.m. and 6.00 a.m. This bill was only amended in 2003. *UURI 13 – 2003*, Article 76 (1) with regard to women's employment and now states that women less than the age of 18 are prohibited from performing night work between 23.00 p.m and 7.00 am, unless otherwise specified by a licence issued by the Department of Manpower. Moreover, this law does not address the issue of men less than 18 years working all night.

In practice, many Indonesian media employers still discriminate against women in job appointments. For instance, although apparently sympathetic, one media employer hinted at his preference,

> *We choose workers more for their work capabilities than for their sex. Nevertheless, from experience, I have seen that men survive better than women in their careers. Women quit easily from positions. I think it is natural because*

women face more barriers in their career than men (Mr BI, radio station director).

However, further on in the same interview with Mr BI, he explained that there was an 'unwritten policy' in his radio station that newly-married women were shifted from their positions as radio DJ or programmer to positions described by Beasley and Theus (1988: 127) as 'support roles' – that do not attract wage bonuses. A female DJ at Mr BI's radio station gave her version of what happened at the initial job interview,

When I was interviewed for my current job as a DJ in this radio station, Mr BI asked me when I wanted to get married. I had to tell him beforehand because he would prepare someone to take over my duties. It seemed like a tradition in this company that if a female DJ married, another girl would take over the job. However, this warning was not given to men who applied for the same position (Miss D, radio DJ).

Mr BI's 'unwritten policy' narrowly avoids the statement in *UURI 7 -1984,* Article 11, paragraph 2(a) which 'prohibit[s], subject to the imposition of sanctions, dismissal on the grounds of pregnancy or of maternity leave and discriminations in dismissal on the basis of marital status', in that he does not dismiss married female workers. However, his 'unwritten' policy marginalises married female workers, implicitly encouraging them to resign. This does seem to contravene in principle the internationally-derived Human Rights Legislation *UURI 39 – 1999,* Article 2(b) which states that 'the worker is to be directed to the position that best suits the worker's capabilities including their skills, talent, and motivation. Placement should be based on dignity, human rights and law'. Yet, on the other hand, Mr BI is acting well within the spirit of the Indonesian Marriage Law – 'an area where blatantly unequal rights still prevail' (World Bank, 2001: 117).

Paragraph one of the Indonesian Marriage Act (*UURI 1 - 1974)* states that the rights and status of the wife are equal to those of the husband both in their married life and in society. However, paragraph three states that the husband is the head of the household and the wife is a housewife, reflecting conventional patriarchal family structure (Ariani and Nilan, 1998: 63; Mariyah, 1995). This impacts upon the perceived legitimacy of married women's careers. The CEDAW report on Indonesia expressed concern about this – 'the predominant view appears to be that married women might provide supplemental income for a family, but that there is very little emphasis on the right of women to develop a career of their own' (1998). Some of the female media/communications graduates in our study who had been able to build up a viable career while single or first married certainly found a change in attitude at home once their family responsibilities increased,

> *I felt sometimes my husband was cranky if I came home late or I had to meet my clients in the night and outside. He suggested I should finish my job in work time and avoided taking it home. It is very hard for me to do, because sometimes I work overtime due to meetings or client appointments. In the first years of my marriage, my husband accepted my working lifestyle. However, now because we have a child, he accuses me if I come home late of not being responsible for our child* (Mrs A, advertising account manager).

This confirms an ILO study which found that in Indonesia still - 'a majority of men and women disapprove of women who continue working after giving birth to a child' (Sziraczki and Reerink, 2003: 48).

The international literature on women and media work acknowledges that the industry tends to be characterised by rough, competitive, masculinized workplaces (Damodaran, 2001), with the exception of certain 'female' niches such as women's magazines. The Indonesian female media workers in focus groups had much to say about how they worked hard to survive in male dominated workplaces. Moreover, while they found most male colleagues to be respectful, helpful and well-mannered, they also identified male colleagues who harassed them sexually. These men would whistle when they came in, come up behind and embrace them, and even squeeze their waist or buttocks. A few viewed these behaviours as *keisengan* [just for fun] – not worthy of attention. Others felt these behaviours constituted harassment and had developed ways of stopping them,

> *If we just keep silent, they will do it all the time. I do not hesitate to tell them off about those behaviours. I don't care if they regard me as* judes *[vicious],*

cerewet [sharp-tongued] or even like a nenek sihir *[witch] because I always scold them if they are behaving badly* (Miss S, newspaper reporter).

Others implied that the risk of sexual harassment just went with the job and had to be endured (MacKinnon, 1979: 1). One overall effect though, is to reinforce the already well-established idea that communications and media workplaces are not suitable for respectable Indonesian women. We note that the increasingly sophisticated ICT area is where male media and communications workers are especially concentrated, and anticipate that the marginalisation of women from this field of workplace responsibilities may well count against their career advancement prospects.

GLOBALISATION AND THE MEDIA AND COMMUNICATIONS WORKFORCE IN INDONESIA

The media and communications sector in Indonesia comprises print media, television, radio, film, advertising, public relations and on-line media. Workers in those industries include journalists, presenters, public relations advisors, photographers, camera operators, sound engineers, production staff, printing workers, ICT and digital media technicians, graphic artists, managers, and technical, secretarial and clerical support staff. Of these workforce sectors, with some exceptions, women are to be found working professionally mainly as presenters, journalists, and in public relations. They constitute the majority in clerical and non-technical support areas. In all but clerical and non-technical support areas, there has been a rapid transformation of media and communications work due to advanced information and communication technologies (Debrah and Smith, 2003). Dahlan (1997) notes the rapid growth of the Indonesian media and communications sector that has occurred since the early 1980s, to the climate of high technology and concentrated capital (see Hill and Sen, 2005) that prevails at present. A recent forum on Indonesian media practices and advertising in Bali concluded that the industry has not only expanded but changed significantly (Widiadana, 2005) in the direction of more advanced ICTs. For example, the number of on-line media providers has grown exponentially while print media output declined. All media forms now target a highly fragmented market of consumers as lifestyles are polarised in the new 'culture wars' that attend Islamisation (Bayuni,

2006). And not only are clients and consumers more demanding of professional standards, the very way of working in the Indonesian media industries has become more globally oriented. This creates particular demands on workers in the media and communications industry, since Indonesia has few media specialists equipped to deal with these challenges (Widiadana, 2005). The training of professional media workers is therefore in the spotlight, particularly in the area of new technologies, where women are likely to feel least confident as practitioners, and potentially will be most exposed to sexual harassment.

According to an ILO (2004) report on the future of work and quality in the media, culture and graphical sector, new ICTs will increase the demand for journalists, editors, artists and multimedia editors and technicians. The same report finds that, in the light of global technological expansion, 'the demand for journalists remains high and will continue', in all countries. For example, in the USA, research quoted by the 2004 ILO report predicts that by 2012, 16 per cent more jobs for writers and editors will have been created. Other predicted increases include: 6.2 per cent more jobs for news analysts, reporters and correspondents, 13.6 per cent more for photographers, 26.4 per cent more for film and video editors, and 21.9 per cent more for graphic designers.

In Indonesia, we find some evidence that similar growth is taking place in this sector. For example, Sen claims that there has been a substantial rise in the number of female filmmakers (directors, producers and scriptwriters) in the post-New Order era (2005), possibly reflecting the greater number of trained professionals in this field. Discussing the recent proliferation of feature films made in Indonesia, it is claimed that young filmmakers demonstrate superior knowledge of their craft, and increased technological skills (Nugroho, 2000; Sulistyani, 2005: 6), indicating, once again, the presence of a youthful skilled labour force in film-making companies.

It can be readily observed that Indonesian newspaper, tabloid and magazine publishing, advertising, online media, television and radio production, public relations and entertainment industries - driven by commercial interests and global competition – make use of the latest ICT equipment and expertise, indicating the work of skilled professionals in these fields. However, an investigation into who these people are, and where they acquired these skills, would be likely to reveal two facts important to the arguments in this chapter – few would be women, despite very high numbers of female communications graduates, and very few workers would have obtained those high-level technology skills during their university training.

The ILO (2004) report quoted above finds that ICT growth presents new challenges in terms of training for jobs in the communication and media industries. Employers interviewed in our study were well aware of this, for example,

> *The prospects are very strong and clear as we move forward into unrestricted world trade. In the global media arena graduates from communication studies must have the capacity to compete with other graduates, especially with regard to skills relevant to professional practice in communications* (Mr. AB, public relations manager of a private television station in Jakarta).

> *Information is the best-selling commodity of the future, especially advertising and product design. The most important thing is how well the graduates anticipate the development of technology, and market demand* (Mrs BD, director of an advertising agency).

Indonesian university communications degrees were already struggling to keep pace with technological change ten years ago (Dahlan, 1997). Evidence suggests that undergraduate degree studies in *komunikasi* [communications] currently offered at most Indonesian universities do not provide anything like adequate technological training for the new media and communications workplaces (Nazara, Wisana and Friawan, 2003: 27). The communications lecturers interviewed for our study readily admitted this,

> *Generally, students are just given basic knowledge or an introduction to the areas of study. As to the mastery of specific skills needed in the work, they are still at the basic level too. It is not possible to expect graduates will be one hundred per cent ready for work, especially in communications-related jobs that depend very much on technology* (Mr. S, communications lecturer).

This was certainly a view shared by many employers, and quite a few of the graduates interviewed during this research project. Some suggested reasons were: teaching staff are out of touch with technology and workplace trends, underfunding of universities so that up-to-date equipment and information technology access is virtually non-existent, and a lack of infrastructure planning relevant to industry needs.

With perhaps five exceptions, universities in Indonesia are notoriously under-funded. Certainly, few advanced technological resources were available for professional training in communication studies at the university where we collected data. And it appeared that male students were explicitly favoured for ICT learning,

> *Yeah we realize that in media jobs they demand people who show mastery of a variety of skills. Usually those skills seem to suit work conducted only by men. For example to be a cameraman, those technologies are basically suited to men* (Mr. BR, communications lecturer).

Even relatively sympathetic explanations of this phenomenon hinted at essentialist discourses of gender that encoded a fixed stereotype of male technical competence,

> *On average, in practical activities most male students do better quality work than female students. I think it is based on men's nature. They are braver than women about operating some media equipment. As a woman, I can understand that generally women do feel not comfortable, or are worried about trying something unfamiliar, like those technologies* (Mrs SI, communications lecturer).

However, female students often gave quite a different account,

> *Sometimes I feel uncomfortable in a group task. Male students often underestimate our abilities. They only let us do things that they consider suitable for females. They don't want to know that we can do it too! Sometimes I feel that it would be better if I could do such tasks in a female-only group rather than in a mixed group* (Miss DH, first year communications student).

Some students reported that their parents also endorsed the idea that females and technological equipment were incompatible,

> *I asked my parents to buy some photographic equipment but they were reluctant. The reason is (in their perception) no woman can be a photographer. Only a man can be a photographer. So it would be useless if they bought it for me. My parents still don't like me doing anything like this. They still seem to think about my life in terms of spending time in the home, which to me is wrong! I never asked them again. I still continue learn journalistic photography using the department's equipment* (Miss D, second year communications student)

The sum effect is that – with a few striking exceptions – female graduates on the whole emerge with less experience and less confidence about their capacity to handle, and learn more about, sophisticated information and communications technology than do males, even though this is exactly what the contemporary media workplace anywhere in the global 'space of flows' (Castells, 1997) demands. This further mitigates against their already reduced chances of obtaining a job, and against later career enhancement.

THE MODERN YOUNG CAREER WOMAN IN ASIA (AND INDONESIA)

The well-educated, smartly-dressed, modern young career woman is one of the transnational commercial icons of globalised late modernity in the region (Gills, 2002). There seems little doubt that, as an icon, this image has a profound effect on the subjectivity of young middle-class women in the transition from school to work. Writing about Australia, Harris maintains that 'unlike previous generations of women, young women today expect a life of paid work in the form of a career that is personally fulfilling' (2004: 41). The apparent opportunities offered by globally altered local labour markets encourage young women to be more independent and self-confident (Rattansi and Phoenix, 1997: 139). This seems no less so in Asia. Certainly Moghadam (1994: 2) claims that in contemporary Asia, women are symbolically linked to progress and modernization (see also Munshi, 2001). In

Indonesia, Sen's (1998: 35) analysis indicates that the smart, young, working woman is one of the icons around which Indonesia's position as a modern nation in a global economy and culture is established. The media itself plays a significant role in promoting the idea of the deserving, glamorous, modern, young, 'can-do' career woman (Harris, 2004), as our Indonesian data indicates,

> *Of course working in the media industry is attractive for me. Like women presenters, for example, who I see on television, their work is identical to secretaries. They write things, they read news to the audience or sometimes they interview someone. Their appearance is so elegant, beautiful and attractive. They work in an office with excellent conditions and so on. I think it is just right for me* (Miss M, first year communications student).

This is similar to findings of the study by Splichal and Sparks (1994) which identified significant differences between male and female students' attitudes towards journalism careers. Female students were less likely to want to become reporters, and much more likely to want to become presenters. It could be argued that this is because the job of presenter seems more promising in terms of conventional femininity than the job of reporter. Becker and Graf's western country study showed that the growth in enrolments in communications education for women has resulted primarily from the increasing appeal of the field to women (1995: 3). They found that women students had some stereotyped ideas about this field of work. Their ideas were tinged by a desire for glamour, fame and wealth. They believed that this program of study would lead to an attractive occupation with high social status and material benefits. In a similar conclusion, Wu (2000: 61) found Chinese communications students reported that they chose this area of study partly because they were attracted by monetary benefits or glamour factors such as quick fame or high social status. In many ways, the career aspirations of young Indonesian women entering communication studies were similar to those identified among Thai village girls who opt to sell beauty products. They were keen to become,

> *Part of a global network, not just through working for a multinational company, but through their participation in defining and exploiting cosmopolitan standards of beauty and desire* (Fadzillah, 2005: 92).

237

In our study, many parents of female communications students did not initially seem to question their daughters' idealised view of a glamorous media career,

> *My daughter chose communication studies because she has seen women who have successful careers in the communications area. These successful women are a mould for her to follow. If I ask her what she wants to be, she just wants to be like Desi Anwar, Zaza Yusharyahya and so on - all successful TV news presenters* (Mr. B, father of a female student).

We argue (Utari and Nilan, 2004) that less well-educated parents were more likely to have unrealistic ideas about what kind of study a communications degree entails, for example,

> *I am not a university graduate. I did not even finish secondary school. So if you are asking me about kinds of courses and the benefits for my daughter, honestly, I will say that I know nothing. I can only comment that I am grateful that my daughter can reach higher education* (Mr. H, father of a female student).

However, once it became clear to parents that communication and media studies was much more than sitting down to write in a nice office and presenting the news, some parents became concerned,

> *If I were to suggest a future job for my daughter, I would prefer her to choose a job that is not related to the profession of journalism. Even though I do not know exactly the nature of journalistic work - I do not have friends or family working as journalists - but from the way it is regarded in society, I have got the idea that the job is not suitable for my daughter* (Mr A, father of a female student).

By the second year of the degree, when they had become more aware of how hard and demanding most work in the media and communications field can be, some of the female students themselves developed misgivings,

The most important thing for me in finding a future media job is that it should not burden me. As long as I can carry out the duties and conform, I will take it, however, if it interferes with my family life in the future, I will forget it. For me, taking care of the family is better than work (Miss Z, second year communications student).

Previous studies have convincingly established that young women everywhere experience problems following graduation from communication studies (see Mariani et al, 2000; Mariani, 1990; Lock, 1991; Cramer, 1993; Beasley 1993; Gallagher, 1995, 2001), even though it is estimated that 'women now make up a third of the world's journalists' (Damodaran, 2001: 1). In Indonesia we find that more than two-thirds of those enrolled at universities in the discipline of *komunikasi* are female, yet after graduation they will account for, at best, perhaps one tenth of skilled media and communications workers, with very few in managerial positions. Globally – 'only 0.6 per cent of women get into decision-making posts in media' (Damodaran, 2001: 1).

In her compiled studies of six Asian countries: Bangladesh, India, Indonesia, Malaysia, Philippines and Sri Lanka, Lock (1991; 2) found there was a wide gap between the number of female graduates of communication studies and the number of them actually working in media industries. Gallagher's study of Indonesia some twelve years ago concluded that the proportion of young women finding employment in the media is by no means the same as their share of training in communication studies. Women accounted for at least 60 per cent of third year communications students but they accounted for only 30 per cent of those holding any kinds of job at all in the media industries (1995: 7-11). Angela Romano's 2002 study of Indonesian journalism also detailed many of the problems encountered by female journalists. Likewise in 2005 Hanitzsch finds that,

The 'typical' Indonesian journalist is young, male, well-educated and earns an above-average salary (2005: 493 our emphasis).

In short, while a career in the field of media and communications initially seemed to match exactly the iconic image of the smart, glamorous young *wanita karir* [career woman] wearing nice clothes in an air-conditioned office, and chatting with famous people, female students at university in Central Java quickly became aware that, for the most part, it did not. Accounts given by women working in various media industries bore testament to the anti-social rigours of most jobs in this typically 'masculine' field of work, for example,

> *This is the craziest work you can imagine. I had just come back from Pontianak after a week of reporting when they sent me off again to cover another news story in Semarang. It meant that just one day after I arrived home I went away again. There is no tradition here that I could refuse the task because I was tired. Yeah...to be a kuli tinta (ink coolie) is to be a super woman* (Miss HS, tabloid reporter).

Although we give a full account of the factors which implicitly exclude female graduates from entering the field elsewhere (Utari and Nilan, 2004), it is sufficient to state here that one reason for some female graduates electing to take jobs outside the sector for which they trained is that most media and communications jobs are not compatible with their socio-cultural identity as women (Damodaran, 2001: 1; Sziraczki and Reerink, 2003) – *kodrat wanita* [women's traditional role]. While research in many countries confirms this as a trend in media and communications, in Indonesia the discourse of *kodrat wanita* - female sex role destined by fate (Sullivan, 1994: 133) - operates as a particularly powerful discourse channelling men and women into separate professional employment fields. In public rhetoric, *kodrat wanita* means having an 'essential' feminine nature of *lemah lembut* [soft and weak]. Women don't speak loudly, and certainly not in their own interests. They don't push their own interests against those of husbands and fathers, but are instead docile wives and mothers and dutiful daughters (Wieringa, 1993: 26). So for example, since women are ideologically regarded as weak, emotional, and incapable of overcoming challenges, by definition women are regarded as unfit for work as journalists (Korvajarvi, 1998: 21), or indeed in most forms of professional media work.

This implicit cultural prohibition against most kinds of media and communications work for women is exacerbated by the fact that workplaces are male-dominated and irregular work hours can be expected. In middle-class conservative Indonesian discourse about women and work (which enshrines many residual elements of New

Order ideology), although they should ideally be 'in the home', women can work, as long as they do so in the moral safety of female-dominated work places - where the kinds of work they do, the positions in the hierarchy they occupy, the hours they work, and the salaries they earn, are all closely related to *kodrat wanita.* The relatively recent cultural Islamisation of Indonesia further strengthens this discourse of implicit prohibition against the kinds of work that typically characterise the media and communications field. At the same time, the apparent discursive link between the circulating image of the smart, 'can-do', young Asian/Indonesian career woman, and the ideal of a female media worker as someone who works in a nice office, is seen on TV, travels and meets interesting people, continues to attract young women into communications degree programs in larger numbers than it does men.

One of the twelve recommendations in the Platform for Action that emerged from the Fourth World Conference on Women in Beijing in 1995 (FWCW, 1995) concerned women and the media. A strategic objective of that recommendation was to increase the participation and access of women to expression and decision-making in and through the media, and new technologies of communication. Yet Damodaran (2001) reports that, despite national programmes by governments that participated in the Women's Conference in Beijing (including Indonesia), the situation of women in media work 'is getting worse, due to globalisation' (2001: 2). Why? It seems to us that not only do Indonesian female media and communications workers suffer from gender discrimination and stereotyping, but that mastery of new information and communication technologies is now considered a vital component of fitness for positions in this field of employment. As we have seen, female job applicants and female workers in the field are much less likely than men to have developed such competencies.

CONCLUSION

At this stage in our discussion we return to our opening comments. Three inter-related aspects of globalisation in Asia were highlighted in this chapter. We considered the global spread of legislative protections for workers and how this affects (or does not affect) the workplace experiences of female media workers. We also looked at how the rapid growth of advanced ICTs in media and communications workplaces impacts on female workers in this occupational field. In the last section above we discussed the transnational icon of the young Asian/Indonesian career woman and how this impacts on both recruitment and the careers of female workers in the field. To signal how these three trends are entwined, we summarise the stages in our discussion as follows:

- Indonesian female media and communications workers are now protected – in theory – by more national labour laws and rights agreements than ever before – but still suffer discrimination and gender stereotyping

- Following global trends, Indonesian media and communications industries are becoming more and more reliant on the information and communication technology (ICT) skills of workers – yet communications degree programs cannot deliver this training effectively. Male students are favoured for mastering the scarce ICT resources that do exist

- Encouraged by the icon of the young Indonesian career woman, young middle-class women seem greatly drawn to the idea of a career in the media and communications field – yet find it is not what they expected.

Accordingly, we suggest the following 'narrative' about these three trends: Many more young women than young men enthusiastically enter communications degree programs in Indonesian universities. Once there, it is unlikely they will receive appropriate training in technology relevant to the media and communications field. While studying the degree program, young women become less and less inclined to follow a career in their chosen occupational field. So following graduation, they seek generalist feminine white-collar jobs such as receptionist or department store sales assistant. Some of them, of course, remain enthusiastic about a career in the media and communications sector and eventually obtain a position. Once in the job though, female workers are likely to find themselves relegated to lower level positions away from the technology side. In these highly masculinised workplaces, there seemed to be little awareness on the part of male bosses of the laws and regulations that are supposed to protect women workers. Although a few young women in our study were able to take up the kind of attractive media and communications careers they originally imagined for themselves, interviews with married female media workers indicated this changed quite dramatically once they married and had children, even though most kept up full-time work to maintain a modern, middle-class, dual-income lifestyle (Robison, 1996: 85).

As media and communications industries in Indonesia become more fully integrated into the global order, they require appropriate best practice professional training of workers so that this important sector of the workforce reflects cultural richness and diversity. It seems critically important in a fledgling democracy that talented young people of both sexes enter university programs to study media/communications, then move confidently into jobs in relevant workplaces according to their talents and interests. However, it appears that, in Indonesia at the present time it is gender, rather than talent and interest, that largely determines this journey, so that male workers are much favoured over women. Moreover, as this sector of work transforms technologically, the challenges for female workers seem to be intensified, rather than diminished.

Drawing some general points from the specific gendered work sector 'narrative' detailed above allows us to see that global – local tensions in Indonesia, and presumably in some other Southeast Asian countries, continue to play a shaping role in the experiences and meaning of work for women in key ICT growth industries. In making these points we refer specifically to female workers in male dominated professional workplaces located in the private rather than the government sector. In fact, the link between media and communications education (in universities), and work in the media and communications sector is unusual, in that the professional education stage is dominated by women, and the professional work/career stage by men. We suspect that this is the case in many Asian countries.

Firstly, while the global icon of the successful, glamorous, professional, young career woman does attract young women into media and communications degrees, the enduring local discourse of appropriate distinct sex roles for men and women (especially married women), strongly mitigates against them ever enjoying the kind of jobs and careers male workers can negotiate in this occupational field. The range of recent – internationally-driven – formal legal protections for female workers seems to be having little effect on this problem. Secondly, at the global level, media and communications as a field is at the forefront of technological change, and local consumers expect the 'products' of national producers to be no less in quality than imported media and communications products and services. However, with a few notable exceptions, the extraordinarily underfunded and archaic professional communications degree programs in Indonesia simply cannot provide training of this kind. Moreover, the extremely scarce ICT resources in university departments are implicitly favoured for the training of male students, even though they constitute the minority of degree enrolments. Lecturers, male students and employers all seem to accept this state of affairs as very much the status quo, reflecting traditional gender discourses and the transferred logic of the national marriage law. This has direct negative implications for the potential – down the line – of the relatively few female media and communications workers to move up as managers, since such positions are frequently linked to technological competencies. Finally, the 'narrative' presented here reminds us that when global work trends, such as the incorporation of advanced ICTs, engage with resilient local discourses such as gender stereotypes, this may result in furthering, rather than diminishing, existing labour force inequities.

REFERENCES

Ariani, I. G. A. A. and Nilan, P. (1998) 'Women's status in marital law within the Balinese sociocultural context', *Journal of Interdisciplinary Gender Studies,* 3(1): 59-74.

Bayuni, E. (2006) 'Porn bill debate exposes culture war fault lines', *The Jakarta Post,* March 28. Available http://www.thejakartapost.com/detailhcadlines.asp?fileid=200603 (accessed 28 March 2006).

Beasley, M. (1993) 'Newspaper: is there a new majority defining the news?', in P. Creedon, (ed.) *Women in Mass Communication.* London: Sage.

Beasley, M. and Theus, K. (1988) *The Majority: A Look at what the Preponderance of Women in Journalism Education Means to the School and the Professions.* Lanham, MD: University Press of America.

Becker, L.B. and Graf, J.D. (1995) *Myths and Trends: What the Real Numbers Say about Journalism Education.* Arlington: The Freedom Forum.

BPS (2005) 'Social indicators', *Biro Pusat Statistik Indonesia.* Available http://www.bps.go.id (accessed 2 April 2006).

Castells, M. (1997) *The Power of Identity, Volume 2, The Information Age: Economy, Society and Culture.* London: Blackwell

CEDAW (1998) *Committee on the Elimination of All Forms of Discrimination against Women: Report on Indonesia.* Online at University of Minnesota Human Rights Library. Available http://www1.umn.edu/humanrts/cedaw/indonesia1998.html (accessed 13 June 2005).

CIRCLE (2002) 'Labour market conditions in Indonesia', CIRCLE-Indonesia – Center for Industrial Relations Research and Labour Education. *Global Policy Network* website. Available http://www.GlobalPolicyNetwork.org (accessed 2 April 2006).

Cramer, J.A. (1993) 'Radio: a woman's place is on the air', in P. Creedon (ed.) *Women in Mass Communication.* London: Sage.

Dahlan, A. (1997) *Pemerataan Komunikasi, Informasi dan Pembangunan.* Jakarta: Universitas Indonesia.

Damodaran, R. (2001) 'Scenting out the gender imbalance in journalism', *New Straits Times* – Life & Times 2, 13 August. Available: http://adtimes.nstp.com.my/jobstory/2001/aug13c.htm (accessed 25 November 2005).

Debrah, Y. and Smith, I. (2003) 'Introduction: globalization and the workplace in Pacific Asia', in Y. Debrah and I. Smith (eds) *Work and Employment in a Globalized Era: An Asia Pacific Focus.* London: Frank Cass Publishers.

Fadzillah, I. (2005) 'The Amway connection: how transnational ideas of beauty and money affect northern Thai girls' perceptions of their future options', in S. Maira and E. Soep (eds.) *Youthscapes: The Popular, the National and the Global.* Philadelphia: University of Pennsylvania Press.

FWCW (1995) *United Nations Fourth World Conference on Women Platform for Action: Women and the Media.* Available http://www.un.org/womenwatch/daw/beijing/platform/media.htm (accessed 5 April 2006).

Gallagher, M. (1995) *Un-finished Story: Gender Patterns in Media Employment.* Paris: UNESCO Publishing.

Gardner, S. (2003) 'Women in trade unions: no big gains for women workers', *Inside Indonesia,* October/December, 76: 7-8.

Gills, D-S. S. (2002) 'Neoliberal economic globalisation and women in Asia: introduction', in D-S. S. Gills and N. Piper (eds) *Women and Work in Globalizing Asia.* London: Routledge.

Hanitzsch, T. (2005) 'Journalists in Indonesia: educated but timid watchdogs', *Journalism Studies,* 6(4): 493-508.

Harris, A. (2004) *Future Girl: Young Women in the Twenty-First Century.* London: Routledge.

Hill, D. and Sen, K. (2005) *The Internet in Indonesia's New Democracy,* London: Routledge

ILO (2002) 'Indonesia tripartite action plan for decent work 2002-2005', *International Labour Organisation.* Available http://www.ilo-jakarta.org.id/ download/decentwork.pdf (accessed 3 April 2006).

ILO (2004) *The Future of Work and Quality in the Information Society: The Media, Culture, Graphical Sector.* Report for Tripartite Meeting on the Future of Work and Quality in the Information Society: Media, Culture, Graphical Sector, Geneva: ILO.

Korvajarvi, P. (1998) 'Reproducing gendered hierarchies in everyday work: contradictions in an employment office, *Gender, Work and Organization,* 5: 19–30.

Lock Y.K. (1991) *Access of Asian Women in Communication Education and Work in Journalism and Communication, an Overview of Six Countries.* Singapore: Asian Mass Communication Research and Information Center.

MacKinnon, C. (1979) *Sexual Harassment of Working Women,* New Haven: Yale University Press.

Mariyah, C. (1995) 'Gender and patriarchy in Indonesian politics,' *Inside Indonesia,* March 42: 18-20.

Mariani, I.R. (1990) *Access of Women in Communication Education and Journalism and in Communication Work in Indonesia.* Singapore: Asian Mass Communication Research and Information Center.

Mariani, I.R., Armando, A., Hasyim, Heri H., Mutmainnah, N. and Ilyas, N. (2000) 'Hope for the future', in Joshi, I. (ed.) *Asian Woman in the Information Age: New Communication, Technology, Democracy and Women.* Singapore: Asian Media Information and Communication Center.

Moghadam, V. (1994) *Gender and National Identity: Women and Politics in Muslim Societies*. London and New Jersey: Zed Books.

Munshi, S. (2001) *Image of the Modern Woman in Asia: Global Media, Local Meaning*. Richmond: Curzon.

Nazara, S., Wisana, I.D.G.K and Friawan, D. (2003) *Determining the Impact of Information and Communication Technology (ICT) on Decent Work in Indonesia: Final Report,* Jakarta: Demographic Institute, University of Indonesia.

Nugroho, G. (2000) 'Eforia sinema Indonesia di tengah Asia', *Kompas Online.* Available at http://www.kompas.com/kompas%2Dcetak/0010/29/hiburan/efor19.htm. (accessed 24 August 2005).

Rattansi, A. and Phoenix, A. (1997) 'Rethinking youth identities: modernist and postmodernist frameworks', in J. Bynner, L. Chisholm and A. Furlong (eds) *Youth, Citizenship and Change in a European Context.* Aldershot: Ashgate.

Republic of Indonesia (1974) *Undang-Undang Nomor 1 1974* [Marriage Law], Jakarta.

Republic of Indonesia (1984) *Undang-Undang Republik Indonesia, Nomor 7 1984 –* Article 11 [Women's Employment], Jakarta.

Republic of Indonesia (1999) *Undang-Undang Republik Indonesia Nomor 39 1999 –* Articles 31- 38 [Human Rights], Jakarta.

Republic of Indonesia (2003) *Undang-Undang Republik Indonesia Nomor 13 2003 –* Article 76(1)[Women's Employment], Jakarta.

Robison, R. (1996) 'The middle class and the bourgeoisie in Indonesia', in R. Robison and D. Goodman (eds) *The New Rich in Asia.* London: Routledge.

Romano, A. (2002) *Politics and the Press in Indonesia,* London: Routledge/Curzon.

Sen, K. (1998) 'Indonesian women at work: reframing the subject', in K. Sen and M. Stivens (eds) *Gender and Power in Affluent Asia.* London: Routledge.

Sen, K. (2005) 'Film revolution? Women are on both sides of the camera now', *Inside Indonesia,* July-September, 2005: 10-11.

Splichal, S. and Sparks, C. (1994) *Journalists for the 21st Century: Tendencies of Professionalization among First Year Students in 22 Countries.* Norwood: Ablex.

Sulistyani, H.D. (2005) 'The construction of women in post-New Order Indonesian cinema', unpublished M.A Thesis. Curtin University of Technology, Western Australia.

Sullivan, N. (1994) *Masters and Managers: A Study of Gender Relations in Urban Java*. Sydney: Allen and Unwin.

Sziraczki, G. and Reerink, A. (2003*) Report of Survey on the School to Work Transition in Indonesia,* GENPROM Working Paper No. 14. Geneva: Gender Promotion Programme, ILO.

Utari, P. and Nilan, P. (2004)'The lucky few: female graduates of communication studies in the Indonesian media industry', *Asia-Pacific Media Educator*, 15: 63-80.

Widiadana, R. (2005) 'First Asia Pacific media forum opens in Bali', *The Jakarta Post,*Monday, 14 March. Available http://www.asiamedia.ucla.edu/article.asp? parentid=21710 (accessed 4 April 2006).

Wieringa, S (1993) 'Two Indonesian women's organizations: Gerwani and the PKK', *Bulletin of Concerned Asian Scholars,* 25(2): 17-30.

World Bank (2001) *Engendering Development.* Washington: World Bank and Oxford University Press.

World Bank (2005) 'Indonesia', *The World Bank 2005 GenderStats.* Available at http://devdata.worldbank.org/genderstats/genderRpt.asp?rpt=profile&cty=IDN ,Indonesia&mh=home (accessed 2 April 2006).

Wu, W. (2000) 'Motives of Chinese students to choose journalism careers', *Journalism and Mass Communication Educator,* 55 (1): 53–65.

Chapter 11

NON-REGULAR WORK IN KOREA

Byoung-Hoon Lee* and Hyunji Kwon**

INTRODUCTION

During the past twenty years, market forces have become more dominant in the shaping of employment relations all over the globe. In the environment of growing global competition, the governments of industrialized economies have commonly taken action to promote the flexibility of labour markets, while firms have tried to reshape existing employment relations to become more market-driven. In the meantime, labour unions in industrialized countries have experienced the shrinkage of their organizational base. Although there is a wide variance of union influence across different countries, political leverage - under the pressure of globalization - has turned many unions into lethargic role-players in re-forging employment relations. Under this context a new division of labour markets has emerged over recent years, which is exemplified by the rapid proliferation of non-standard employment patterns. This includes temporary or fixed-term labour, part-time workers, temporary agency or dispatched labour, on-call workers, contract labour, independent contractors, and home workers, as noted in Lee and Frenkel (2004). The new fracture line that divides labour markets by workers' employment status (regular versus non-regular) is commonly identified in industrialized countries, which have experienced intensified market competition fuelled by globalization, deregulation, and propelled technological breakthroughs (Houseman & Osawa 2003).

---

* Professor of Sociology, Chung-Ang University, e-mail: bhlee@cau.ac.kr

** Research fellow, Korea Labour Institute, e-mail: sk248@cornell.edu

Korea is not an exception to this experience. In the 1990s, the country was baptized a neo-liberal economy, manifesting itself in the governments' globalization strategy and market-oriented economic restructuring policies. This occurred under the context of the integrated WTO market and, particularly, its foreign exchange crisis (Lee 2003a). In the neo-liberal economy, the increased use of non-regular labour is a core component of the changing trend of employment relations, generating a new dividing line in the labour market in Korea. Compared to other industrialized economies, the growth of non-regular employment in Korea has been remarkable, particularly under the context of the economic crisis that broke out at the end of 1997. Specifically, the share of non-regular workers in the wage labour population of the country exceeded that of regular (permanent and full-time) employees from the period beginning 1999 onwards. More importantly, the employment conditions of non-regular workers are quite inferior and the workers quite vulnerable, in comparison with the regular workers. As a consequence, there are two layers of working classes that coexist in the polarized labour market – regular workers as the first-class citizens and non-regular workers as the second-class. Consequently, the new segmentation of the labour force by employment status has become a core issue for policy makers and governments as, in its current form, it undermines any possibility of achieving an equitable quality of life for working people.

Given this background, this chapter aims to delineate the segmentation of working life in Korea by outlining the growing trends and employment conditions of the non-regular workforce and discussing the key reasons for the polarization of the labour market. A brief sketch of two industrial cases is also presented – banking and auto – by focusing on the recent trends and working conditions of non-regular labour in those sectors. The reason why the banking and auto sectors were selected as case examples is because the two sectors can provide an interesting contrast in labour segmentation: that is the female-dominated services versus male-dominated manufacturing. In conclusion, some policy implications are addressed that are designed to tackle the issue of segmented work.

NON-REGULAR WORK IN GENERAL

Trends and Composition

As displayed in figure 1, the share of non-regular labour among the total waged workforce in Korea has grown since 1994, soaring sharply during the period of the economic crisis (1997-1999) and slightly declining in 2003-2004. The proportion of non-regular workers in the waged labour force, estimated through the annual Economically Active Population Survey (EPS) by the National Statistical Office (NSO), increased from 41.9 % in 1995 to 52.1% in 2000, and then dropped to 48.8% in 2004. During this period, both male and female non-regular employment demonstrated identical trends. Note, however, that non-regular employment is much higher among the female waged labour force (63.3 % in 2004) than that (37.5 %) of the male waged workforce.

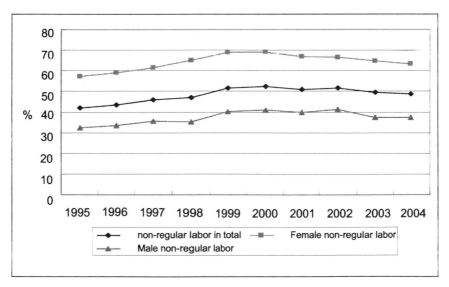

Source: Korea Labour Institute (KLI) (2005).

Figure 1. Trends in the Share of Non-regular Labour

Table 1 summarizes a detailed composition of the non-regular labour force, which is estimated by the 2005 EPS additional survey. The total number of non-regular workers in the EPS additional survey, which was conducted in 2000, is higher than the figure in the EPS, because the former includes on-call, dispatched, contract, home workers and independent contractors, in addition to the latter's temporary and part-time employees. Among various non-regular employment patterns, the share of temporary workers is over 63 %. It is also noteworthy that the vast majority of temporary workers are characterized as quasi-permanent, in that employers use them by renewing their short-term employment contract regularly in order to gain the reduction of labour costs and numerical labour flexibility. Yet, those permanent temporary workers (or perma-temps), termed by Tsui, Pearce, Porter & Hite (1995) and Way (1992), are observed as suffering from insecure employment status, since the renewal of their contract can be unilaterally refused by employers without a legal constraint (Lee & Kim 2004).

Table 1. Composition of Wage Labour Force by Employment Status and Gender in 2005

	Total (1,000)	Male (1,000)	Female (1,000)
Regular Workers	6,564 (43.9 %)	4,648 (53.5 %)	1,916 (30.5 %)
Non-Regular Workers	8,404 (56.1 %)	4,034 (46.5 %)	4,370 (69.5 %)
Composition of Non Regular Workers			
Temporary Workers	5,323 [63.3 %]	2,716 [67.3 %]	2,603 [60.0 %]
Part-time Workers	1,044 [12.4 %]	309 [7.7 %]	736 [16.8 %]
On-call Workers	717 [8.5%]	466 [11.6 %]	252 [5.8 %]
Independent Contractor	633 [7.5 %]	239 [5.9 %]	394 [9.0 %]
Dispatched Workers	117 [1.4 %]	43 [1.1 %]	75 [1.7 %]
Contract Workers	430 [5.1 %]	247 [6.1 %]	183 [4.2 %]
Home Workers	140 [1.7 %]	14 [0.0 %]	127 [2.9 %]

Source: Kim, Y. (2005) The figure in the parenthesis is the percent of total wage labour force, while that in the square bracket is the percent of total non-regular employees.

As shown in Table 2, the primary industries (agriculture, fisheries and forestry) have the highest share of non-regular labour, followed by construction and the wholesale-retail-food-hotel sectors. Non-regular workers in the finance-real estates-renting business sectors account for over 50% of total employment in those sectors, while the manufacturing (and mining) sector employ less than 40% of labour force in non-regular employment (next to the lowest share in the utilities sector).

Table 2. Composition of Labour Force by Employment Status and Industry in 2005

Industry	Regular Labour ('000)	Non-regular Labour ('000)
Agriculture, Fishery, Forestry	13 (0.9 %)	135 (99.1 %)
Manufacturing & Mining	2,179 (61.7 %)	1,354 (38.3 %)
Electricity, Gas, Water Supply	55 (80.9 %)	13 (19.1 %)
Construction	323 (19.6 %)	1,329 (80.4 %)
Wholesale & Retail, Food, Hotels	591 (19.9 %)	2,375 (80.1 %)
Transport, Storage, Communication	535 (60.2 %)	354 (39.8 %)
Finance, Real Estates, Renting	442 (43.9 %)	565 (56.1 %)
Social & Personal Service	2,427 (48.3 %)	2,601 (51.7 %)

Source: Kim, Y. (2005) The figure in the parenthesis is the percent of total employment in each industrial category.

There are two notable features of the non-regular workforce in Korea. First, according to Nam and Kim (2000) and Ryu (2001), who examine the job transferability of non-regular workers through a time-series analysis of the EPS data, those peripheral workers in Korea are trapped in non-regular jobs, rather than being able to step into regular jobs. Nam and Kim (2000) note that only 1 % of non-regular workers succeed in being permanently transferred to regular jobs, while over 80 % of them, exiting from their marginal jobs, tend to return to non-regular employment status within two years. These findings highlight that the Korean labour market is, to a certain extent, fragmented between regular and non-regular jobs. In a similar vein, Ahn et al. (2002) indicate that the segmentation of labour markets between the two worker groups is a structural problem, rather than a temporal phenomenon under the context of economic crisis. Secondly, a substantial portion of the non-regular workforce in Korea is employed in precarious jobs against their will. That is, although many non-regular workers want to have regular jobs, they are employed as 'disposable labour', because employers have increasingly avoided increasing their regular employment contracts. The involuntary employment of non-regular workers is evidenced by industry-level case studies regarding non-regular jobs. For instance, the Korea Metal Workers Federation (KMWF) (2003) reports that 61.6 % of surveyed contract workers in the metal industry have no chance of obtaining regular jobs and, therefore, are forced to take non-regular employment. Another study on the banking industry presents a similar story, that married women who have banking experience and want to be re-hired after childbirth or childcare stand little chance of obtaining regular jobs, because most banks constrain female job applicants from being re-employed as regular employees (Kwon 1996).

Polarized Working Life between Regular and Non-regular Workers

The polarizing quality of working life by employment status is exemplified by the wide wage gap that is evident between regular and non-regular workers. As illustrated in figure 2, the relative ratio of non-regular workers' average monthly wages, compared to regular workers (=100) has declined steadily from 53.7% (840 thousand won vs. 1,570 thousand won) in 2000 to 50.9% (1,120 thousand won vs. 2,200 thousand won) in 2005.[1] The discrepancy of hourly wages between the two work groups has been further widening from 57.0 in 2000 to 51.9 in 2005.

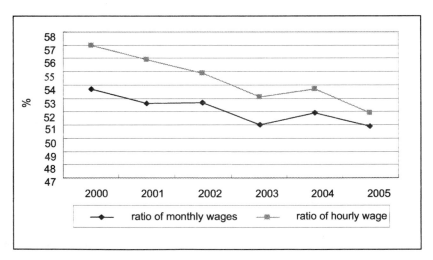

Source: Kim, Y. (2005).

Figure 2. Relative Ratio of Wage Gap between Regular and Non-regular Workers

When applying EU LoWER(Low Wage Employment Research Network) criteria, which defines a low wage as being less than two thirds of the median earnings of waged workers, 42.1% of the non-regular workforce (3,540 thousands) is placed under the category of 'low wage earners', while only 6.8% of regular workforce (440 thousands) belongs to this category. In accordance with the statutory minimum wage, which was set at 3,100 won per hour in September 2005, the number of workers who are below the minimum wage is 1,730 thousand in total, and the share of non-regular workers below the minimum wage is 94.8% (1,640 thousand). This means that one in every five non-regular workers is not protected by the statutory minimum wage.

The proliferation of cheaper non-regular labour is accompanied by the deepening inequality of wage earnings among the workforce. As demonstrated in figure 3, Gini coefficients and the ratio of wage earnings dispersion[2], both of which are indicative of wage inequity in urban households, abruptly soared in 1998 to the highest level during the past 15 years, and have since remained at that level. In light of the trend of wage earnings inequity this appears to match that of non-regular employment and the segmented working life between the regular and non-regular workforce has resulted in the increase of income inequity and social disintegration in the country.

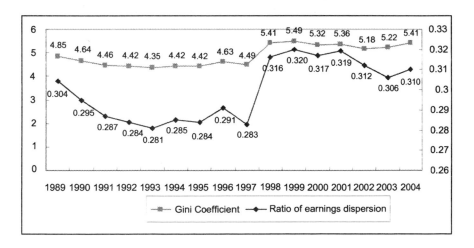

Source: KLI (2005)

Figure 3. Trends of Earnings Inequity in Urban Households, 1989-2004

Moreover, the vast majority of non-regular workers are excluded from social welfare and statutory working conditions. As shown in table 3, in 2005 only around 30% of non-regular workers were given social welfare programs, such as the national pension (32.8 %), medical insurance (33.4 %), and employment insurance (30.7 %), despite the universal coverage of the social welfare to the entire workforce by law and a gradual increase of the coverage between 2001 and 2005. This contrasts with the regular worker group, whose coverage of those welfare plans ranges from 81.6 % to 98.3 %. The case of statutory working conditions, such as severance pay (a legal payment given to employees, when they leave after one year of service) and extra work allowances (a legal premium payment for overtime (50 %) and holiday (100 %) work), is even worse (See Table 3). Besides, according to Lee, Kim, Ryu & In (2002), while a luxurious list of corporate-level benefit plans are offered to regular workers, non-regular workers are limited or totally excluded from corporate welfare benefit plans. As such, non-regular workers have suffered from the social exclusion of statutory and corporate welfare benefits as well as wages inequity.

Table 3. Beneficiary Rate of Social Welfare & Statutory Protection in 2002 & 2005

[Unit: %]		National Pension	Medical Insurance	Employment Insurance	Severance Pay	Extra Work Allowances
Regular Worker		92.7	94.8	80.0	94.3	75.6
	2005	98.0	98.3	81.6	98.2	80.6
Non-Regular Worker	2001	19.3	22.2	20.7	13.6	9.7
	2005	32.8	33.4	30.7	19.6	14.6

Source: Kim (2005).

Given these circumstances, the question is why has this disadvantaged group of non-regular employees grown so dramatically since the late 1990s. There are three main factors that explain the growth of non-regular labour. The first and most important factor to explain the growth of non-regular work is employers' market-oriented HRM strategy on the labour demand side. During the 1990s, employers pursued the externalization of employment relations, including downsizing, outsourcing, spin-offs, and the utilization of non-regular labour. In particular, employers carried out a massive downsizing of regular employees in response to the economic depression of

1997-1999, and re-filled those regular jobs with non-regular workers during the period of economic recovery (occurring since 2000). The growing use of 'external' non-regular labour by firms has been a main part of their strategic effort to gain a reduction in labour costs and numerical labour flexibility, tailored to market demand.

According to the KLI workplace panel survey, which was conducted in 2002, 32.1 % of surveyed establishments (N=832) use non-regular employment to save labour costs, while 30.3 % employ 'disposable labour' so as to be able to easily adjust in response to business situations (Ahn, Kim & Lee 2003). An additional hidden reason for the use of non-regular labour may be employers' intentions to avoid unionization, in that those marginal workers cannot be easily integrated into the current enterprise-based union structure.

A second factor that explains the growth of non-regular labour is the government's policy to promote labour market flexibility. Since the early 1990s, and particularly since the economic crisis, the government has made a sustained effort to promote the flexibility of labour markets as a key means to enhance the competitiveness of the national economy. This has occurred under the context of globalization and liberalized domestic markets, and subsequent attempts to reform labour laws have permitted employers to bring about massive lay-offs and introduce non-regular labour in the face of labour unions' strong opposition (Lee 2003a). The government's neo-liberal policy for labour market flexibility has provided favorable conditions that indirectly promote the increasing utilization of non-regular labour. Moreover, the government has expanded its use of non-regular labour, since it was obliged to employ a number of cheaper workers under budget constraints, following the massive downsizing of the public sector during the economic crisis. In fact, the increasing use of non-regular labour in the public sector (that is in schools, hospitals, post offices, and many public enterprises) helps them to justify these employment practices by utilizing flexible workers in the private sector.

A third factor is the weakening of union power regulating employers' use of non-regular labour. This is illustrated by a sharp decline in union density. Union density peaked at 18.6 % in 1989, following political democratization in mid-1987, and has since fallen to 11 % in 1997 and continued on a downward trend thereafter. Although the union movement in Korea has been militant, unions have not been able to effectively constrain employers from using non-regular labour and pressure the government to protect those vulnerable workers. Lee (2005) argues that Korean labour unions are trapped in a crisis of solidarity, through protecting 'insiders (regular workers)' within the narrow boundary of enterprise unionism and therefore reinforcing workforce segmentation.

NON-REGULAR LABOUR IN THE BANKING SECTOR

Although employers' effort to introduce flexible, less costly, and performance based systems had already started in the early 1990s, the intensity of changes in employment relations triggered by the financial crisis was unprecedented. The banking industry in particular suffered from the crisis as so many companies went bankrupt due to the enormous debts they carried. Together with other institutional and market changes, including increasing foreign investments, mergers, and deregulation, the industry has undergone the most dramatic industrial restructuring process in the economic crisis period. For example, foreign share has dramatically increased in the banking industry and more than 55% of share was owned by foreign investors as of 2004. This increase appears to affect managerial strategies and restructuring plans which now lean towards short-term, cost-containment and profit maximization.

A rapid increase in non-regular workforce has been the most conspicuous result of the cost-driven restructuring process. In the banking industry, the existence of a former gender based, dual career and wage structure within a firm's internal labour markets existed until the early 1990s. Since that period there has been a slow growth of direct-hire temps between 1993 (just after the former dual structure) and 1997. This led employers to choose the option of re-building a secondary employment subsystem with temporary or fixed term workers as the option gave benefits to employers of reducing additional costs which were attached to the uncertainty of other flexibility options.

Fixed term work has been the dominant type of nonstandard employment in the retail banking industry to date (Ahn, Kim, Chun & Kim 2004).[3] By definition, fixed term employment means that employers hire some workers directly on a contract basis with a fixed ending point, determined by the completion of a task or date (Kalleberg, Reskin & Hudson 2000; Houseman 1999). A fixed term contract tends to mean short-term employment but this is not the case in the Korean banking industry. Banks have replaced regular jobs with fixed-term hires mostly for frontline customer service positions. Moreover, they often get the fixed-term contracts renewed over time as they still require stable quality services from renewed fixed-term employees. Hence, direct-hire fixed term workers are more likely to become perma-temps (employed for years as "temporary," without equivalent benefits to those enjoyed by permanent employees).

The period between 1997 and 2000 saw the most significant changes in employment relations, accompanying massive downsizing and increases in temps. It is notable that the restructuring pressure was harsh enough for the banking unions to finally agree with 32 percent in employment reduction even after their first strike ever in union history. The results of this first round of restructuring significantly decreased both the number of banks and the number of employees. Five banks were ordered to close their business by the Financial Supervisory Committee and five small banks were merged with larger ones. This means that the number of banks decreased by 30 percent (30 into 20). At the same time, approximately 40,000 fulltime regular employees (out of 130,000 employees) lost their jobs by either getting discharged or accepting early retirement package.[4] In contrast, temporary workers increased: 5,400 contingent workers were hired in the same period.

Table 4 shows the changes in the employment composition of the major nation-wide retail banks before and after the crisis (between 1996 and 2002), It demonstrates just how dramatic were the changes that have followed the restructuring process in the industry.

Table 4. Employment Changes in the Retailing Banking Sector:

between 1996~2002.

Changes of employment between '96~'02	Bank A	Bank B	Bank C	Bank D	Bank E	Bank F	Bank G	Bank H
% of Changes in regular jobs	-35	-21	-35	-44	-48	-39	-42	-29
(% of changes in employment)	(-15)	(-31)	(-31)	(-45)	(-43)	(-35)	(-35)	(-26)
Upper manager	-44.3	-50.5	-35.9	-77.6	-37.0	-59.3	-46.4	-41.8
General managers: 3rd grade	60.6	22.2	118.8	16.8	-27.0	-10.1	-23.1	-14.1
Team managers: 4th grade	2.4	-6.2	-54.4	-20.9	-5.6	-4.6	-29.2	-13.5
Clerks and Tellers 5/6th grade	-56.5	-48.9	-39.7	-54.6	-63.1	-49.8	-49.8	-47.6
Temps	260.7	-14.4	38.1	-41.8	-0.9	16.4	70.4	69.9
% of temps in '02	34.2	25.1	21.7	14.3	20.8	21.3	24.9	32.0
Total employees in '02	27,910	5,993	6,875	11,905	5,403	8,456	9,471	4,392

Source: Financial Supervisory Services (1996-2000), Annual Statistics of Bank Management, each year

Table 4 suggests that employers substituted fixed-term employees for regular front-line service jobs. In fact, the first row in Table 4 shows the percentage of changes in regular jobs as well as in all jobs. This confirms that employers buffered the shock of sudden and massive scale downsizing by hiring a great number of fixed-term employees. This implies that banks reshuffled their internal labour markets by bringing about the separation of teller jobs that had been incorporated into the internal labour market during the last decade from the core internal labour market. Another implication from the table is that the employment restructuring process is closely linked to gender structure. This is because the uneven discharge based on job rank reflects gender differentiation as well as skill differentiation evidenced by the fact that fixed-term employees hired for the front-line service jobs were nearly all women.

As mentioned above, it is also noteworthy that banks have attempted to stabilize the secondary employment subsystem with direct-hire-temps. The evidence is twofold: a) the secondary subsystem continues to grow and b) the workers' tenure in the secondary subsystem has been longer than is usually expected for fixed term workers. Moreover, nation-wide banks increased the number of female temps by 30%, from 14,324 in December 2002 to 18,460 in June 2003. This trend moved in the opposite direction from the hiring trend of regular employees which increased merely 0.7% during the same period. As shown in table 5, the number of direct-hire-temps working less than a year with their employers is fewer than the temps with more than 5 years of service (18.6% versus 21.3%) in the financial industry. Although workers with 1~2 years of tenure still consist of the largest group (25.7%) of temps, it appears that long term employment of more than 3 years is also fairly common in the financial industry (42%), which may stem from the customary employment practice of multiple contract renewals.

Table 5. Tenure of Temporary Workers in the Financial Sector (2003)

Less than a year	1~2 years	2~3 years	3~4 years	4~5 years	5+ years
18.6	25.7	13.5	10.5	10.5	21.3

Source: Contingent Work Supplement of Economically Active Population Survey (NSO, 2003)

Table 6. Employer Motivations for Using Non-regular Work Arrangements

	% of Positive Response			Primary Reason (%)		
	All	Large firm	Banking Industry	All	All Manufac	All Service (financial)
Cost containment	**54.6**	**63.1**	**70**	**23.2**	**23.6**	**23.0(26.8)**
No bonus pay	38.0	34.5	30	1.5	2	1.6(0.0)
No soc welfare	16.4	12.6	-	0.5	0.9	0.2(0.0)
No benefit	25.8	26.3	40	0.1	0.0	0.2(0.0)
Employment Flexibility	**76.0**	**73.4**	**70**	**30.6**	**34.5**	**28.2(26.8)**
Seasonal/temporal needs	28.8	28.3	10	0.9	0.9	9.2(2.4)
Easier dismissal	**66.4**	**74.7**	**80**	**21.2**	**18.9**	**22.7(26.8)**
Job simplicity	50.4	54.3	30	6.6	4.4	7.9(4.9)
Short term tasks	21.9	19.8	10	1.5	2.1	1.1(0.0)
Jobs avoided by regular workers	50.9	51.2	40	8.6	7.7	9.2(7.3)
Special knowledge/skill	21.6	24.2	30	3.2	3.8	2.9(4.9)
Avoid labour disputes	8.9	11.3	-	0.5	0.9	0.2(0.0)
N	895	293	10	895	339	556(41)

Source: KLI Workplace Panel Survey (2005)

As the data in table 6 shows, employers in the banking industry had higher positive responses to 'cost containment (70%)' and to 'easier dismissal (80%)' for explaining the use of nonstandard workers than those given by other large firms in general. Hence, in the banking industry, employers' main purpose for expanding the secondary employment subsystem was to reduce the burden of high wage costs and to make their organizations leaner. Managers claimed that they found it hard to respond effectively and swiftly to soaring competition and the extending boundaries of the product market with their existing costly and rigid internal labour market systems.

One of the main reasons for banks to use a significant level of temps may be the lower costs of wages and benefits paid to temps. As a result, significant wage disadvantages have become the hallmark of secondary employment subsystems where perma-temps are dominantly placed. In the Korean banking sector: regular workers have obtained a significant wage premium relative to the wages of direct-hire-temps..

Table 7. Worker Characteristics, Union Coverage, and Wages in the Banking Sector

	Temp_ Female	Regular_ Female	Regular_ Male
Average Tenure	3.1	7.1	10.3
Average Age	34.0	28.8	37.2
Average Schooling Years	12.8	13.7	15.2
% of working in Nonunion workplaces	56.4	37.4	28.9
% of non-union members in union workplaces	33.6	5.6	10.4
% working in union without choosing membership	7.9	11	10.8
% of Union Member	2.0	45.6	49.8
Average Monthly Wages (1,000 won)	126.4	169.2	286.2

Source: Korea National Statistical Office, Contingent Supplement to Economically Active Population Survey, 2003.

Table 7 compares some basic conditions between temporary female workers and regular employees such as individual characteristics and union representation while also comparing their average wages. As displayed in Table 7, workers' outcomes differ greatly along the lines of employment status, and temps are disadvantaged in wage terms to a great extent. Female temps — only females are shown in the table because women are the overwhelming majority among temps in the financial sector — are paid only 55 percent of regular workers' wage.

Table 7 also shows that, the proportion of temps with union representation is far lower than that of regular employees. It is worth observing that currently 33.6 percent of temps are working at unionized workplaces but do not have the opportunity to become a union member. While 45.6 percent of the regular employees are unionized, only 2 percent of the temps are.

The Korean Financial Industry Union recently conducted a survey on temporary employment and their working conditions (KFIU 2003), and found that temps annually earned 16,460,000 won on average (approximately 15,000 dollars), which is 41.4 percent of average regular employees' annual wages (39,900,000 won). Also, while the percentage of temps who earned less than 18,000,000 won was about 70%, regular employees, whose annual wages were less than 25,000,000 won, were only 9.7%. In general, other things being equal, a temporary workers' wage level is about 40 percent of regular employees. The gap concerning company-provided benefits is even wider between direct-hire-temps and regular employees than that of the wage gap. This is an important point because company-provided benefits are a crucial welfare source in Korea. At the same time they have been a key source of differentiation between large firms core labour markets and others. The banks have developed the most generous benefit structure among all Korean firms. Indeed, as Houseman (2001) discussed, savings on benefit costs are regarded as one of the most important factors in employer decisions for using flexible staffing arrangements. In fact, around 40% of bank employers gave a positive answer when asked if they use non-regular workers because they said that they do not need to pay (many) benefits to such employees. The claim that firms, which have developed a better benefit structure, are more likely to use temporary work is applicable to Korean banks (Houseman and Osawa 2003). According to a survey conducted by the Financial Industry Union, the difference in benefits seems to be a more crucial reason for using temps when employers seek to pursue a cost containment policy: Some of the potential benefits are as follows and indeed this shows a large gap between temps and regular employees: support for private pension plan (93.9% vs. 16.6%), monthly one day paid leave (84.2% vs. 42.5%), annual bonus (99.3% vs. 19.4%), annual profit sharing (76.8% vs. 20.1%), support for housing loan (94.8% vs. 4.4%), support for education costs for children (94.4% vs. 2.4%), and support for employee's own educational costs (86.7% vs. 4.6%). If one considers the amount of support for each item, the differences may be even greater.

The results of both wage and benefit differentials imply that saving compensation was the major motivation for implementing a secondary subsystem concerning the internal labour market and for filling out the subsystem with temporary workers in the retail banking industry. Moreover, Korean labour laws that do not effectively regulate employment arrangements and that lack strong wage parity regulations contribute to employers decision to increase the numbers of temporary workers (Lee 2003b). Recently, as the issue of wage discrimination against non-regular workers has been often brought up to public, employers have attempted to reorganize workplaces by separating regular workers' tasks from temporary workers' ones. By doing this, employers attempted to advocate that the wage differentials between the two result from separate work units and tasks. Yet, the separation of work processes and products is not obvious in retail banks.

NON-REGULAR WORK IN THE AUTO SECTOR

One of the most prominent non-regular employment patterns in the manufacturing industry, including the auto sector, is contract work. The KLI Workplace Panel survey revealed that 57.2% of 682 manufacturing firms claimed to use contingent labour, including 31.4% who specifically used contract labour (Ahn et al. 2003). This may be a conservative estimate for the auto industry: according to a Korea Metal Workers' Union Federation survey of large (+400 employees) metal manufacturing establishments, the share of contract workers among contingent labour in the sampled firms was 71% (KMWF 2001). This section sketches the trends and working conditions of contract workers in the auto sector, by focusing on a major Korean auto company, MOTOR K (alias). Given the lack of sufficient industry-level data concerning non-regular labour in the auto sector, Motor K is an interesting case, in that it is the largest auto maker having nearly 50% of domestic market share and has played a role of pattern-setter in employment relations of the auto sector as well as the metal industry. This company is also a typical case to illustrate how to use contract labour in auto production lines.

Contract workers are employed by small contracting firms who allocate the workers to Motor K with whom they have contracted to supply labour. The employment arrangement for contract workers is often referred to as triangular. In terms of the legal framework of employment relations, contract workers belong not only to the subcontract firm which employs them as an official employer and pays for their labour services, but also to the client company (i.e. Motor K) that uses their labour services as a real employer.[5] The client company pays for work or labour services provided by the subcontractor during the contracted period. In Korea, the client company's remuneration to contract work is determined in one of the following three ways: by production output (the volume contract), or by hourly pay rates (the pay rate contract), or by fixed pay amount per worker (the headcount contract). Motor K pays for contract work in the form of pay rate contract.

Motor K began to use contract workers in manufacturing plants in 1986. Up until 1997, the number of contract workers increased steadily to over five thousand (including four thousand for main production and production support), while regular workers stabilized. The 1998 economic crisis led to a sharp decline in the numbers of both kinds of workers, as illustrated in Table 8. The size of the contract workforce dropped to around three thousand in 1998, when the company took unprecedented action to downsize the number of regular employees by over ten thousand (Lee 2002). Owing to rapid economic recovery and the accompanying expansion of auto production since 1999, Motor K increasingly hired contract workers, more than doubling their number between 1999 and 2003. This reflects Motor K's policy of hiring contract labour rather than regular workers as demand expands, a policy which management justify on the grounds that to do otherwise (hiring regular employees) would reduce labour flexibility and increase labour costs, as well as increase the organizational power of the labour union (Lee & Frenkel 2004). By 2003, contract workers at Motor K comprised 22.9% of the total production workforce, compared to 13.4% in 1998. In addition, there are secondary contract workers who are employed by subcontract firms affiliated with auto parts companies and working inside the plant area of Motor K for feeding auto parts into production lines. The size of those secondary contract workers is around 750.

Now, contract labour has been deployed in the following three areas: i) main production (i.e. departments of manufacturing), ii) production support (i.e.

departments of maintenance, material handling, quality assurance, and distribution), iii) indirect operation (i.e. cleaning, dining, and plant guards). Prior to 1997, the company allocated contract work to sub-production lines, yet has deployed newly employed contract workers to main production lines from 1999 in order to deal with the shortage of regular production labour, that derived from the 1998 downsizing. As a result, assembly plants have a blended arrangement of both contract and regular employees working side-by-side on the main production lines.

Table 8. Trends in Regular and Contract Production Workers, Motor K, 1997-2003

Workers' status	1997	1998	1999	2000	2001	2002	2003
Contract	5,334	3,034	3,173	5,787	6,476	6,650	6,980
Regular	26,265	19,602	22,332	22,465	22,409	22, 449	23,563

Source: Lee & Frenkel (2004).

Subcontract firms, totalled 125 at the end of 2003. They are generally small in size working with an average of 55.8 contract workers. The size of contract employment at subcontract firms ranges from less than 10 to 129 at maximum (Lee 2004). The averaged duration of their operation with Motor K was only 42.4 months at the end of 2003, which indicates that a majority entered the subcontracting business between 1999 and 2000. It is also worth noting that owners of many of the subcontract firms are former managers and supervisors retired from Motor K.

Now, the subcontract management team of the personnel policy division[6] supervises subcontract firms and their contract employees in production areas, while the general operation department deals with contract workers for general operation areas. It should be noted that the company's policy emphasis in the use of contract labour has shifted from the reduction of labour costs to the increasing of labour flexibility since 1999. According to a senior manager, top management at Motor K, who experienced the tumultuous process of the 1998 downsizing due to the union's tough opposition, began to recognize the significance of subcontracting, which enables them to flexibly adjust and deploy contract labour on production lines in response to the fluctuation of market demand and the rigid work practice of regular employees. In 1998, the company suffered a heavy production loss of 101 thousand units (amounting to 983.4 billion won), resulting from the union-led 36 day strike action against the downsizing (Lee 2002).

As illustrated in Table 9, an employee survey, conducted in 2002, shows that contract workers are younger and have much shorter service years (about 2 years) than regular workers. Compared to regular employees in production, who are male and mostly married, the contract workforce comprises a substantial portion of unmarried and female workers, while educational background is identical between the two worker groups. The female contract workers are mostly deployed to such production support areas as final testing and export shipping, which requires their sharp-eyed quality inspection. Note that the monthly turnover rate of contract workers has sharply declined from over six percent in 2002 to below one percent in 2005. This is largely because of the steady improvement of their economic and working conditions.

Table 9. Comparison of Regular and Contract Employees

		Regular workers (N=95)	Contract workers (N=450)
Length of tenure		160.6 months	23.6 months
Age		38.8	31.1
Marriage	Married	94.7%	43.0%
	Unmarried	5.3%	57.0%
Gender	Male	98.9%	87.8%
	Female	1.1%	12.2%
Education	Middle school	3.2%	11.5%
	High school	78.9%	74.5%
	College	17.9%	14.0%

Source: Lee (2004)

Contract workers at Motor K have suffered from discriminatory working conditions in many aspects, although their work is similar to, and even more difficult than, those of regular workers. Above all, as shown in Table 10, wide wage differentials exist between regular workers and contract workers. The hourly wage of contract workers is approximately 60% below that of regular workers on average. Even though contract workers' service is around two years on average, their hourly wage is lower than the entry-level hourly wage of newly hired regular workers. In light of additional compensation, such as bonuses and cash incentives, the wage gap is even wider, as displayed in Table 10. In 2003, the average monthly pay of contract workers was below 50% of regular workers pay. When comparing the two worker groups with the same length of service years (two years), the pay for contract workers was approximately 70% of regular workers pay. Although social welfare plans, such as unemployment insurance, occupational accident insurance, medical insurance, and national pension, are guaranteed for contract workers, fringe benefit plans, which subcontract firms provide, are inferior to those offered by Motor K to regular workers. As a result, the low pay and inferior company welfare programs are a core source of discontent among Motor K contract workers.

Table 10: Comparison of Wages between Contract and Regular Workers

(Unit: Won)

		2002		2003	
		Hourly wage	Monthly pay	Hourly wage	Monthly pay
Contract workers		2,786 (100)	1,088,348 (100)	3,090 (100)	1,222,596 (100)
Regular Workers	Entry-level	3,387 (121.6)	1,562,177 (143.5)	3,795 (122.8)	1,731,825 (141.7)
	Average	4,905 (176.1)	2,355,104 (216.4)	5,313 (171.9)	2,524,753 (206.5)

Note: The figure in the parenthesis is the relative ratio of regular workers' wages, compared to contract workers. Monthly pay is calculated, based on 232 working hours per month, including bonuses and other cash incentives.

Source: Lee (2004)

Another discrimination that contract workers have experienced concerns their lack of union representation. In Motor K, there is an enterprise union representing hourly production workers and salaried employees of low rank (below deputy manager). Contract workers are excluded from membership of the Motor K union, and are unable to organize their own unions in subcontract firms, since management at Motor

K has taken a tough stance on the unionization of subcontract firms. For instance, Motor K cancelled work assignments for two subcontract firms, which were unionized early in 2000. In 2003, however, contract workers finally succeeded in organizing their labour union, and put many demands, including direct negotiation, to Motor K management. The demands made by the contract workers union have been disregarded by Motor K management, and the core union leaders were dismissed due to their illegal work stoppages. Now, only 600 contract workers maintain the membership of their union, in the face of the suppression of Motor K management. As a result, the majority of contract workers are not represented or protected by labour unions, in contrast to regular workers whose interests have been enhanced by the Motor K union. This is a key source of differentiation in employment conditions between the two worker groups. At the same time, it is noteworthy that the Motor K union administration has made efforts to improve contract workers' employment conditions during recent years. In fact, union leaders were confronted with pressure from nation-wide labour organizations and NGOs to demand the protection of non-regular labour over the precarious working conditions of contract workers within Motor K. They discussed the enhancement of employment practices through joint meetings with the company's senior management. From 2000 until the present time the regular workers union has undertaken collective bargaining with Motor K management on behalf of the contract workers, and this has resulted in substantial wage increases and improvements in working conditions. Because the economic conditions for regular workers have also been enhanced as a result of annual negotiation during recent years, the discriminatory gap between the insiders (regular workers) and outsiders (contract workers) has not been greatly reduced.

Another discriminatory point is in the relationship between regular and contract workers. In most places, contract workers assume the least desirable part of their production lines, because they are deployed to the so-called 3D jobs (difficult, dirty, dangerous jobs) as a result of shopfloor-level labour-management bargaining. Regular workers (and union stewards) have used contract labour as a buffer to ease their work burden and dump the undesirable jobs. Moreover, contract workers have experienced social discrimination at workplace, in that they are excluded from the use of resting lounges and work supplies assigned for regular workers. In short, contract workers have suffered from moral exclusion from regular workers' shopfloor community (Lee & Frenkel 2004).

CONCLUSION: POLICY IMPLICATIONS

Now, Korea is confronted with a grave social problem of growing labour segmentation and polarized working life, mainly derived from the proliferation of the non-regular workforce and their discriminatory employment conditions. The fact that non-regular workers have commonly experienced workplace discrimination that differentiates their working life from those of regular workers, albeit with some variation of non-regular work across industries (that is the perma-temps in the banking sector and contract labour in the auto sector), creates dissatisfaction among working people and, as a result, draws attention from the labour unions and the government. In order to tackle this problem, the authors make several policy suggestions, based on the analysis of the factors discussed here that influence the widening gap in employment conditions between regular and non-regular workers. First, the government, which pursued the neo-liberalistic restructuring of labour markets over the past decade, needs to re-align its labour policy to harmonize economic efficiency and social equity from the long-term perspective, in that the market-driven policy is likely to produce the polarization of QWL in the working population and result in social tensions. In a word, the government needs to constrain employers' excessive use of non-regular labour, which is currently damaging social integration in Korean workplaces.

Secondly, the reform of labour laws to protect non-regular labour is a matter of utmost urgency. A tripartite dialogue to tackle the issue of non-regular labour has thus far failed to produce relevant labour law reform, due to a conflict of interest between labour unions and employers. Therefore, the government needs to take the initiative for balancing the interests of organized labour and employers and persuading both parties to accept the need to restructure the existing segmented labour market. Revised labour laws should include protective provisions to reduce the gap in employment conditions between regular and non-regular workers. The functional flexibility of regular workforce also needs to be promoted in order to ease employers' burden of rigid and expensive utilization of regular labour, which led them to increasingly use non-regular employment. Furthermore, statutory regulation should strictly enforce employers' infringement of non-regular workers' labour rights, and a policy plan to enable labour unions and NGOs to supervise employers' illegal use of non-regular labour could be implemented in light of the shortage of government resources.

Lastly, labour unions will need to transform their bargaining and organizational structure from the current enterprise-based model to a more centralized one in order to effectively represent the interests of non-regular labour. This is affirmed by research findings in Lee and Kim (2003) and Kim (2003), arguing that a centralized bargaining structure is likely to limit employers' use of non-regular labour. In this vein, the government needs to be supportive of labour unions' strategic move towards centralized bargaining as an indirect means to regulate employers' excessive reliance on non-regular labour.

The proliferation of non-regular work in Korea is closely associated with the influence of globalization, which became salient in the 1990s and has, to a certain extent, transformed the contour of employment relation practices, particularly since the economic crisis of 1998. In the context of globalization, the growing use of non-regular labour has been commonly observed in every industrial sector of the country. In fact,, the banking and auto sectors have seen management's increasing utilization of non-standard workforce, which has mainly targeted on the cost reduction and labour flexibility, yet also created crucial workplace problems, such as bipolarized employment structure and intensified tension among management, regular workers and those marginal workers in the recent years. Given the commonality of non-regular work in terms of the increasing size and problematic issues, the two sectors differ in the specific form of non-regular employment in use: direct-hire fixed-term workers in the banking sector versus contracted workers in the auto sector. This difference is chiefly attributed to management's strategic choice of each sector, conditioned by the production processes and labour relations.

In short, the baptism of globalization has transformed the Korean economy in the neo-liberal direction, and, as a consequence, posed crucial challenges of labour segmentation to working people. The bipolarization between regular and non-regular workers is the most critical policy issue to be tacked by the government and civil society in Korea.

REFERENCES

Ahn, J., Cho, J. and Nam, J. (2002) *Situation of Non-regular Labour and Policy Issues (II)*, Seoul: Korea Labour Institute. (in Korean).

Ahn, J., Kim, D. and Lee S. (2003) Situation of Non-regular Labour and Policy Issues (III), Seoul: Korea Labour Institute. (in Korean.

Ahn, J., Kim, D., Chun, B, and Kim, J. (2004*), Labour in the Financial Industry before and after the Recent Economic Crisis*, Seoul: Korea Labour Institute.

Financial Supervisory Service (1996~2002) *Annual Statistics of Bank Management.*

Houseman, S. (1999) *Flexible Staffing Arrangements: A Report on Temporary Help, On-Call, Direct-Hire Temporary, Leased, Contract Company, and Independent Contractor Employment in the United States*, www.upjohn.org

Houseman, S. (2001) 'Why employers use flexible staffing arrangements: evidence from an establishment survey', Industrial and Labour Relations Review, 55 (1), 149-160.

Houseman, S. and Osawa, M. (2003) *Nonstandard Work in Developed Economies*, Upjohn Institute.

Kalleberg, A., Reskin, B. and Hudson, K. (2000) 'Bad jobs in America: standard and nonstandard employment relations and job quality in the United States', American Sociological Review, 65 (2); 256-278.

Korea Financial Industry Union (KFIU) and Korea Contingent Workers Center (2003) Employment Conditions of Nonstandard Workers and Union strategies of Unionization. (in Korean)

Kim, Y. (2003) 'The forces propelling the growth of the nonstandard workforce in the Korean labour market: cross-section and time-series analyses', Ph.D. Dissertation of Economics Dept., Korea University. (in Korean).

Kim, Y. (2005) 'Size and situation of non-regular labour: analysis of EPS additional survey', *Labour and Society*, 105, 10-49.

Korea Labour Institute. (2005) *2005 KLI Labour Statistics*, Seoul: KLI.

Korea Metal Workers Federation (2003) *A Study on the Situation of Contract Workers in the Metal Industry*, Seoul: Korea Contingent Workers Center. (in Korean)

Kwon, H. (1996) *Situation of Non-regular Workers and Labour Movement*, Seoul: FKTU Research Center (in Korean).

Lee, B. (2002) 'Industrial restructuring and employment relations in the Korean auto industry', *Bulletin of Comparative Labour Relations*. 45, 56-94.

Lee, B. (2003a) 'Globalization and industrial relations in Korea'. *Korea Journal*, 43 (1): 261-88.

Lee, B. (2003b) 'Case Study on the Infringement of Non-regular Workers Labour Rights', in FKTU Research Center (ed.), *Problems of Non-regular Labour and Unions*, 21-70. (in Korean)

Lee, B. (2004) 'Employment relations of subcontract firms in the auto industry', in S. Cho (ed.), *Subcontract Structure and Hierarchical Employment Relations in the Korean Auto Industry*. Seoul: KLI. (in Korean)

Lee, B. and Kim, Y. (2004) 'Segmented quality of working life, regular vs. non-regular workers in Korea', in W. Glatzer (ed.), Challenges for Quality of Life in the Contemporary World. Dordrecht: Kluwer Academic Publishers.

Lee, B. and Frenkel, S. (2004) 'Divided workers: social relations between contract and regular workers in a Korean auto company', Work, Employment and Society, 18 (3): 507-530.

Lee, B., Kim, Y., Ryu, M. and In S. (2002) *A Study on Labour Policy to Promote Corporate Infringe Benefits*. Working Paper presented to the Ministry of Labour. (in Korean).

Nam, J. and Kim, T. (2000) 'Non-regular labour, bridge or trap?', *Korean Journal of Labour Economic*, 23 (2): 85-105 (in Korean).

Ryu, K. (2001) 'Situation of nonstandard workers: analysis of workforce survey. Presented at the 2001 KLEA Conference, Seoul. (in Korean).

Tsui, A., Pearce, H., Porter, L., and Hite, J. (1995) 'Choice of employee-organization relationship: influence of external and internal organizational factors', *Research in Personnel and Human Resources Management,* 13: 117-51.

Way, P. (1992) 'Staffing strategies: organizational differences in the use of temporary employment', Industrial Relations Research Association 44th Annual Proceedings, 332-39.

[1] As of early 2006, the exchange rate of 1,000 Korean won is approximately equal to one US dollar

[2] The ratio of earnings dispersion is calculated by the sum of top 20 % workers' wage earnings divided by that of bottom 20 % workers' wage earnings.

[3] Because the Contingent Work Supplement of Economically Active Population Survey administered by NSO (National Statistical Office) in 2003 only provides one-digit industrial categories, we unfortunately can not provide exact information of the distribution of nonstandard workers in order to support our general observation in the retail banking industry. However, there is a clue as to recognizing how predominant the fixed-term hires are. Only the two categories, direct-hire temps and independent contractors explain 98% of nonstandard work arrangements in the financial sector including the retail banking industry. Given the fact that independent contractors who are prevalent in the sales occupations in the insurance industry have never been used in the retail banking sector, we can conclude that direct-hire temps is the dominant type of nonstandard employees in the retail banking industry as we portrayed earlier.

[4] This number also includes the employees who worked for the bankrupted banks. Some of the employees were rehired by other banks by some agreements between the banks.

[5] Temporary help agency (or dispatched) and on-call workers are under the similar employment arrangement. Yet, these non-regular work patterns are different from contract labour, in terms of who to control them at workplace. The former is controlled by the client firm's managers, while the latter is supervised by the subcontract firm's management.

[6] The subcontract management team, was affiliated with the production support division prior to late 2004, moved to the personnel policy division, considering increasing labour relations issues among contract workers.

Chapter 12

EMPLOYMENT IN TRANSITION:
CHANGES IN JAPAN SINCE THE 1980s

Kunio Hisano[1]

A SUCCESSION OF CHANGES SINCE THE 1980s

In the 1980s the Japanese economy experienced a succession of changes which had a significant impact on the employment and occupational structure of the workforce. These included: the rapid adoption and diffusion of microelectronic technologies in the machinery sector during the 1980s; and the appreciation of the yen, followed the Plaza Accord in 1985. Japanese firms reacted by increasing their offshore production, particularly in China and East Asia. This contributed to the greater globalization of the Japanese economy. Finally, nearly two decades of union movement reorganization occurred with the formation of the national union centre 'Rengo' (*Nippon Rodo Kumiai Sorengokai*, Japanese Trade Union Confederation) which was formed in 1989. Section one of this chapter discusses these changes, section two examines the changes in the composition of workers by industry and occupation, while the final section concludes that the impact of these changes has been the degradation of employment, leaving enterprise unions at a crossroads.

The Micro-Electronics and Information Technology Revolution

The Micro-Electronics and Information Technology revolution led to the convergence of the numerical control of machine tools in line with the development of computer technology. The transition from the tool to the machinery stage in the development of technology has broken, in the technological sense, the dependence on the skill of the tradesperson, which has been replaced by machinery. In other words, machinery has substituted the role and skill of the worker. Previously, in the machinery sector however, the substitution of machinery in the place of workers was limited. This is because the production process still needed a quasi-craftsman's skill to transform the metals, even with the aid of machine tools. Therefore, the automated machine factory without skilled workers was not *economically* viable for all types of manufacturing. The enormous cost of building up a machine-based manufacturing operation could only be sustained in the consumer durable industries such as automobiles and household appliances where the economies of scale attained through mass production could be exploited.

Conversely, microelectronics, particularly Integrated Circuit technology, made it possible to extend the automated manufacturing process to the machinery sector. The recent advent of the System on Chip symbolizes this trend because microprocessor technology allows for the automatic control of production, which contrasts with machinery production. At best, this achieves an automatic operation. Microelectronic technologies, along with the development of Numerical Control (NC) technology, have made it possible to develop automatic control devices for machines. In this sense, a series of machines that are NC machine tools, Machining Centres (MC), which is an NC machine tool with an automatic tool changer, and Industrial Robots (IR) embody different types of technology from the manufacturing plant, which represents a further stage in the technological development[1]. While the technological development of microelectronics continues, the aim of this technology in manufacturing is the development of a factory that does not need to be touched by human hands. It should be noted that the recent attention given to Information and Communication Technology (ICT) relies on the Micro-Electronics Technological Revolution, because the application of ICT is possible on the condition that the information is changed into the binary system.

---

[1] I am grateful to Kaye Broadbent for her helpful suggestions.

Figure 1 shows the trend of the share by industry of NC machine tools and MC as the total of machine tools. The source is the Ministry of International Trade and Industry's (1995) survey *Kôsaku-Kikai Setsubi Tôkei Chôsa*. This concerned machine tools that were installed in fabricated metal products and machinery factories, which included general machinery, electrical machinery, transport equipment and precision instruments. The average percentage of NC machine tools and MC in these sectors in 1981 was just 3.48 percent which increased to 10.93 percent in 1987 and 20.97 percent in 1994. From the technological point of view, it is clear that the NC percentage was relatively high even in 1981. This was particularly the case in the following industries: the manufacture of aircraft and parts, ship-building and the repair and manufacture of marine engines, other transportation equipment, machinery and equipment for agriculture, construction and mining, metal machine tools, optical instruments and lenses, industry machinery, boilers, engines and turbines, communication equipment, electronic appliances and parts[2]. It is interesting that NC and MC rapidly diffused in the motor vehicles, parts and accessories and household electric appliances industries in the 1980s. These industries represented the Japanese industrial sector's competitive edge internationally.

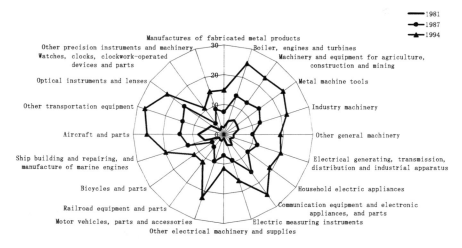

Source. The Ministry of International Trade and Industry

Figure 1. Numerical Control and Machining Centre's Share of Total Machine Tools by Minor Group of Industry (%, units)

CHANGES TO WORKFORCE SKILLS AND THE LABOUR PROCESS

The immediate impact of the introduction of NC technology was the deskilling of the workforce. Thus, it was likely that the diffusion of Micro-Electronic (ME) technology based on NC would contribute to the shrinking of skilled workers in the machinery sectors. A further impact was that it weakened the strength of trade unions, because those skilled workers were well represented in trade unions. In addition, the design change caused by ME led to changes in the end product – a shift to the semiconductor circuit. The impact of this was to open up semi-skilled jobs in the manufacturing sector to unskilled workers, which included outside contractors and women. In addition, the labour process, such as the assembly of the printed circuit board or wire harness, was both physically lighter and deskilled.

Japanese FDI Inflows into China

The appreciation of the yen since the Plaza Accord in 1985 compelled Japanese companies dependent on the export market to seek out cheaper labour sources overseas in order to remain competitive and to set up operations in the United States and Europe. The exchange rate value of the Japanese yen against the US dollar averaged 235 yen in 1985 but rose approximately 100 per cent to 128 yen in 1988.

Conversely, wages in Asian countries were low by Japanese standards and China initiated the 'open door' policy in the late 1970s. Indeed, Japan's direct investment particularly in China, where wages were only one-seventieth of those in Japan in 1990[3], has increased significantly since this time. According to table 1, China's share of total foreign direct investment by Japanese firms, with respect to number of cases, was only 1.9 percent in 1989. However, it has continued to rise from 13.1 (1992), 20.1 (1993) 25.7 (1994) and 26.9 (1995) percent. As far as the total amount of capital stock measured in yen is concerned, the figures were 3.1 (1992), 4.7 (1993), 6.3 (1994) and 8.7 (1995) percent respectively. This means that Japan's foreign direct investment into China in the early 1990s came from small and medium-sized enterprises[4]. Japan's trade balance with China has been in deficit since 1988 and has expanded from 50 billion yen in 1988 to 3.1 trillion yen in 2005[5]. Although, foreign direct investment in Japan by other countries remains small, Japan imports clothes and daily necessities and reimports electronic machinery from manufacturing affiliated companies in Asia, particularly China. Thus, the overseas production ratio of Japanese manufacturing corporations has risen from 3 percent in 1985 to 17 percent in 2002[6].

Table 1. Trends of Japan's Foreign Direct Investment

Year	Japanese FDI Inflows into China by Year Number of Cases, and Total Capital Stock in Yen 100million						Yen to US Dollar Rate	Inward Direct Investment Yen 100million
	Cases			Yen 100 million				
	China	%	Total	China	%	Total		
1989	126	(1.9)	6,589	587	(0.6)	90,339	138.20	3,857
1990	165	(2.8)	5,863	511	(0.6)	83,527	145.14	4,046
1991	246	(5.4)	4,564	787	(1.4)	56,862	134.29	5,896
1992	490	**(13.1)**	3,741	1,381	(3.1)	44,313	126.51	5,306
1993	700	**(20.1)**	3,488	1,954	(4.7)	41,514	110.53	3,586
1994	636	**(25.7)**	2,478	2,683	(6.3)	42,808	101.39	4,327
1995	770	**(26.9)**	2,863	4,319	(8.7)	49,568	93.83	3,697
1996	365	**(14.6)**	2,501	2,828	(5.2)	54,095	109.18	7,707
1997	258	**(10.3)**	2,495	2,438	(3.7)	66,236	121.76	6,782
1998	114	(7.0)	1,637	1,377	(2.6)	52,780	131.19	**13,404**
1999	79	(4.5)	1,744	858	(1.1)	75,292	113.22	**23,993**
2000	106	(6.2)	1,717	1,114	(2.1)	54,193	108.34	**31,251**
2001	189	**(10.6)**	1,786	1,819	(4.5)	40,413	122.15	**21,779**
2002	263	**(12.2)**	2,164	2,152	(4.8)	44,930	124.55	**21,863**
2003	332	**(13.8)**	2,411	3,553	(8.7)	40,795	115.58	**21,161**
2004	361	**(13.2)**	2,733	4,909	(12.8)	38,210	107.74	**40,265**

Sources: Ministry of Finance a

Japan's Labour Movement Post 1980

This section surveys the reorganization of Japan's labour union movement in the 1980s. Two major national centres, Sohyo (General Council of Trade Unions of Japan) and Domei (Japanese Confederation of Labour), dominated Japan's postwar union movement. Sohyo, affiliated with the World Federation of Trade Unions was a 'left-leaning' national centre for organized labour, whose membership mainly comprised government and other public sector workers' unions including the National

Railway Union. Domei was a conservative national centre affiliated with the International Confederation of Free Trade Unions. It drew its membership mainly from private sector unions. After the dissolution of Domei and two other minor national centres in 1987, a new national labour federation, Rengo (Japan **Private Sector** Trade Union Federation) was formed. Rengo comprised 55 industrial federations and 5,390,000 workers. Two years later after years of public sector privatisation in Sohyo, it dissolved and many of its affiliates followed suit and joined a new unified national centre Rengo (Japanese Trade Union Confederation). The new Rengo comprised 74 industrial federations and 7,980,000 workers representing the interests of both public and private sector workers. A small number of Sohyo's unions formed Zenroren (*Zenkoku Rodo Kumiai Sorengokai*, National Confederation of Trade Unions) or Zenrokyo as competing national centres[7].

With the birth of the unified national centre Rengo, expectations were that unions would gain greater political power but the Rengo was, in reality, a conservative organisation dominated by the major private sector industrial federations rather than a nationally representative organisation for all workers. The deregulation of labour rules was further accelerated in the 1980s as legislation was passed which continued to deregulate labour practices. The Law for Dispatch (Labour Hire) Workers was passed in 1985[8] with the law at first only applying to 26 professional jobs. This increased the scope for employers to offer and utilise short-term employment contracts. Changes to the Labour Standard Law (LSL[9]) in 1987, allowed employers to use flexible working time practices, but this could apply to a limited range of jobs. Successive changes to the LSL and Law for Dispatch Workers, widened the range of jobs where the laws could apply. Next, this chapter will discuss the changes that have occurred since the 1980s and the impact this has had on the employment structure in the following sections.

The Shift from a Manufacturing to a Service Economy

In the two decades from 1980-2000, Japan's employment has shifted from a concentration in manufacturing towards service sector occupations. Table 2 separates the industries between the goods production and services sector, and then divides the services sector into four including the distributive, producer, public-social and personal services. However, the goods-producing sector excludes the primary industries because this would exaggerate the decline in employment in this sector. Unlike other goods producing industries, the dramatic decline in agricultural employment occurred in the 1960s-70s.

Increases in the Producer Services

Between 1980-2000, the increase in total employed persons 15 years of age and over, excluding the primary industries, was 9,495,901, compared with only 20,742 in the goods-producing sector. As a result, 99.8 percent of the increase in the workforce between 1980 and 2000 came from industries in the service sector. Furthermore, of the approximate 9.5 million increase in the service sector workforce, almost half of this came primarily from producer services, then public and social services. In summary, the majority of employment shifted to the services sector. The shift occurred specifically in the manufacturing industries. Approximately 60 percent of producer service industries consist of the following: information services and research - such as computer programming and other software services, data processing, information services and news syndicates; detective agencies and credit bureaus, engineering and architectural services and other professional services, building maintenance services, security guard services, labour hire agencies and business services not classified elsewhere. There is a disparity however in the working conditions between industries in this sector. For example, while the working conditions of professional services such as information services are relatively good, those of the other business services such as building maintenance services, security guard services, and labour hire agencies, that rely heavily on outsourcing, are poor (Table 3)[10].

Table 2. Transition of Employment by Industrial Sector and Occupation in Japan (1980-2000, Employed persons 15 years of age and over, Except the Primary Industry)

Industry / Occupation	Change, 1980-2000	Total	Goods-producing 1)	Distributive services 2)	Producer services 3)	Public and social services 4)	Personal services 5)
Total		9,495,901	20,742	1,717,457	**4,328,523**	2,592,097	837,082
	2000	59,066,116	18,932,309	15,665,072	9,169,430	9,409,107	5,890,198
	1980	49,570,215	18,911,567	13,947,615	4,840,907	6,817,010	5,053,116
Crafts and Operators 6)		369,794	**-1,087,892**	754,323	957,379	1,568	-255,584
	2000	18,102,933	12,626,057	2,829,800	1,712,702	454,485	479,889
	1980	17,733,139	13,713,949	2,075,477	755,323	452,917	735,473
Indirect workers 7)		3,118,594	216,926	824,812	1,328,528	646,742	101,586
	2000	15,553,239	3,033,860	5,404,525	3,313,910	3,298,895	502,049
	1980	12,434,645	2,816,934	4,579,713	1,985,382	2,652,153	400,463
Managers & officials		-806,832	-446,902	-324,308	12,581	-31,406	-16,797
	2000	1,842,780	698,597	503,154	364,313	182,090	94,626
	1980	2,649,612	1,145,499	827,462	351,732	213,496	111,423
Sales workers		1,403,137	462,246	162,815	619,584	23,922	134,570
	2000	9,383,488	1,074,474	6,268,423	1,421,558	32,965	586,068
	1980	7,980,351	612,228	6,105,608	801,974	9,043	451,498
Professional & technical workers		**3,692,624**	922,243	118,838	1,186,038	1,433,643	31,862
	2000	8,561,158	1,470,164	275,899	2,039,354	4,634,470	141,271
	1980	4,868,534	547,921	157,061	853,316	3,200,827	109,409
Service workers		1,712,761	-47,134	180,047	221,932	516,803	841,113
	2000	5,616,331	27,878	382,079	315,071	805,338	4,085,965
	1980	3,903,570	75,012	202,032	93,139	288,535	3,244,852

Notes: 1) Mining; Construction; Manufacturing; Electricity, gas, heat supply and water.

2) Transport and communication; Wholesale and retail trade, except Eating and drinking places.

3) Financing and insurance; Real estate; Machine, upholstery, furniture, etc, repair services, except otherwise classified; Goods rental and leasing; Motion picture and video production; Broadcasting; Information services and research; Advertising; Professional services not elsewhere classified; Other business services.

4) Waste treatment services; Medical and other health services; Social, insurance and social welfare; Education; Scientific research institutes; Religion; Political ,business and cultural organizations; Other services; Foreign governments and international agencies in Japan; Government.

5) Eating and drinking places; Hotels, boarding houses and other lodging places; Other Domestic and personal services; Laundry, Beauty and bath services; Amusement and recreation services, except motion picture and video production; Automobile parking; Automobile repair services;

6) Agricultural, forestry and fisheries workers; Mining workers; Production process workers and labourers.

7) Clerical and related workers; Workers in transport and communications occupations; Protective service workers.

Sources: Ministry of Internal Affairs and Communications Statistics Bureau (2004).

Table 3. Number of persons engaged in work and features of main 6 producer services

	1989	%	1999	%	Other parties that establishments got income %		Employment status %		Wages and salaries (annual) per employee (Yen, 10thous)		
					General consumers	Enterprises and associations	Part-timers, arubaito, and so on	Temporary employees	Total	Self employer	Companies
All employees							17.4		497		
Services	8,495,968	(100.0)	11,716,691	(100.0)	41.5	56.3	24.8	4.1	398	232	415
Personal services	3,441,371	(40.5)	4,453,092	(38.0)							
Public and social services	1,779,807	(20.9)	2,471,490	(21.1)							
Producer services	3,274,788	(38.5)	4,792,107	(40.9)							
Information services and research	540,927	(6.4)	769,772	(6.6)	2.1	93.7	8.1	1.1	616	162	613
Engineering and architectural services	320,301	(3.8)	459,489	(3.9)	5.9	91.8	7.6	2.1	562	281	572
Other professional services	206,792	(2.4)	356,144	(3.0)	6.8	85.8	9.3	2.0	536	314	560
Building maintenance services	506,000	(6.0)	666,284	(5.7)	7.2	90.0	45.9	3.2	324	147	325
Guard services	171,142	(2.0)	303,664	(2.6)	3.7	95.1	30.7	11.1	335	210	335
Business services not elsewhere classified	293,647	(3.5)	613,992	(5.2)	5.7	90.8	35.4	6.6	398	194	389

Sources: Ministry of Internal Affairs and Communications Statistics Bureau a, Ministry of Health, Labour and Welfare

Decreased Crafts and Operator Workers in Manufacturing

The occupation column of Table 2 shows the changes in employment by occupation. The largest increase in the number of workers occurred in professional & technical workers, which almost doubled in the years from 1980 until 2000. Professional & technical workers include those employed as public health and medical workers and teachers. What is noteworthy is that the increase in workers in the goods production sector is in sharp contrast to the decline of the crafts and operators in these sectors. Closer inspection reveals that professional & technical workers in the manufacturing sector, which is the largest sector in the goods production sector, mainly comprised engineers and technicians.

From the above data, some conclusions can be drawn as to the impact of economic changes on employment by industry and occupation. The most obvious has been the severity of the impact of the Micro-Electronics and Information Technology Revolution on employment. This technological revolution directly affected the craft and operator occupations in the manufacturing sector and resulted in a weakening of the enterprise unions. It is difficult, however, to establish a causal relationship because it could just as easily be said that because Japan's unions are predominantly enterprise based, they have enabled the widespread diffusion of microelectronics and information technology at the factory-level. If trade unions in Japan were general unions, then the introduction of new technology, which can lead to the disappearance of some trades in factories, would have potentially met with greater resistance.

The union movement was weakened by the formation of the unified national centre Rengo, which accepted, without resistance, the labour displacement, which occurred with the introduction of ME and IT. Combined with the deregulation of working rules as part of the Japanese government's economic rationalist policy, both developments have accelerated the employment shift and weakened the union movement described above. As a result, employment conditions in the manufacturing sector are sharply segmented   along occupational lines. These comprise professional & technical workers who constitute an upper stratum and other assembly operators who occupy a lower stratum. In short, this has led to a rise in outsourcing and agency hire workers across a wide range of jobs in the manufacturing sectors, which had been difficult as a machine-based labour process. While information software services and computer programming have been outsourced to high cost operators, non-skilled jobs in the workshop and indirect work have been outsourced to contracting companies. Meanwhile, many full-time workers have been replaced by labour hire workers. These factors have also had a significant impact on the increase in business services. The workers in business services, not classified elsewhere, numbered 2,144,303 in 2000. Of this number, 878,755 are employed in the crafts and operators category[11], which represents the numbers employed from contracting companies.

THE IMPACT OF GLOBALISATION ON EMPLOYMENT

The trade pattern in post-war Japan has been characterised by export-oriented industrialization where raw materials are imported and transformed into processed manufactured exports. Japan-US trade frictions have occurred frequently, because the main export market for Japan has been the United States. Although the transition to an open economy in Japan has been slow, the appreciation of the yen following the Plaza Accord in 1985 progressed the opening up of the Japanese economy. Japan has been importing manufactured goods and machinery since the 1990s, as table 4 shows[12]. Furthermore, inward direct investment in Japan increased sharply in the late 1990s, as shown earlier in table 1. Moreover, foreign workers in Japan have been increasing since the 1990s, rising to 709,240 in 2000[13].

Over the past two decades, growth in the manufacturing workforce in Japan has been stagnant. The workforce involved in the manufacture of textile products, which is a typically labour-intensive industry, sharply declined from 972,414 in 1980 to 279,041 in 2000. Conversely, the industries in the manufacturing sector that have increased their workforce are the following: food, general machinery, electrical machinery, transportation equipment and publishing. Other industries which encompass the manufacturing sector have declined, with the textile industry experiencing the greatest decline[14]. However, it is difficult to conclude that globalization has resulted in a hollowing-out of the manufacturing sector. The machinery sectors have increased their employment numbers and a definitive horizontal division of labour between Japan and other Asian countries has not occurred. Moreover, Japan has still maintained a trade surplus in manufacturers. Rather, it could be said that a vertical division of labour, or segmentation has developed[15] over time. This issue will be further developed later on in the chapter. The following section examines employment status in greater depth.

Table 4. Trade Statistics Values by Commodity

	Import	Food and Live Animals	Crude Material	Mineral Fuels	Chemicals	Manu-factured Goods	Machinery
1980	319,953	33,264	54,322	159,324	14,126	23,058	24,864
	%	(10.4)	**(17.0)**	**(49.8)**	(4.4)	(7.2)	(7.8)
1985	310,849	37,188	43,435	133,864	19,390	26,880	32,741
	%	(12.0)	**(14.0)**	**(43.1)**	(6.2)	(8.6)	(10.5)
1990	338,552	45,724	41,344	80,832	23,208	49,743	64,091
	%	(13.5)	(12.2)	(23.9)	(6.9)	**(14.7)**	**(18.9)**
1995	315,488	47,838	30,843	50,229	23,092	47,615	86,571
	%	(15.2)	(9.8)	(15.9)	(7.3)	**(15.1)**	**(27.4)**
1999	352,680	50,401	25,508	56,463	26,369	44,973	120,734
	%	(14.3)	(7.2)	(16.0)	(7.5)	**(12.8)**	**(34.2)**
2004	492,166	53,022	30,789	106,706	38,162	48,625	151,752
	%	(10.8)	(6.3)	(21.7)	(7.8)	(9.9)	**(30.8)**
2005	569,494	55,588	35,052	145,597	43,212	54,168	165,790
	%	(9.8)	(6.2)	(25.6)	(7.6)	(9.5)	**(29.1)**

Yen 100 million

Source: Ministry of Finance c

The Fragmentation of Employment and Growing Non Standard Employment

Table 5 shows the growth in non-regular employees in manufacturing and services that occurred between 1982 and 2002. A regular employee refers to full-time employees who are engaged consistently by the company and who work on a contract with an unspecified period of employment. Non-regular workers cover other forms of employment and experience unstable employment security. The number of non-regular workers has increased 2.4-fold during the 20 years prior to 2002, namely from 6.7 million in 1982 to 16 million in 2002. In the category of non-regular workers are part-time workers[16]. In common with other countries, women dominate Japan's part-time workforce. In 2002, 7.2 million (or 92 percent) of all part-time workers were women, the majority of whom were housewives. The high proportion of married women employed part-time relates to Japan's tax system where a wage earner who earns less than 1,030,000 yen annually is exempt from income tax. In addition, their spouse can receive a tax deduction. Moreover, a wage earner with annual pay of less than 1,300,000 yen is exempt from social insurance contributions, which typically includes an employee's pension insurance and health insurance, to which employers have to co-contribute half the amount. In turn, this has contributed to the serious financial crisis in the Japanese pension system due to the ageing population and an increase in part-time employees who are exempt from pension insurance contributions.

Arubaito derives from the German 'Arbeit' (work) and in Japan it refers to temporary workers who are on a contract which may vary from a duration of less than a month to being employed on a daily basis. Whereas part-time workers are often housewives earning the family's second income, *arubaito* are mainly students who work for pocket money. Dispatched (Labour hire) workers are a recent phenomenon, as mentioned earlier, coming about because of the 1985 Law. Labour hire workers are classified into two types, general (or registration) labour hire workers and specified labour hire workers. The former register with any employment agency and work on a contract of a specific period as and when the client needs them. About 80 percent of labour hire workers are included in this category. Specified labour hire workers on the other hand, are regular employees of any employment agency that deals with 26 professional jobs such as programmers or translators. Contracted employees are workers who work on contracted jobs under the direction of a contracted company.

Table 5. Growth of Non-regular Employees, Manufacturing and Service 1982 and 2002

Thousand persons

		Employees	Executive of company or corporation	Employees, excluding executives of company 1	Regular staffs 2	Part-time workers 3	Arbaito (temporary workers) 4	Contract employees or entrusted employees 5	Dispatched workers from temporary labour agency 6	Other 7	Non-regular employees 3-7 8	Non-regular employees as a % of regular staffs 8/2	Non-regular employees as a % of employees, excluding executives of company 8/1
All industries													
1982	Both sexes	42,454	2,751	39,704	33,009	4,675		695		1,325	6,695	20.3	16.9
	Male	27,455	2,269	25,186	23,101	774		458		853	2,085	9.0	8.3
	Female	14,999	481	14,518	9,908	3,902		237		472	4,611	46.5	31.8
2002	Both sexes	54,733	3,895	50,838	34,557	7,824	4,237	2,477	721	946	16,206	46.9	31.9
	Male	32,201	2,957	29,245	24,412	628	2,096	1,309	204	544	4,780	**19.6**	16.3
	Female	22,531	939	21,593	10,145	7,196	2,141	1,169	517	402	11,426	**112.6**	52.9
Manufacturing													
1982	Both sexes	12,008	751	11,257	9,573	1,367		150		167	1,684	17.6	15.0
	Male	7,849	632	7,217	6,885	130		107		95	332	4.8	4.6
	Female	4,159	119	4,040	2,688	1,237		43		73	1,353	50.3	33.5
2002	Both sexes	11,411	753	10,659	8,144	1,500	346	374	200	80	2,500	30.7	23.5
	Male	7,734	592	7,142	6,395	150	195	245	96	49	735	**11.5**	10.3
	Female	3,677	161	3,517	1,749	1,350	151	129	103	31	1,764	**100.9**	50.2
Services													
1982	Both sexes	8,929	419	8,510	7,032	995		228		255	1,478	21.0	17.4
	Male	4,489	350	4,139	3,753	168		131		89	388	10.3	9.4
	Female	4,440	69	4,371	3,280	827		97		167	1,091	33.3	25.0
2002	Both sexes	15,977	817	15,160	10,105	2,382	1,076	189	1,016	373	5,037	49.8	33.2
	Male	7,387	626	6,760	5,398	198	498	48	469	141	1,354	**25.1**	20.0
	Female	8,591	191	8,400	4,707	2,185	578	141	547	233	3,683	**78.2**	43.8

Growing Wage and Reward Differences from Work

An important feature of the Japanese economy has been the fact that there is a wide divergence in wages, employment conditions, and fringe benefits between those employed in large companies and those employed in small companies. For example in 2004, the annual average wage of those who work in firms of ten to 99 employees was around 60 percent of those who work in firms of more than 1000 employee[17]. Related to this is the multi-stratified sub-contracting structure or pyramidal structure that is peculiar to Japanese manufacturing and which generates large discrepancies in the wages and conditions that are associated with work. In iron mills and shipyards, more than half the workers come from outside sub-contracting companies. Japanese electronics firms often choose to form an affiliated firm when they set up a new branch factory, particularly in rural areas, where employees receive lower wages and fewer benefits. This is because large companies can make more use of cheaper labour from their sub-contracting companies than they can by increasing the employment of full-time employees in their own company. This is because they would have to pay full time workers higher wages[18].

A serious issue for employment in Japan has been the wage differentials of employees based on the size of the firm. However, the situation has changed because of the differential in working conditions between regular employees and non-regular employees. This is particularly due to a wide expansion in the number of non-regular employees throughout the manufacturing sector. The number of non-regular women employees exceeded the number of regular employees in 2002. While previously most non-regular employees were female workers, numbers are now increasing among male workers with the number of non-regular male employees accounting for 20 percent of regular male employees in 2002.

THE EROSION OF THE JOB FOR LIFE MODEL

The 'job for life model' of employment practices which came to be synonymous with employment in Japan - that is long-term employment, seniority based wage payments and enterprise unions - is collapsing[19]. Working conditions in general have been eroded in the two decades since 1982. Moreover, the number of suicides per year continues to exceed 30,000 and the unemployment rate has risen to 4 percent since 1998. Although this is low compared with international figures, it is high by Japan's standards[20]. The long-lasting economic stagnation since the burst of the 'bubble' boom in 1991 has also aggravated the decline in employment conditions. The years where negative economic growth has been recorded since 1991 are 1998, 1999 and 2002[21]. Still, there seems to be a widespread sense of uneasiness about employment among workers in Japan mainly because the workers cannot adjust to the new type of employment practices. Japanese firms are likely to continue to limit the employment of regular employees and the wage system is changing from one based on seniority to a performance-based pay system. This system is being overseen by the Japanese Federation of Economic Organizations. The national centres representing Japan's labour unions have devised the annual Spring Wage Offensive (Shunto) tactic in order to restore some level of power to the Japanese enterprise unions because this tactic aims for a general increase in seniority-based wages. However, it is difficult in today's economic climate for them to continue this tactic under a performance-based pay system. Primarily this is because an individual employee's pay will vary depending on the individual employee's performance.

TRADE UNIONS UNDER PRESSURE

While unions are expected to prevent any further degradation in employment conditions, their potential effectiveness is limited. Japan's unions are largely enterprise-based where only regular employees are eligible for membership. Almost all enterprise unions in large companies have reached union-shop agreements. However, while there is significant disparity in the pay and conditions between regular and non-regular workers, their job content is virtually indistinguishable. In this way, members of enterprise unions are becoming a type of privileged worker. The privileges enjoyed by one group of workers at the expense of another has led to worker disenchantment with unions. Currently, the Japanese enterprise unions stand at a crossroads; they have become a kind of pressure group for regular employees in common with the old craft guilds. That said they could try to encourage contingent employees to unionise and aim for improving overall working conditions which include them.

CONCLUSION

Since the 1980s the Japanese economy has experienced a succession of changes which have had a significant impact on employment structures. Namely, the rapid diffusion of Micro-Electronic and Information & Communication Technologies in the machinery sector, the appreciation of the yen and the birth of the unified national centre Rengo. The ME and I & C Technology Revolution brought about the deskilling of the workforce and weakened the strength of trade unions. The appreciation of the yen while progressing globalisation in Japan, has resulted in the decline of labour-intensive industries and a weakening of worker's bargaining power. The Rengo is, in reality, a conservative national centre, which subordinates the left-leaning national centre and is dominated by the major private enterprise unions. Thus, it is helpless against the deregulation of labour rules.

Japan's employment has shifted from a concentration in manufacturing to the services sector, in particular, the business supporting producer services. Although the working conditions of the professional services, such as information services, are relatively good, the other business services such as building maintenance services, security guard services, and labour hire agencies that rely heavily on outsourcing are comparatively poor.

Furthermore, employment conditions in Japan are fragmenting with the growth of non-standard employees. This has meant a virtual end to the employment practices, which were synonymous with employment in Japan that is long-term employment, seniority based wage payments and enterprise unions. This is largely because the employment security of non-standard workers is unstable, and the wage system is changing to a performance-based pay system. The Japanese enterprise unions expect to try organising contingent employees into unions in a bid to improve overall working conditions which include them. Just how successful such a move will prove to be remains to be seen.

REFERENCES

Broadbent, K. (2002) *Women's Employment in Japan: The Experience of Part-time Workers*. Curzon Press.

Hisano, K. (1998) 'The Japanese Model of the Transition from an Industrial to Information Society', *Keizaigaku=Kenkyu* (Journal of Political Economy, Kyushu University), Vol. 64, No. 5-6, p.215-23.

Hisano, K. (2000) 'Globalisation, Sub-contracting Structures in Japan and Women's Working Conditions' *UNEAC Asia Papers* (E-journal), No.3.

(online at http://www.une.edu.au/asiacenter/UNEAC_Asia_Papers_3.html.)

Hisano, K. (ed.) (2004) *Sangyo to Rodo no New Storii (The Unexplored Proposals of Industry and Work)*. Horitsu-Bunka Sya.

Kamii, Y. and Nomura, M. (eds.) (2004) *Japanese Companies: Theories and Realities*. Trans Pacific Press.

Kubo, B. (2004) "Rodo-shijo no kokusaika" in Hisano, K. (2004) *Sangyo to Rodo no New Storii (The Unexplored Proposals of Industry and Work)*. Horitsu-Bunka Sya.

Kumazawa, M., Hane, M., Gordon, A. and Selden, M. (1996) *Portraits of The Japanese Workplace: Labor Movements, Workers, And Managers*. Westview Press.

Ministry of Economy, Trade and Industry, *Survey of Overseas Business Activities*. (online at http://www.meti.go.jp/english/statistics/data/h2c4tope.html)

Ministry of Finance a, *Foreign Direct Investment*. (online at http://www.mof.go.jp/english/fdi/reference01.xls)

Ministry of Finance b, *Financial Statements Statistics of Corporations by Industry*. (online at http://www.mof.go.jp/english/e1c002.htm)

Ministry of Finance c, *Trade Statistics*. (online at http://www.customs.go.jp/toukei/info/index_e.htm)

Ministry of Health, Labour and Welfare, *Wage Structure of Japan*. (online at http://www.mhlw.go.jp/english/database/db-l/index.html)

Ministry of Internal Affairs and Communications Statistics Bureau (2004) *Population Census of Japan*. (online at http://www.stat.go.jp/english/data/kokusei/index.htm)

Ministry of Internal Affairs and Communications Statistics Bureau a, *Survey on Service Industry*. (online at http://www.stat.go.jp/english/data/service/index.htm).

Ministry of Internal Affairs and Communications Statistics Bureau b, *Employment Status Survey*. (online at http://www.stat.go.jp/english/data/shugyou/index.htm)

Ministry of International Trade and Industry (1995) *Kôsaku-Kikai Setsubi Toke Chôsa*.

Mouer, R. and Kawanishi, H. (2005) *A Sociology of Work in Japan*. Cambridge University Press.

Noble, David F. (1984) *Forces of production : a social history of industrial automation* New York : Alfred A. Knopf.

Price, J. (1997) *Japan Works: Power and Paradox in Postwar Industrial Relations*. Cornell University Press.

---

[1] See Hisano (1998).

[2] See Noble (1984).

[3] See Hisano (2000).

[4] Ministry of Finance a.

[5] Ministry of Finance c.

[6] Ministry of Economy, Trade and Industry. Overseas production ratio = sales amount of overseas affiliates / sales amount of domestic corporations $\times$ 100, Domestic corporation: The Ministry of Finance b.

[7] On the reorganization of union movement in recent Japan, see chapter 9 of Mouer and Kawanish (2005).

[8] Law Concerning Securing the Proper Operation of Workers Dispatching Undertakings and Improved Working Conditions for Dispatched Workers

[9] The Labour Standard Law was enacted in April 1947 along with the Trade Union Law in December 1945 and the Labour Relations Adjustment Law in September 1946, as a part of the Postwar Democratic Reform by the Occupation Army. See Price (1997) chapter 2 in detail.

[10] See Hisano (2004). Though the original source is the Ministry of Internal Affairs and Communications Statistics Bureau a, the data in 2004 do not link with those in 1999, because of the change of the Standard Industrial Classification for Japan in 2003.

[11] Ministry of Internal Affairs and Communications Statistics Bureau (2004).

[12] The export structure in Japan is still same, machinery occupies most of all. It increases its share from 59.4 in 1980 to 71.3 percent in 2004.

[13] See Kubo (2004), p.122.

[14] Ministry of Internal Affairs and Communications Statistics Bureau (2004).

[15] The manufacturing offshore by Japanese firms might be for exporting to third countries, particularly the USA.

[16] The part-time worker in Japan is a worker who works less than 35 hours a week. For further details on part-time workers in Japan, see Broadbent (2002).

[17] Ministry of Health, Labour and Welfare.

[18] See Hisano (2000).

[19] On the Japanese employment practices, their problems and their history, see Kumazawa *et al*. (1996), Price (1997).

[20] Although this is often considered a distortion because of the suspected high rates of disguised unemployment.

[21] Kamii and Nomura (2004) criticizes the analysis by Koike, Aoki, Asanuma and others to praise the Japanese style management during the 'bubble' boom.

Chapter 13

GLOBALISATION AND THE EMERGENCE OF
NON-TRADITIONAL EMPLOYMENT IN SINGAPORE

Rosalind Chew and Chew Soon Beng

This chapter aims to analyze the emergence of non-tradition employment in a society characterized by a social safety net which is based on employment. In Singapore, non-traditional employment is represented by part-time workers, employers, own account workers, family contributing workers and contingent workers. The chapter begins with an overview of the Singapore economy and describes the salient features of its social safety net which essentially comprises the Central Provident Fund (CPF), supplemented by the flexible wage system to ensure maximum employment. Next, it discusses the extent to which firms can adopt various non-traditional employment methods instead of resorting to outsourcing and the use of foreign workers. After analyzing the supply side of non-traditional employment, the chapter then discusses the incentives that attract Singaporeans to choose various forms of non-traditional employment as well as the factors affecting non-traditional employment trends in Singapore. Finally, the chapter uses regression analysis to determine whether there is any correlation between the size of the part-time and contingent workforce and also to determine whether healthcare costs and the adoption of the flexible wage system affect their size.

OVERVIEW

Over the past 40 years, Singapore's economic performance has generally been sterling. Per capita income increased by more than 25 times from $1,618 in 1965 to $41,513 in 2004. Singapore's first recession in the last quarter of the 20th century occurred in late 1985, but the economy rapidly recovered by 1987. This rapid recovery was largely due to the reduction in employers' Central Provident Fund contribution rate from 25% to 10%. Unwilling to rely on the social security scheme as a macro-economic instrument, the Government and National Wages Council (NWC) has since then actively promoted the flexible wage system.

The Singapore economy enjoyed another period of strong growth until the onslaught of the 1997 East Asian Currency Crisis. In contrast to the neighboring countries, the Singapore economy was able to withstand the Crisis better than the other Southeast Asian economies (Lim Chong Yah, 2000). However, in 1998, the Singapore economy, too, succumbed. The unemployment rate in Singapore increased from 2% in 1996 to 3.6% in 1999. The hope of relying on the flexible wage system to bail Singapore out was thwarted, however. This is because the implementation of the flexible wage system was not sufficiently widespread, and the timing and quantum of the bonus were not coordinated for policy purposes.

Under the flexible wage system, employers award above-average workers with an annual bonus of one or more than one month's pay (depending on the size of the performance measure adopted) which was paid out at a time mutually agreeable to both employer and workers. This flexible wage system was promoted by the National Wages Council and the Government in an attempt to increase the flexibility of labour cost to make it more responsive to business conditions so as to enable firms to weather the tide of economic conditions. Bonus payments may be made at the end of the calendar year, or at the end of the Chinese lunar year, or even at mid-year. However, if the need to reduce labour cost at a specific time were to arise, not all firms may be able to do this as the bonus may not be due at that time. Hence, the attempt to increase the flexibility of labour cost by means of bonus pay was not effective as most firms do not pay the bonus at the same time. Therefore, the CPF employer's contribution rate was again reduced from 20% to 10% in 1999.

The desire to ensure that the CPF need not be used as a macroeconomic instrument caused the government and the NWC to devise a more effective "flexible wage system". This brought about the promotion of the Monthly Variable Component (MVC). With the MVC, the income of a typical worker is divided into three components: a fixed monthly income component, the MVC which should account for

10% of the wage cost, and the bonus which should account for about 20% of the wage cost. The MVC can be easily reduced if there is need for a concerted effort to reduce labour cost at the national level. This means that workers must be educated concerning the wisdom of not including the MVC in determining the financing of housing mortgages and other loans.

According to a report of the Ministry of Manpower (MOM, 2004), 81% of employees in Singapore were employed under a wage system that incorporated at least one of the three features: the MVC, the performance-based bonus and reduced wage range between entry level pay and maximum pay. This means that 37% of employees were under a wage system that did not have any flexibility. The implication for these firms is that, if the demand for their products/services were adversely affected by recession, the only option to save their business would lie in retrenchment.

The impact of economic recession is most obvious in the employment scene. Table 1 shows that, in 1994, there were 34,000 unemployed in Singapore, about 4,000 (11.76%) of whom were graduates. In 2004, there were 116,400 unemployed, of whom 21,400 (18.38%) were graduates. Thus, not only were there more unemployed workers in 2004, but the structure of unemployment had also changed. Among the unemployed, those with primary education more than doubled from 1994 to 2004 while those with university education quadrupled. Another point which should be noted is that the number of unemployed in 2004 was the same as the number of unemployed in 2003 but the rate of GDP growth in 2004 was 8.1%. A closer examination of Table 1 shows that the high growth occurring in 2004 reduced the proportion of lowly educated among the unemployed, while the proportion of tertiary educated among the unemployed increased. This shows that Singapore's effort in helping lowly educated workers find jobs through the job redesign effort has paid off handsomely. The objective of job redesign is to convert low-paid jobs into higher-paid jobs by introducing the use of equipment into the job design, which necessitates the training of workers in the use of the equipment at work. The National Trades Union Congress, Singapore's labour movement has been the prime mover of this effort and has been able to create 4000 jobs on the basis of the job redesign effort. This was unfortunately achieved at the expense of jobs for unskilled foreign workers. Thus, the impact of the high growth of 2004 showed in 2005 when the number of unemployed fell to 60,000.

Table 1. Unemployed by Education, Singapore ('000)

Year	Total	Primary	Lower Secondary	Secondary	Upper Secondary	Diploma	Degree
1994	34.0	10.0	6.4	8.9	2.7	2.2	3.8
1995	34.9	10.5	5.8	9.9	2.7	2.3	3.6
1996	37.7	10.5	5.9	10.6	2.7	2.5	5.0
1997	34.8	9.4	6.6	9.1	2.6	3.2	3.8
1998	62.7	16.1	13.6	17.4	3.3	5.5	6.9
1999	69.5	18.0	13.7	19.2	5.0	5.2	8.3
2000	65.4	17.9	12.4	17.7	5.6	4.2	7.6
2001	71.9	17.1	12.4	19.1	6.2	7.2	9.8
2002	94.0	20.3	15.6	25.3	8.9	8.4	15.4
2003	116.4	23.2	18.9	29.5	11.5	12.2	21.1
2004	116.4	21.5	17.6	29.9	12.7	13.4	21.4

Source: *Report on Labor Force in Singapore 2004*, Ministry of Manpower, Singapore.

There is no unemployment benefits scheme in Singapore. Those who are unemployed are not allowed to withdraw their CPF balances during the period of unemployment. This is because CPF balances can only be withdrawn at the age of 55, although CPF members are allowed to use their CPF balance to finance their housing mortgages. This means that the unemployed must find work. Generally, Singaporeans are less selective over jobs, and hence the emergence of non-traditional employment modes in this context of zero welfare support is apparent.

GLOBALISATION AND THE SUPPLY OF NON-TRADITION EMPLOYMENT

Firms in Singapore, as in most other countries, are greatly affected by globalization. The value of the annual trade volume is about three times the GDP for Singapore. Singapore is one of the few countries for which monetary policy to accommodate the exchange rate policy is more effective in increasing employment and decreasing inflation because of such an open economy. About 50% of the workforce in the manufacturing sector is employed in firms under foreign ownership.

Wage costs in Singapore are high, yet Singapore has been able to compete for foreign investment due to lower unit labour and unit business costs (Chew and Chew, 2005). Most firms will want to explore all possible ways to increase their flexibility in managing their workforce and business. The following options are available to most firms in Singapore:

1. Employ part-time workers when firms experience difficulties in recruiting full-time workers. There are, however, pros and cons to employing part-time workers. Part-time workers tend to be less efficient because among other factors, they receive less training (Arulampalam and Booth 1998, for example, find a negative correlation between technical efficiency and the proportion of temporary jobs at the firm level in Spain). On the other hand, they generally cost less in terms of pay and fringe benefits such as medical coverage. Full-time workers are, in general, placed under the seniority-based wage system while part-time workers are on the flexible wage system. In the early 1990s, firms employed part-time workers because they experienced difficulties in getting full-time workers. However, since the 1997 Currency Crisis, firms have employed part-time workers because they are cheaper in terms of healthcare and fringe benefits, although, as discussed later, part-time workers also enjoy significant medical benefits. Of course, the implementation of the flexible wage system for full-time workers reduces the incentive to employ part-time workers, but the trend to employ part-time workers is gaining momentum. The labour market in Singapore is also free from regulation on minimum pay, working hours and restriction on dismissals. Hence, the creation of low-paid, part-time and temporary jobs is unconstrained, which is similar to the experience of OECD countries (OECD 1992). However, as Arulampalam and Booth (1998) show, people who are in marginal forms of employment, which include part-time employment, do tend to receive less training. Diaz-Mayans and Sanchez (2004) also find a negative correlation between technical efficiency and the proportion of temporary jobs at the firm level in Spain.

2. Outsource certain business activities to save costs and increase business competitiveness. For instance, in 2004, Singapore International Airline (SIA) outsourced its entire IT department to IBM. About 131 IT workers in SIA were offered employment by IBM under so-called comparable terms. It is reported that SIA saved $15 million a year from the decision to outsource its IT department (Straits Times 2004a, 2004b). Although outsourcing is not under the scope of the present chapter, it does affect firms' decisions to employ part-time workers because the more firms outsource, the less they reliant they need to be on both full-time and part-time workers.

3. Employ foreign labour. Firms in Singapore benefit from the inflow of three types of foreign personnel: global talent on employment passes for jobs that pay more than $2,500 in monthly wages; specialist manpower on an S pass (which is for semi-skilled foreign workers) for jobs that pay more than $1,800 in monthly wages (but less than $2500); and semi-/unskilled workers on work permits for jobs that pay less than $1,800 in monthly wages. At present, the total number of foreign manpower in Singapore stands at 620,000, of whom 72,000 are employment pass holders, 540,000 are work permit holders including 150,000 domestic maids and 8,000 are S pass holders. Firms in Singapore employ foreign workers when they experience difficulties in recruiting native full-time and part-time workers. According to a report on the motivation of promoting flexible work arrangements (Chew et. al., 1993), the ease of employing foreign workers has also affected firms' attitudes towards employing part-time workers and implementing flexible work arrangements, especially in the Construction Industry where 5 foreign workers can be employed for every native worker, implying that fewer full-time native workers are employed.[i]

The above issues are also relevant when firms consider employing contingent workers which will be discussed later in the chapter. In the case of contingent workers, firms do not provide any work benefits at all. Issues concerning the contingent workforce are similar to those of outsourcing except that the work is done at the workplace in the case of the former.

In terms of analysis, it is not possible to assert that one mode of non-traditional employment will be more popular than another as they are, in fact, substitutes for each other.

DEMAND FOR NON-TRADITIONAL EMPLOYMENT

Singaporeans need to earn a living in a sustainable manner. Due to the volatility of the labour market, many Singaporeans now resort to the following types of non-traditional employment; employers, own account workers, contributing family workers, part-time workers, flexi-place workers, contingent workers who are temporary workers and other similar job arrangements. Hence, globalization has given rise to multiple job arrangements.

Part-Time Employment

Few people, especially males, actually opt for part-time work. Even females who do not have young children want to work full-time as the cost of living is high in Singapore. In Hong Kong, for instance, most part-time workers (44%) are males who cannot find full-time work (Ngo, 2002). To a certain extent, part-time employment is disguised unemployment. Some people try to use part-time employment as a stepping stone towards full-time employment. Blank (1998) notes that, in the US, part-time work does not always increase the probability of getting full-time jobs. We believe that Singapore's experience is similar to that of the US.

Table 2 shows the proportion of employees in Singapore working in various types of flexible working arrangements. The most significant form of flexible employment is part-time employment. Indeed, the share of part-time employment has increased from 2% in 1998 to 3.6% in 2004. Part-time employment could be involuntary, as some of these workers are those who could not get full-time jobs. In terms of employee type, about 5% of rank and file workers engaged in part-time employment, while the corresponding figure for management staff was only 0.5%. Among the various industries, the services industry sees the highest proportion of part-time workers (see Table 3). The construction industry does not use much part-time employment because

301

it is one of the very few industries which have been allowed to import foreign workers. Within the services industry, hotels and restaurants rely heavily on part-time staff, which account for about 30% of the workforce.

Table 2. Proportion of Employees on Flexible Working Arrangements

Type of Flexible Working Arrangements	1998	2000	2002	2004
Total	2.6	3.0	3.8	4.1
Office-based	2.5	2.9	3.6	4.0
(i) Part-time	1.9	2.6	3.4	3.6
(ii) Flexible time	0.6	0.3	0.2	0.3
(iii) Job sharing/Splitting	-	-	-	-
Flexi-place	0.1	0.1	0.1	0.2
Teleworking	-	0.1	0.1	0.2
Home working	-	-	-	-

Source: *Conditions of Employment 2004*, Ministry of Manpower, Singapore.

Table 3. Proportion of Workers in Part-time Employment, 2002 and 2004

Type of Employees	2002	2004
All Employees	3.4	3.6
Manufacturing	0.6	0.6
Construction	0.9	0.6
Services	5.7	6.0
(i) Wholesale and Retail Trade	5.2	8.8
(ii) Hotels and Restaurants	27.2	30.7
(iii) Financial Services	1.0	1.3
(iv) Business and Real Estate Services	2.3	2.1
(v) Community, Social and Personal Services	5.4	5.5
(vi) Transport and Communications	2.0	1.1

Source: *Conditions of Employment 2002, 2004*, Ministry of Manpower Singapore.

In Singapore, the Employment Act stipulates that certain labour standards must be applied, such as the number of paid days of holiday leave annually. But many firms extend significant fringe benefits beyond the legal minimum even to part-time workers, as shown in Table 4. In the early 1990s, firms offered fringe benefits in order to attract part-time workers. Today, firms have no problem recruiting part-time workers. Hence, it is expected that fringe benefits for part-time workers would decline as firms want to save costs in order to remain competitive.

Table 4. Proportion of Establishments Which Extended Benefits to Part-Time Employees in 2004.

Type of Benefits	Part time workers in 2003
Compassionate Leave	48.0
Marriage Leave	39.9
Paternity Leave	42.0
Paid sick leave for Father	55.2
Paid sick leave for Mother	60.1
Paid Sick Leave for Spouse Leave	54.9
Paid Sick Elderly Parents Leave	56.9
Paid Exam Leave	35.9
Unpaid Exam Leave	24.3
Paid Study Leave	34.1
Unpaid Study Leave	38.9
Meal benefits	45.3
Transport Benefits	37.8
Housing Benefits	3.9
Childcare Benefits	45.7
Holidays and Travel Incentives	32.9
Country Club Benefits	5.6
Family Relocation/Orientation Benefits	13.9
Stock Options	30.1
Housing Loans	24.7
Car Loans	12.7
Education Loans	24.7
Flexible Benefits Plans	29.4

Source: *Conditions of Employment 2004*, Ministry of Manpower, Singapore.

Employers

While some people are born entrepreneurs, most people become self-employed out of economic necessity (Chew and Azlan, 1995). When jobs are plentiful and pay well, as was the case in the early 1990s, most Singaporean graduates preferred to either work for the public sector or for multi-national corporations (MNCs). But things have changed since 1997 as a result of adverse labour market conditions. Consequently, many Singaporeans, especially graduates, took the plunge and became self-employed. Indeed, the number of employers has increased steadily from 95,000 in 2002 to 100,400 in 2004. Moreover, about 80% of employers are male.

Table 5 shows that about 70% of employers are engaged in services, such as trade and business services, where entry is relatively less resource-based. In terms of education level, almost 24% of employers are university graduates and 8% have a diploma (see Table 6.). Increasingly, we expect employers to be more educated as they find it increasingly harder to get good jobs, which is one potential consequence of globalization.

Table 5. Employers, Own Account Workers and Contributing Workers by Industry in 2004

Type	Employers	Own Account Workers	Contributing Family Workers
Total	100,400	174,200	14,700
Manufacturing	14,500	6,400	600
Construction	13,500	10,400	800
Services	-	-	-
(i) Wholesale and Retail Trade	31,700	33,900	6,300
(ii) Hotels and Restaurants	7,500	14,900	5,300
(iii) Financial Services	1,700	12,600	100
(iv) Business and Real Estate Services	15,200	20,400	500
(v) Community, Social and Personal Services	-	-	-
(vi) Transport and Communications	5,100	46,700	200

Source: *Report on Labour Force in Singapore, 2004,* Ministry of Manpower, Singapore.

Table 6. Employers, Own Account Workers and Contributing Workers by Education Level in 2004

Type	Employers	Own Account Workers	Contributing Family Workers
Total	100,400	174,200	14,700
No Formal Education	10,900	33,800	4,000
Primary Education	4,100	11,700	1,400
Lower Secondary	18,500	36,000	3,600
Secondary	24,700	44,300	4,000
Upper Secondary	11,000	17,600	1,000
Poly Diploma	7,900	11,200	200
Degree	23,500	19,600	500

Source: *Report on Labour Force in Singapore, 2004*, Ministry of Manpower, Singapore.

Own Account Workers

As the term implies, employers are people who are self-employed and who also employ other workers. However, there also are those who are self-employed and do not employ other workers. This group is referred to as own account workers. Very little is known about this group of workers, but we do know for a fact that they do not benefit from the Central Provident Fund (CPF) scheme (a scheme which is contributed to by both employers and workers themselves) in contrast to full-time workers and part-time workers. With few restrictions on entry into self-employment, and without minimum conditions, there is a good chance that people become own account workers due to a lack of employment choice. The number of own account workers increased from 167,000 in 2002 to 174,000 in 2004. About 76% of own account workers are male. Own account workers generally work in trade and transport lines and about 72% have, at most, upper secondary education.

Contributing Family Workers

Contributing Family Workers refers to those persons who assist another member of their family in the operation of their family business or farm, such as farm assistants, shop assistants, hawker assistants and the like. They do not receive wages on a regular basis. They refer to those employed on an informal basis, and hence they typically have no CPF contributions. As a result, young people have a tendency to shy away from working for their families unless they cannot find decent alternative employment outside the family. Table 7 shows that the number of contributing family workers has decreased from 15,800 in 2002 to 14,700 in 2004. Most of the contributing family workers are female, perhaps because females have less of a pressing need to be the breadwinner in the family. They generally work in the trades and in restaurants, and are lowly educated. .

Table 7. No of Contributing Family Workers by Gender, 2002-4

	2002	2003	2004
Total	15,800	15,100	14,700
Male	3,800	3,700	3,800
Female	12,000	11,400	10,900

Source: *Report on Labour Force in Singapore, 2004*, Ministry of Manpower, Singapore.

Contingent Workers

Workers in contingent employment generally include those who are employed and supplied by third parties (employment agencies) to establishments under contract for service, and employees on short-term contracts who are directly employed by the establishments, as well as those who are engaged on a causal or freelance basis. In Singapore, some firms may prefer to employ contingent workers as they can save on employee benefits (compared to core employees and part-time staff, who are eligible for the full range of staff benefits (see Table 4 above)).

Irini (2004) argues that employers will only use temporary or contingent workers if it is easy to control output and to train the workers. For highly specialized and infrequent jobs, employers are likely to use contractors. But employers also use contingent workers for low skilled functions such as cleaning, security and non-core services.

In Singapore, contingent workers are welcome to join the union, and if a workplace is not unionized, contingent workers can join the General Branch Union. This union is for workers employed at non-unionized firms who can, through this union, join the labour movement so as to enjoy non-collective bargaining benefits (Chew and Chew: 2003a).

Table 8 shows that contingent employment has been quite stable over time and has increased from 3% in 2000 to about 3.6% of the workforce in 2004. However, the usage of contingent workers varies from industry to industry and varies even within the industry. This is because the contingent workforce has been used as a buffer by firms against business fluctuations. In 2000, which was a good year for the Singapore economy, about 20% of the workers in hotels and restaurants used a contingent workforce. However, due to poor business prospects, the share of the contingent workforce has declined in this industry to 5% in 2004. As to be expected, most firms' usage of the contingent workforce is higher among rank and file workers than among management staff, as shown in Table 9.

**Table 8. Proportion of Workers on Contingent Employment,
2000, 2002 and 2004**

Type of Employees	2000	2002	2004
All Employees	3.02	3.63	3.6
Manufacturing	1.07	5.84	4.5
Construction	0.58	1.61	1.3
Services	5.00	2.80	3.6
(i) Wholesale and Retail Trade	6.8	2.16	2.0
(ii) Hotels and Restaurants	20.19	3.09	4.9
(iii) Financial Services	1.10	3.45	4.8
(iv) Business and Real Estate Services	3.19	2.07	3.3
(v) Community, Social and Personal Services	5.23	3.29	4.4
(vi) Transport and Communications	1.25	3.29	4.2

Source: *Conditions of Employment, 2000, 2002, 2004*, Ministry of Manpower, Singapore.

Table 9. Proportion of Contingent Workforce by Employee Type, 2004

Type of Employees	Percentage of Contingent Workforce of Total Workforce	Workers Supplied by Employment Agencies	Freelance or Casual Basis	Short-term Contracts
All Employees	3.6	2.3	0.7	0.6
Rank and File Employees	4.6	3.0	0.9	0.7
Management Staff	1.4	0.7	0.3	0.5

Source: *Conditions of Employment, 2004*, Ministry of Manpower, Singapore.

Generally, contingent workers are supplied by employment agencies. There were 957 employment agencies in Singapore in 2004, most of which deal with foreign maids and workers on work permits, and to a certain extent, contingent workers as well. Houseman, Kalleberg and Erickcek (2003) find that employment agencies have three important roles to play: they enable a speedy job match with economies of scale, employers can pay contingent workers lower wages without upsetting existing full-time workers (in terms of hot having them directly on staff), and the cost of hiring unsuitable workers is much lower.

At the industry level, large firms, such as those in the manufacturing and transport industries, use employment agencies to supply contingent workers but small firms such as those in hotels, restaurants and business services employ contingent workers on a casual basis upon request or demand (see Table 10). Thus far, it is too soon to say whether contingent employment will become a permanent feature of the labour market in Singapore.

Table 10. Proportion of Contingent Employment by Sources and by Industry, 2004

Type of Employees	2004	Workers Supplied by Employment Agencies	Freelance or Causal Basis	Short-term Contracts
All Employees	3.6	2.3	0.7	0.6
Manufacturing	4.5	4.0	0.1	0.4
Construction	1.3	1.0	0.2	0.1
Services	3.6	1.6	1.1	0.9
(i) Wholesale and Retail Trade	2.0	0.8	0.5	0.6
(ii) Hotels and Restaurants	4.9	0.9	3.7	0.4
(iii) Financial Services	4.8	2.8	0.3	1.7
(iv) Business and Real Estate Services	3.3	1.7	0.7	0.8
(v) Community, Social and Personal Services	4.4	0.4	2.9	1.1
(vi) Transport and Communications	4.1	3.2	0.2	0.8

Source: *Conditions of Employment, 2004*, Ministry of Manpower, Singapore

FACTORS AFFECTING NON-TRADITION EMPLOYMENT TRENDS

The Wage System

As explained earlier, the wage system can affect the popularity of non-traditional employment such as part-time work, outsourcing and contingent work. Specifically, firms will have less incentive to employ a temporary workforce if they implement a flexible wage system. Table 11 shows the degree to which the flexible wage system has been implemented in terms of the number of months of monthly pay extended under the variable component of pay. The number of months of the variable component increased from 1.76 in 2003 to 1.87 in 2004. This implies that many firms have intensified the flexible wage system in terms of giving bigger bonuses. For instance, some firms do reward excellent workers with more than six months' pay as bonus. The intensive implementation of the flexible wage system can weaken the trend to employ part-time and contingent workers alongside rank and file workers.

Table 11. No of Months of Variable Component

Type of Employees	2003 All employees	2004 All employees	2004: Rank and File	2004: Management Staff
All Employees	1.76	1.87	1.70	2.13
Manufacturing	1.90	1.97	1.86	2.14
Construction	0.86	0.96	0.87	1.09
Services	1.79	1.91	1.70	2.24
(i) Wholesale and Retail Trade	1.76	1.85	1.64	2.16
(ii) Hotels and Restaurants	0.87	0.81	0.78	0.87
(iii) Financial Services	2.79	3.00	2.58	3.32
(iv) Business and Real Estate Services	1.31	1.39	1.05	1.83
(v) Community, Social and Personal Services	-	-	-	-
(vi) Transport and Communications	2.22	2.29	2.28	2.33

Source: *Conditions of Employment, 2003, 2004*, Ministry of Manpower, Singapore

Occupational Structure

Table 12 shows that the number of management and professional staff among the employed has been rising over time while the number of rank and file workers has declined in Singapore. It was also shown earlier that there is less incidence of part time and contingent work amongst management staff. Hence, on account of occupational structure, which is moving towards more management and professional staff and less rank and file workforce as the economy restructures, the part-time and contingent workforces will be smaller and self-employment among graduates may rise.

Table 12. Employed Persons Fifteen Years and Over by Occupation and Sex
1990, 1995, 2001 and 2004

Occupation	1990	1995	2001	2004
	Persons	Persons	Persons	Persons (in thousands)
Legislators, Senior Officials and Managers	119,804 (8.15)	218,036 (12.81)	275,512 (13.46)	271.0 (13.11)
Professionals	80,306 (5.47)	124,745 (7.33)	241,745 (11.81)	249.6 (12.08)
Technicians and Associate Professionals	173,888 (11.84)	269,097 (15.81)	339,881 (16.61)	359.0 (17.37)
Clerical Workers	206,829 (14.08)	220,002 (12.93)	274,905 (13.43)	271.7 (13.15)
Service Workers	219,531 (14.94)	209,973 (12.34)	230,648 (11.27)	228.2 (11.04)
Production Craftsman, Plant and Machine Operators, Cleaners and Laborers, Agricultural and Fishery Workers	605,492 (41.21)	589,567 (34.63)	607,330 (29.67)	606.1 (29.32)
Workers Not Classified by Occupation	63,344 (4.31)	70,670 (4.15)	76,724 (3.75)	81.4 (3.94)
Total	1,469,194 (100.00)	1,702,089 (100.00)	2,046,744 (100.00)	2,066.9 (100.0)

Source: *Report on Labor Force in Singapore, 2004,* Ministry of Manpower, Singapore.

Healthcare Costs

It is argued here that if the healthcare bill increases, there will be more incentive for firms to employ contingent workers. Table 13 shows that the average days of outpatient leave in Singapore increased from 1.7 days in 1997 to 4.2 days in 2004. At the same time, the average Days of Hospitalization Leave per Employee increased from 10 days in 1997 to 15 days in 2004, and the Proportion of Staff on Sick Leave increased from 10% in 1997 to 52% in 2004 (Table 14). Thus, there seems to be a large increase in the healthcare bill in 2004 compared to 2003. It is not too clear whether the high usage of sick leave was due to SARS or whether it is the beginning of a rising trend in Singapore. In Singapore, employers must purchase healthcare insurance for their employees subject to a minimum percentage. For instance, the public sector will pay for 85% of the cost of hospitalization, and the percentage of entitlement varies in the private sector. However, if the entitlement is insufficient, workers can use their CPF balances to buy additional healthcare insurance coverage. Although it is not compulsory, most Singaporeans would use their CPF balances to buy healthcare insurance.

Table 13. Average Days of Outpatient Leave per Employee

Industry	1997	2000	2002	2003
All Employees	1.7	1.6	1.5	4.2
Manufacturing	1.6	1.6	1.5	4.1
Construction	1.7	1.5	1.6	3.2
Services	-	1.6	1.6	4.4
(i) Wholesales and Retail Trade	1.6	1.7	1.5	4.1
(ii) Hotels and Restaurants	1.7	1.7	1.6	3.8
(iii) Financial Services	1.7	1.7	1.7	5.0
(iv) Business and Real Estate Services	1.6	1.5	1.6	3.9
(v) Community, Social and Personal Services	2.2	1.8	1.6	5.0
(vi) Transport and Communications	1.7	1.6	1.6	4.7

Source: *Conditions of Employment, 2004*, Ministry of Manpower, Singapore

Table 14. Proportion of Staff on Sick Leave

Industry	1997	2000	2002	2003
All Employees	10.1	8.5	11.1	52.4
Manufacturing	10.0	6.3	10.3	60.5
Construction	10.1	13.2	12.3	32.0
Services	-	10.2	11.3	52.3
(i) Wholesale and Retail Trade	10.5	10.6	11.1	52.6
(ii) Hotels and Restaurants	12.0	10.7	10.6	37.7
(iii) Financial Services	10.4	9.6	15.1	60.4
(iv) Business and Real Estate Services	10.7	9.4	9.4	58.0
(v) Community, Social and Personal Services	10.1	11.1	10.8	54.3
(v) Transport and Communications	9.4	9.6	11.6	47.5

Source: *Conditions of Employment, 2004*, Ministry of Manpower, Singapore.

ANALYSIS OF CORRELATION BETWEEN THE CONGINGENT AND PART TIME WORKFORCES, THE FLEXIBLE WAGE SYSTEM AND HEALTHCARE COSTS

For this analysis, we focus on 12 sub-industries in the manufacturing and 18 sub-industries in the services industries.[ii] It is assumed that the sub-industries within each industry have a similar propensity to outsource and a similar degree of reliance on foreign workers, except for the propensity to use contingent and part-time workforces. For instance, the proportion of the contingent workforce was 8% for Electronics but only 0.1% for Textiles within the manufacturing industry. In the case of the services industry, the contingent workforce constituted 10% for postal services and 0.5% for air travel. A similar pattern can be seen in the usage of part-time workers.

We put forward the following hypotheses:

1. We expect that the contingent and part-time workforces are substitutes for each other in that if firms use more contingent workers, they would employ fewer part-time workers. We know for a fact that firms have more than these two ways to increase flexibility in their operations. Two other main ways they can do so are to employ foreign workers and to outsource certain operations. Nevertheless, we want to determine, based on regression analysis, whether the contingent workforce is negatively related with the part-time workforce.

    Null Hypothesis 1: The Proportion of the contingent workforce is not correlated with the proportion of part-time staff.

2. When firms experience an increase in healthcare cost, which is measured in terms of the proportion of regular (non-contingent) workers on sick leave, some firms will use more contingent workers as they are not entitled to medical benefits. Hence, we expect the proportion of the contingent workforce to be positively correlated with the proportion of regular workers on sick leave.

    Null Hypothesis 2: The proportion of the contingent workforce is not correlated with the proportion of staff on sick leave.

3. When firms adopt the flexible wage system, which is measured in terms of the number of months of bonus, firms have less incentive to employ contingent workers. Hence, we expect the proportion of the contingent workforce to be negatively correlated with the number of months of bonus.

> Null Hypothesis 3: The proportion of the contingent workforce is not correlated with the number of months of bonus.

4. The employment of part-time workers is slightly different from the employment of contingent workers, even though, as shown in Table 5, part-time workers also enjoy significant medical benefits. Hence, when there is an increase in healthcare costs, firms may employ more part-time workers as their medical coverage is not so extensive. But there is also a possibility that firms may employ less part-time workers when there is an increase in healthcare cost measured in terms of the proportion of workers on sick leave. Whether the part-time workforce is positively or negatively correlated with the proportion of workers on sick leave is an empirical question.

> Null Hypothesis 4: The proportion of the part time workforce is not correlated with the proportion of staff on sick leave.

5. Again, when firms adopt the flexible wage system as measured by the number of months of bonus, there is less incentive for firms to employ part-time workers because full-time workers who are more committed to the firms are paid according to their contribution. Full-time workers have a career because they enjoy longer job tenure than part-time workers. We expect the proportion of the part-time workforce to be negatively correlated with the number of months of bonus.

> Null Hypothesis 5: The proportion of the part time workforce is not correlated with the number of months of bonus.

RESULTS

We estimate equation 1 for the Manufacturing Sector:

$$\text{Contingent Workforce} = a + b.(\text{Part-time Workforce}) + c.(\text{Healthcare Cost}) + d.(\text{Bonus}) \qquad (1)$$

The regression gives the value of coefficient b as -0.21. It is only significant at 72% level of confidence. Coefficient c is -0.05, but it is only significant at 62% level of significance. Coefficient d is 2.59 but it is only significant at 18% level of confidence. R Square for the equation is 0.37.

Hence, for the manufacturing industry, there is weak evidence that the contingent workforce is negatively related to the part-time workforce and negatively related to healthcare cost. Null hypothesis 1 is rejected at 72% level of confidence and Null hypothesis 2 is rejected at 62% level of confidence. The results based on equation 1 for the services industry are statistically insignificant.

We estimate equation 2 for the services industry:

$$\text{Part Time Workforce} = a + b.(\text{Healthcare Cost}) + c.(\text{Bonus}) \qquad (2)$$

The regression yields the value of coefficient b as -0.90 which is significant at 95% level of confidence. Coefficient c is -3.51, and is significant at 90% level of significance. R Square for the equation is 0.73.

Hence, there is strong evidence for the services industry that the part-time workforce is negatively related to healthcare cost and negatively related to implementation of the flexible wage system. Null hypothesis 4 is rejected at 90% level of confidence and Null hypothesis 5 is rejected at 95% level of confidence. Moreover, the results based on equation 2 for the manufacturing industry are statistically insignificant.

CONCLUSION

There is an increasing trend for firms to employ part-time workers and contingent workers in Singapore because of increasing labour costs, including healthcare costs, and also because of the increasing intensity of competition due to globalization. However, there are other factors which will discourage firms from employing part time and contingent workers, such as the promotion of the flexible wage system and an increase in the proportion of management staff in Singapore. As we expect that healthcare costs will continue to increase, firms may be further discouraged from employing part-time workers over time.

There is also a growing trend for graduates to be self-employed as the salary of an employee tends to decrease with globalization and the increasing shift in Singapore towards the knowledge economy. Hence, we expect the number and proportion of employers and own account workers to increase over time. As the level of education of Singaporeans increases, we also expect the proportion of contributing family workers to fall. Hence, in conclusion, as Singaporeans become more educated and a greater proportion work as management staff, we expect non-traditional employment to grow, although not all forms will enjoy the same degree of growth, as Singapore transforms into a knowledge economy.

REFERENCES

Arulampalam, W and Booth, A.L. (1998) "Training and Labour Market Flexibility:Is there a Trade-off". *British Journal of Industrial Relations*, 36:4, Dec, pp 521-36.

Blank, R.M. (1998) "Labour Market Dynamics and Part-time Work". *Research in Labour Economics*, 17, pp 57-94.

Chew Soon Beng and Azlan Ghazali (1995) "Entrepreneurial Propensity of Singaporean Graduates". In *The Southeast Asian Chinese: Culture, Economy and Society*, Institute of Southeast Asian Studies, pp 100 - 130.

Chew, Soon Beng and Chew, Rosalind (2003a) "Trade union orientation and macro-economic management". *Review of Pacific Basin Financial Markets and Policies,* 6:3, pp. 381-403.

Chew, Soon Beng and Chew, Rosalind (2005) "Singapore's Responses to Globalisation and Regional Competition." In *Globalisation and World Economic Policies* edited by Clem Tisdell, India: Serial Publications, pp. 287-309.

Chew Soon Beng, et. al. (1993) *A Study of Flexible Work Arrangements in Singapore*, National Trades Union Congress, Singapore.

Diaz-Mayans, M.A. & Sanchez, R (2004) "Temporary Employment and Technical Efficiency in Spain", *International Journal of Manpower*, vol 25, #2 pp 181 -195

Lim Chong Yah (2000) "Postmortem on Asian Currency Crisis". Keynote address presented at the *Seventh Conference, East Asian Economic Association*, 17-18 November, Singapore.

Ministry of Manpower (1999a) *Explanatory Note on MVC*. Singapore: Ministry of Manpower Labour Relations Department.

Ministry of Manpower (1999b) *Explanatory Note on MVC*, Singapore: Ministry of Manpower Labour Relations Department.

Ministry of Manpower (2002. *Report on Wages in Singapore*. Singapore: Ministry of Manpower Research and Statistics Department.

Ministry of Manpower (2005) *Report on Labour Force in Singapore 2004*. Singapore: Ministry of Manpower Research and Statistics Department

Ministry of Manpower (2003) *Highlights on Annual Wage Changes*. Singapore: Ministry of Manpower Research and Statistics Department

Ministry of Manpower (2004a) *Employment Trend and Structure*. Singapore: Ministry of Manpower Research and Statistics Department.

Ministry of Manpower (2004b) *Wage Restructuring Outcome*. Singapore: Ministry of Manpower Research and Statistics Department.

Ministry of Manpower (2004c) *New Challenges to the Workplace: Workers' Expectations and Socio-economic Adjustments*. Singapore: Ministry of Manpower Research and Statistics Department.

Ministry of Manpower (2005) *Conditions of Employment 2004*. Singapore: Ministry of Manpower Research and Statistics Department

Ngo Hang-Yue (2002) "Part-time Employment in Hong Kong: Gendered Phenomenon: *International Journal of Human Resource Management*, vol 13, #2, March, pp 361-377.

OECD (1992) "The Job Study, Part II". *The Adjustment Potential of the Labour Market*, Paris, 207.

Straits Times (2004a) "Big firms' outsourcing trend". 4/10/04, p. A16, Money Section.

Straits Times (2004b) "SIA to outsource IT jobs to IBM". 27/10/04, p. H7.

---

[1] However, it can be argued that, without foreign workers on work permits, firms in the construction industry will not have the ability to tender for large projects as their labour costs would be too high, which would result in less employment opportunities for native workers.

[2] The 11 sub-industries in the manufacturing sector are food, textiles, paper, petroleum, fabricated metal, machinery, electrical, electronic, medical, transport and others. The 18 sub-industries in the services sector are wholesale, retail, hotels, restaurants, land transport, water transport, air transport, supporting transport, postal services, financial services, insurance, real estate, IT, R&D, other business, education, healthcare and other services

INDEX

flexibilization, 17, 19, 21, 28–33
flexible
  labour market, 42
  production, 96
  staffing arrangement, 263
  wage adjustments, 34
  wage system, 295–6, 299, 314
  work arrangements, 300
Flexicurity strategies, 33
Florida, 75
Forced distribution system, 214–15
Foreign capital flows, 9, 93, 122
Foreign Direct Investment (FDI), 2, 7, 8, 10, 17, 151, 155, 157, 164, 172
  inflow, 158, 163
    Japan, 278–9
Foreign Employment, 104–6
foreign funded enterprises (FFEs), 52
foreign investment policies, 151
foreign investment, 6
foreign labour, 300
foreign trade liberalisation, 108
formal sector, 115
  employment, 35, 119
Fourth World Conference on Women in Beijing in 1995 (FWCW), 241
Fragmentation of Employment, 286–7
Free Trade Agreements, 10, 155
  regional economic integration, 151
free trade zone (the ASEAN Free Trade Area), 24, 160
Freeman, R., 19
Frenkel, S., 249, 265, 270
Friawan, D., 234
Friedman, S., 73, 80
Functional flexibility, 31–2

Gallagher, M., 239
Gamble, J., 41, 198
Garment Industry Growth, 100–3
GATT, 158
GDP, 1, 105, 153, 156
  growth, 17, 297
Gender Development Index, 119
Gender Distribution, Malaysian Labour Force, 166
gender variations, in labour force, 28
General Agreement on Trade in Service (GATS), 189

General Branch Union, 307
General Council of Trade Unions, 279
Generalised System of Preferences (GSP), 104, 109
Gereffi, G., 198
Ghoshal, S., 198, 200, 202
Gini coefficients, 20, 37, 38, 255
Gita Sen 179
global economy, 1, 25
  Impact of, 179–96
global production system, 41
Globalization, 17, 19
  dual factors of, 7
  effects of, 19, 42
  on Employment Impact of, 285–8
  impact of, 162–3
Goel, S., 72, 75
Goka, K., 5, 15
Graf, J. D., 237
Great Leap Forward Period (1958–62)
Greater Economic Integration, 24–5
Green, 19
Growing Non Standard Employment, 286–7
Growing Wage and Reward Differences from Work, 289
Guest, D., 202
Gunter, B. G., 19
Gupta, A., 70

Hajinoor, S. M., 153
Hall, P., 198
Hallak, J. C., 19
Hamid, Abdul, 153
Hamilton, G. G., 198
Harris, A., 237
Harrison, A., 20
Hasyim, 228
HCL
  BPO, 73
  nasscom, 73
Healthcare Costs, 311–13
Heckman, J., 18, 21
Heri, 228
Hill, D., 232
Hirst, P., 202
Hisano K, 12, 275
Hite, J., 252
Hollingsworth, R. J., 198

322